Lynn Figueroa

The cover illustration, *I'll Be Singing Up There*
by Brother Michael O'Neill McGrath, was inspired
by the life of Sister Thea Bowman.
Credit: Bee Still Studio.

Our Mission

The primary mission of Harcourt Religion Publishers is to provide the Catholic and Christian educational markets with the highest quality catechetical print and media resources. The content of these resources reflects the best insights of current theology, methodology, and pedagogical research. The resources are practical and easy to use, designed to meet expressed market needs, and written to reflect the teachings of the Catholic Church.

Printed in the United States of America

ISBN 0-15-900505-1

10 9 8 7 6 5 4 3 2 1

Contents

Introduction

Have you ever wondered, as you sat in church or in a religion class, why the history of the Church seems to be exactly that—a "HIS story" rather than a full and complete story of the Body of Christ? Could it be that women did not have an active or significant role in the early Church? According to Scripture and tradition, there seems to be ample evidence that women were deeply immersed in the experience of equal partnership within the earliest Christian faith communities. This reality may escape notice, however, if you are not familiar with the Bible or if the only Scripture readings you hear are the readings that are proclaimed at Mass.

Or could it be that the stories about women in the Church have less relevance to us today than do the stories about what men have said or done? This is an even less-likely probability, since so many stories of women in Scripture are stories of courage and faithfulness, often at great personal cost. These are stories of women who believed in a vision of the kingdom yet to come, a kingdom where the "last will be first" and where love of God and love and compassion for all God's creation prevail. This is the message the world so desperately needs to hear today. The history of women within the Catholic Church is a vibrant and exciting story, and it is one that you may not have heard. It is also a story that deserves to be told, over and over again, until it becomes a familiar and beautiful part of the Catholic faith story.

But if women have really had such an influential and exciting place in the history of the Church, where have they been? Why do we know so little about them? Part of the problem may be as simple as discerning the answers to two questions—Exactly who wrote the book? and When was it written? Stories in the Gospels lead us to surmise that the good news Jesus announced to his followers was meant to overturn systems of oppression and discrimination. But, in the post-Pauline letters of the New Testament, we find some teachings that seem to be at variance with the example Jesus gave his followers. Later we will look in more detail at how this happened and its effect on developing Christian doctrine.

Even if you may feel that you do not have a complete understanding of the role of women within the history of the Catholic Church, you probably know more than you realize. For example, some names of women who have been especially important to the Church probably come quickly to mind. There was Mary, the mother of Jesus, and there were other Marys, too. Of course you may know the names of many of saints and holy women, even if their life stories are not completely familiar to you. For example, there were Saints Thérèse of Lisieux, Teresa of Ávila, Catherine of Sienna, and Bernadette of Lourdes. And in more recent times, there were Dorothy Day and Mother Teresa of Calcutta.

Surely there were more women of significance than this! There were, and their names read like a beautiful litany of faithfulness and devotion to Jesus and to the Church. But even if you know a few details about some women who made significant contributions to the Church, you may never have had a chance to really know them or feel close to them or see them as real people—people just like you, people with a story.

Of all the fascinating women who have graced the Church, perhaps none are as intriguing as the women who actually knew the historical Jesus. Some of their names, just mentioned, are familiar to us. There was Mary, the mother of Jesus, Mary Magdalene, perhaps his dearest woman friend, and the sisters Mary and Martha. There were other women who financed his ministry and who supported him in all he did—Salome, Joanna, and Susanna. These were the women who were his family and his dearest friends, the women who followed him, were healed by him, and, in turn, ministered to him in his times of greatest need. These women heard his words of compassion and acceptance. And it was to some of them that Jesus chose to appear first after his resurrection. These women looked into the very eyes of the Son of God.

Then there were the women of the early Church, the Church of the first few centuries following the resurrection. These women played an important role in the spread of Christianity. Phoebe, for example, may have been the Church's first deaconess, and Priscilla was a coworker of Paul. The fact that these long-ago women were mentioned by name in the Bible indicates their importance to the early Christian community. But there were so many others whose names have been lost to us through time, among them women who were leaders and partners in the developing Church. Some names are "lost" just because the Bible is not a complete, or even always an accurate, historical record of the Church. Sometimes the best we can do is to work the puzzle with the pieces we have and hope that the result will be a picture whose beauty and intricacy we can understand and appreciate.

A more disturbing factor, however, is the absence of most women's names and a lack of acknowledgement of their

ministries within the early Church. This is due to the fact that women of that time were held in low regard. They were often marginalized within a society and a culture that saw little value in their presence. Whether our modern sensibilities are offended by this or not is really of little importance. Understanding that this marginalization occurred, however, is important. Because we know that the human authors of the Bible saw little reason in recording women's names and accomplishments, unless it absolutely could not be avoided, we can understand that an absence of names does not necessarily equal an absence of a true and historical presence of women.

Actually, the history of women in the Church is fascinating. It is a history that is filled with centuries of mystics, martyrs, poets, artists, and ecologists—many of them saints. Frequently their stories have only recently become known and appreciated. But their stories are true, and their place in history cannot be denied. They were women of courage who were willing to risk everything, all because of their belief that Jesus is truly the Son of God and our Savior. They are wonderful models for us today, at a time when the Church, as always, desperately needs models of faith for both women and men.

But first we must reclaim women's stories. Recognizing that the diminishment of the experience of women occurred, we can better understand why there often is a poverty of feminine images and stories within the Church today. Digging deeply into the wealth of the history and tradition of the Church, we can find these stories. These women were real, and their presence and contribution to the Church was, and is today, significant.

In the Book of Galatians in the Bible, the early Church was instructed that there should not be any separation within the Church because of who a person was or was not: "There is no longer Jew or Greek, there is no longer slave or free, there is no longer male and female; for all of you are one in Christ Jesus" (3:28). In other words, wealth, social status, nationality, and gender made absolutely no difference. This was a radical departure from the way society was structured. Imagine how hope-filled and empowered people living on the edge of society must have felt to hear this news proclaimed.

It is always a difficult task to attempt to interpret a time and a culture that is not our own. What easily happens is that our personal feelings and biases get in the way. Without meaning to do so, we often superimpose our attitudes and ideas onto a different time and culture, and end up with erroneous interpretations. Also, when looking into the past, we often attempt to make logical assumptions and conclusions from incomplete data. This, too, can cause misinterpretations. In fact, it should be noted that there is considerable controversy among some historians and biblical scholars over whether or not women were truly oppressed during the time of Jesus.

Some experts feel that the oppression of women that was a part of Hebrew society lessened with the influence of Greek culture and education in first-century Palestine. Others argue that Greek culture, like most ancient systems, was itself patriarchal and dominated legally, socially, and economically by men. Perhaps a middle ground can be found by acknowledging that patriarchy existed and women were indeed oppressed in

Hebrew society. However, there probably was some diminishment of patriarchal law, especially in cities, in later centuries. During the life of Jesus, however, gender equality under the law, and in most other areas of society, was not the general experience of women.

Jesus preached and lived a radical equality that was meant for his followers then, just as it is meant for the Church today. Jesus valued and respected his friendships with women. He included many women in his closest circle of friends and treated them as equals. Jesus trusted women. It was to women that Jesus chose to appear first after his resurrection.

Jesus had compassion for the physical and emotional suffering of marginalized women. Jesus healed women who were considered ritually "unclean," demon-possessed, or otherwise sinful. And perhaps most comforting, Jesus never refused to heal a woman who came to him. Because of their faith, he cured them with his healing touch.

This book is about women of faith—women who made a difference in the history of the Church and women whose faith is shaping the Church today. Whether you are a woman or a man, aspects of your faith journey will resonate with theirs. Come find yourself in the pages. As a person of faith, you deserve to know your story.

A Survey of Your Thoughts and Opinions

It might be a good idea, before you go any further, to spend some time with your own thoughts about what you have just read and to acknowledge your opinions, feelings, or even biases. By this point in your life, you probably have some pretty strong feelings about certain matters of faith. Spend some time with these open-ended questions and see where your thoughts take you. Perhaps use a journal to reflect on some of your feelings, or, if you are comfortable doing so, share your thoughts with another person. Feel free to add to this survey any questions that speak to your heart.

1. To me, religion means . . .

2. If I were asked to describe the Catholic Church in one sentence, I would say . . .

3. It seems as if almost every Christian religion has a different understanding of the Bible. To me, the Bible . . .

4. I wonder if Jesus really liked / disliked some people more than others?

5. When I think about Jesus, I wish I knew what his laughter sounded like, or what made him sad, or . . .

6. If Jesus were to appear physically in the world today, I think I would find him at . . .

7. Jesus identified himself with people of faith who also were often marginalized by society. I wonder who Jesus would feel is truly "keeping the faith" today?

8. To me, a Church of equality means . . .

9. If someone asked me to draw a symbol of my relationship with God and I could use no words, I would draw . . .

10. The most significant religious event that ever happened to me was . . .

Chapter One

Naming the Women

Christ Healing the Woman Who Was Hemorrhaging

Life in First-Century Palestine

Imagine for a few moments that you are a person living in Palestine during the time of Jesus. Whether you are a male or a female, you would have learned obedience from an early age, based on the examples found in the Torah (the first five books of the Hebrew Scriptures). Teachings such as the Ten Commandments, as well as many found in other books of Scripture, such as the Book of Proverbs, contained much of the wisdom that comprised the Hebrew moral code for life. These teachings stressed, first and foremost, love of God and then respect and love of parents.

Parents, on the other hand, were instructed through some biblical texts to chastise and even physically punish their children if they truly loved them. To do otherwise was seen as nothing short of neglect. It is from writings such as these, found in Proverbs, that parents were admonished not to "spare the rod" unless they were willing to have their children become willful and self-indulgent. This must not be interpreted, however, to mean that Hebrew parents did not love their children. In their society, children were seen as nothing less than blessings from God, and to be childless was a terrible misfortune.

Of course at that time there was also a not-so-hidden agenda in Hebrew society when it came to children. Like their mothers, children were considered the property of their fathers. Large families, especially families with many boys, increased a

father's standing in his community and provided the necessary laborers for all the work that had to be done. But even more important to the male head of the household provided the continuation of the family line and name. Since daughters were generally destined for marriage and would thus become a part of their husbands' households, the family that had only daughters was in a difficult place. For this reason alone, the birth of sons was especially desirable.

Boys began their formal education at around the age of five or six, with the reading of the Torah providing the basis for all subjects. In addition, sons generally were taught the trade of their fathers. Association with an honest trade was very important in Hebrew society, which might be one reason that Jesus was so frequently identified as a carpenter's son or as being a carpenter himself. For boys who were able to receive it, secondary education, provided by a rabbi, was generally available. These boys sat around the rabbi's feet as ideas and questions were presented to them.

As Carla Ricci notes in her book *Mary Magdalene and Many Others, Women Who Followed Jesus* (Minneapolis: Augsburg Fortress Press, 1994), girls were not totally excluded from learning the Torah. Those sections that pertained to the things that females were not to do, those things that began with "Do not," were to be learned by all young women. With this one exception, however, the Torah was considered basically off limits to girls. "If anyone teaches his daughter the Torah, it is as though he were teaching her obscenity . . . the words of the Torah should be destroyed by fire rather than be taught to girls . . . a girl should not be taught anything except how to use a spindle."

Words such as these sound so harsh and demeaning that it is difficult to even imagine how they could have been written, let alone given any importance. We can only wonder if these words sounded as harsh and hateful to young girls of that time and place as they do to us today. It is probable that young women and men would have just accepted that this was how things were meant to be. After all, they would not have had many models or options for change. Also, from an early age, they would have been told that this was how God ordained things. We do the same sometimes, usually without realizing it. (We will see how our own attitudes affect our understanding of our present experience of Church in chapters 8 and 9.)

While it is true that using a spindle to make cloth was one of the things about which young girls were educated, it certainly was not the only thing. However, almost all of what a girl did learn would have been associated with homemaking. For example, young women learned how to faithfully observe all the strict dietary regulations from the Torah regarding the preparation of food. According to Hebraic Law, it was forbidden to cook meat dishes together with milk or to eat the meat of swine (pigs). Foods such as these were considered ritually unclean. In addition to the great number of such dietary laws that were necessary for girls to know, they would also have been trained in all the other aspects of caring for a home and a family. Grinding grain and making bread, sewing, weaving, mending, caring for children, and sometimes also tending livestock—all were considered part of a proper education for young girls. Of course generally their mothers would have trained the girls in these skills so that one day their daughters would be able to assume their responsibilities as good wives and mothers.

In the Hebrew culture of first-century Palestine, both boys and girls had much to learn in a relatively short time. There was no such thing as adolescence or being a teenager, since adulthood came about the age of thirteen. In the time of Jesus, there was only the time of being a child and then the time of being an adult. Since the average life span probably was around forty-five years of age, people did not have the luxury of delaying marriage nor of postponing the birth of their children. Therefore, shortly after reaching the age of adulthood, young girls generally were betrothed. A betrothal could be compared to an engagement of today, but only in the most casual sense, for a betrothal was more of a contractual arrangement. It consisted of an agreement to marry, an exchange of gifts, and the paying of the "bride price."

The bride price, to our modern sensibilities, sounds a great deal as if a young girl was being sold to her prospective husband. Perhaps, considering the lack of personal choice involved, she really was being sold. But actually, the purpose of the bride price was to provide compensation to the girl's family—to make up, in some small way, for the family's loss of their daughter's labor. Since marriage was considered such a serious matter, parents arranged almost all marriages. Our relatively modern idea of "marrying for love" would, no doubt, have been considered very foreign to the people of this time—probably even quite dangerous. It was believed that marriage was best entrusted to those who knew. No doubt, parents felt that a good marital match would ultimately lead to love between the new husband and wife.

Of course the fact that the betrothed's father was receiving payment for his daughter probably had something to do with the serious and contractual nature of the matter. But the bride price may also have acted as a sort of insurance policy for the new wife. If she should be widowed, or if her husband wanted to divorce her (women had no rights to ask for divorce, even if they were being abused), then the bride price would provide a temporary source of financial support for her. Quite often, however, the bride price for a daughter was what the father used to secure a good wife for his son. In other words, the money or property or goods that were acquired through the betrothal and subsequent marriage of a man's daughter could be used for the betterment of his son.

It is evident, even from such a cursory look at life in the time of Jesus, that it was not an easy existence for persons of either gender. Work was hard and long, but life usually was not long. Disease, natural disasters, and lack of adequate sanitation and medical care took their toll. But in a very significant way, the oppression of females within the Hebrew culture was a type of oppression that was so pervasive and so much a part of society that it generally was not even recognized as such. Unlike other factors of life in first-century Palestine, such as those just mentioned, this element targeted persons of only one gender. For example, while anyone could fall victim to a serious illness and everyone had to endure rather primitive medical care by modern standards, only women carried the added burden of having normal bodily functions, such as menstruation, labeled as "disease." In fact, because women had a monthly flow of blood and thus broke the "blood taboo," they were considered ritually unclean during that time.

Blood taboos were found frequently in ancient cultures. Since blood flow was recognized as a powerful force of life, anything associated with loss of blood was a very serious matter. For the Hebrew people, the blood taboo forbade, for example, the drinking of any blood of an animal as well as the improper slaughter of certain animals or the improper preparation of meat. But regarding women, the blood taboo had a deeper, darker significance. Here, the blood flow of menstruation was seen as a punishment from God, a belief that was reinforced by rabbinic authority.

> *According to Jewish rabbinic tradition, three precepts are incumbent only on women: the lighting of candles at the onset of the Sabbath, the separation and burning of a small piece of dough prior to baking bread, and the observance of the laws of menstrual purity, called* Niddah*. . . Concerning menstruation: The first man was the blood and life of the world, and Eve was the cause of his death; therefore has she been given the menstruation precept. The same is true concerning* Challah *(leaven): Adam was the pure* Challah *of the world . . . and Eve was the cause of his death; therefore has she been given the* Challah *precept. And concerning the lighting of the [Sabbath] lamp: Adam was the light of the world . . . and Eve was the cause of his death; therefore has she been given the precept about lighting the [Sabbath] lamp. Failure to observe these precepts causes women to die in childbirth.*
>
> Ross S. Kraemer, *Her Share of the Blessings* (New York: Oxford University Press, 1992).

It's evident, from this brief look at just some of the aspects of life in first-century Palestine, that life was very regimented for women. Even before birth, a girl's very existence was less desired than that of a male. Women's access to education was controlled and limited. Life choices were not necessarily theirs to make, as in the area of marriage. Even a woman's right to the privacy of her own body was denied, as she was blamed and shamed for her God-given ability to share in the natural cycles of fertility and procreation. As a final indignity, she would have been taught to believe from her earliest days that all of these things, all of these ways of being, were because God simply desired that they should be so.

Having some sense of what women of this time and place in history would have believed, or at the very least would have had to endure, imagine how liberating the message of Jesus must have been. News of his powerful and impassioned preaching, his working of miracles in God's very name, his associating with the people that society shunned, must have burst across the region like the good news that it was! For some women, it was enough to allow them to break free of religious and cultural barriers that had contained and shaped their entire lives. These women became part of the inner circle of Jesus' closest friends. Their lives were changed forever.

The Women Who Walked with Jesus as His Companions

You may be familiar with the term *follower of Jesus* because it is one used frequently. A follower of Jesus would have been anyone, male or female, who believed in the teachings of Jesus, who followed him, and who sought to imitate his way of life. In the New Testament there are many references to Jesus as "rabbi" or "teacher," and teachers of the time frequently had their followers. Jesus certainly did, and in the most common understanding of the term, the women who were with Jesus were his "followers." But sometimes it can be helpful to take a new look at the way we choose our words to describe such important aspects of our faith. Perhaps an even more descriptive term, and one closer to historical reality, would be to describe the women who were with Jesus as "those *companions* who walked *with* him," not *behind* him, as is suggested by the image of a follower. All of this may sound quite trivial until we look at the origin of the word *companion*.

Remember that words can convey powerful meaning and significance. If someone special ever praised you as a child, you learned this lesson long ago. Conversely, if you have ever been hurt by someone's thoughtless words, then they may have echoed those words in your mind for a long, long time. Words are powerful shapers of our thoughts, even sometimes of our identities. They also, of course, help shape our theology—how we understand God and how we understand ourselves in relation to God.

The word *companion* comes from the Latin *companio*, which is a compound noun formed from the Latin words *com* ("with") and *panis* ("bread") (John Ayto, *Dictionary of Word Origins* [New York: Arcade Publishing, Inc., 1991]). Therefore, a companion is someone with whom you share your bread. To our modern way of thinking, this probably seems of little significance, since, for many people, mealtimes have become so casual. But in the time of Jesus, sharing your bread with someone implied a relationship of trust and closeness.

Since Jesus traveled extensively through Galilee and Judea and really had no home to call his own, his companions would have been those people whom he most trusted. They would have been his inner circle of friends and his support. They would have known him best, loved him, and believed in his mission, even financing it out of their own means. They would have been like family to each other, a family comprised of women and men of faith. We can be certain of this because of one significant clue regarding women, which we find in the Bible in Luke 8:1–3. Here, some of the companions of Jesus are mentioned by name, and their importance to his ministry is stressed.

> *Soon afterwards he went on through cities and villages, proclaiming and bringing the good news of the kingdom of God. The twelve were with him, as well as some women who had been cured of evil spirits and infirmities: Mary, called Magdalene, from whom seven demons had gone out, and Joanna, the wife of Herod's steward Chuza, and Susanna, and many others, who provided for them out of their resources.*

Knowing how restrictive life was for Hebrew women of this time, it seems nothing less than amazing to think that these women were able to journey with Jesus at all. We can only wonder what consequences they may have faced either within their own families of origin or within society in general. Remember that single women would have been under the control of their fathers and married women under the control of their husbands. Did their close association with Jesus damage their relationships with their families? Were their reputations as good and decent women harmed? Scripture gives us no answers but actually generates even more questions.

For example, were some of the women's family members also disciples of Jesus? Would they, too, have been part of the group that traveled with him? Or were some of the women without family members at all and, thus, adrift in Hebrew society? And some of the women must have had access to money, as we are told that they provided for Jesus out of their own resources. (Perhaps the women who had some financial resources had been city dwellers, where the slightly less restrictive influence of Greek culture might have allowed them to have some personal property and goods.) Unfortunately, the answers to these questions are probably lost in time, but at least from the clues we can find in Scripture and in the early tradition of the Church, there is still plenty of information to be gained. Let's start with Mary of Magdala (Mary Magdalene).

Mary of Magdala

There probably is no woman in Scripture who has been more demeaned than Mary Magdalene. (Unless, of course, you consider the unnamed woman of Luke 7:36–50, who anointed Jesus' feet, first with her tears and then with ointment, and whose sins Jesus freely forgave.) The fact that this woman and Mary Magdalene are so frequently thought of as being the same person no doubt accounts for part of this association. Carla Ricci, in her book *Mary Magdalene and Many Others, Women Who Followed Jesus*, suggests a very plausible reason for the confusion. The sinful woman of the anointing story immediately precedes the introduction of Mary Magdalene as a companion of Jesus in his ministry and as the woman "from whom seven demons had gone out" (Luke 7:36–8:3).

On this rather sketchy association, biblical scholars of the past have identified the two women as one and the same, and this identification, until recently, has been readily accepted by many. How ironic that perhaps the dearest female friend that Jesus had would have been identified as a sinful woman (probably a prostitute, since women's sinfulness was generally associated with sexual sins of some nature, whether or not that was actually the case). Then, too, Mary Magdalene is sometimes mistaken for Mary of Bethany, who was also a good friend of Jesus and who, like the sinful woman of Luke 7:36–50, anointed him with expensive perfumed oils.

Who Mary Magdalene actually was, historically, was a woman of great faith who did her best to be a true disciple of Jesus. She managed to do this so well that even the writers of Scripture,

Mary Magdalene

who hardly ever mentioned women at all, let alone named them, always listed her first whenever any women's names were given. As Jesus ministered in the land of Galilee, she was by his side. Since women of that time were generally limited to roles of domestic service, it would be understandable if assumptions were made, however incorrectly, that Mary and other women were there merely to care for the daily needs of Jesus and the Twelve (the men). In fact, we do a great disservice to her memory and to the memory of the other women disciples if we diminish their contributions in this manner. This is especially true since nothing in Jesus' contact with women leads us to the conclusion that he would differentiate in this way between his disciples, relegating women into roles of servitude to the everyday needs of the men. In fact, all that Jesus ever modeled for his followers was a discipleship of equality.

From Luke 8:1–3, Mary Magdalene and several other women were seemingly there in partnership and solidarity with Jesus. And Mary Magdalene, who was with Jesus in his life-giving ministry, was also brave enough to stand at the foot of the cross as Jesus died. Even as so many of the other disciples fled the horror of his tortured death by crucifixion, Mary stayed, and so did some other women, as recorded in Mark 15:40–41.

> *. . . among them were Mary Magdalene, and Mary the mother of James the younger and of Joses, and Salome. These used to follow him and provided for him when he was in Galilee; and there were many other women who had come up with him to Jerusalem.*

What Mary Magdalene did was incredibly compassionate, for the comfort of her physical presence was all that she could give Jesus as he hung on the cross, slowly dying. It was also incredibly brave, for to be identified in any way as a follower, or a disciple, or even just as someone who knew Jesus, was dangerous to the extreme. (If you are familiar with the biblical account of the events leading up to the crucifixion, you will remember Peter's fearful denial of Jesus.) Terrified of being recognized as one of Jesus' disciples, Peter let his fear temporarily win out over his love for his friend. He finally understood what the fate of Jesus was to be, and he recoiled at the thought of meeting a similar destiny. His choice, and the choice of all the other male disciples except John, was to flee, to hide. This makes Mary Magdalene's choice, and the decision of the other women who stayed, all the more remarkable.

We can assume that they must have felt abandoned, too. As they watched Jesus die, they must have felt as if all of their

hopes for a different way of life, a life of equality and respect and dignity was dying, too. Still, they did not run and hide but stayed with their friend until the end. Finally, it was to the women that Jesus chose to appear upon his resurrection, and then it was these very same women whom he sent as apostles to testify to the other disciples of his rising from the dead. This is all the more astounding when we know that, according to Hebraic Law, women were not allowed to give testimony. The four Gospels all list Mary Magdalene as being the first witness to the resurrection, but they differ somewhat on who else was present.

- The Gospel according to Matthew records that "the other Mary" was also with Mary Magdalene (Matthew 28:1–10).

- The Gospel according to Mark tells us that Mary Magdalene, Mary, the mother of James, and Salome were present (Mark 16:1–8).

- The Gospel according to Luke explains that Joanna, Mary, the mother of James, and "the others who accompanied them" were with Mary Magdalene at the tomb (Luke 23:55–24:11).

- The Gospel according to John names only Mary Magdalene (John 20:1–18).

These differences in lists of who was actually present are understandable when we remember that the Gospels were written at different times by human authors who sought to emphasize different aspects of the story. What is remarkable is that the male authors of the Gospels mentioned any of the women by name at all.

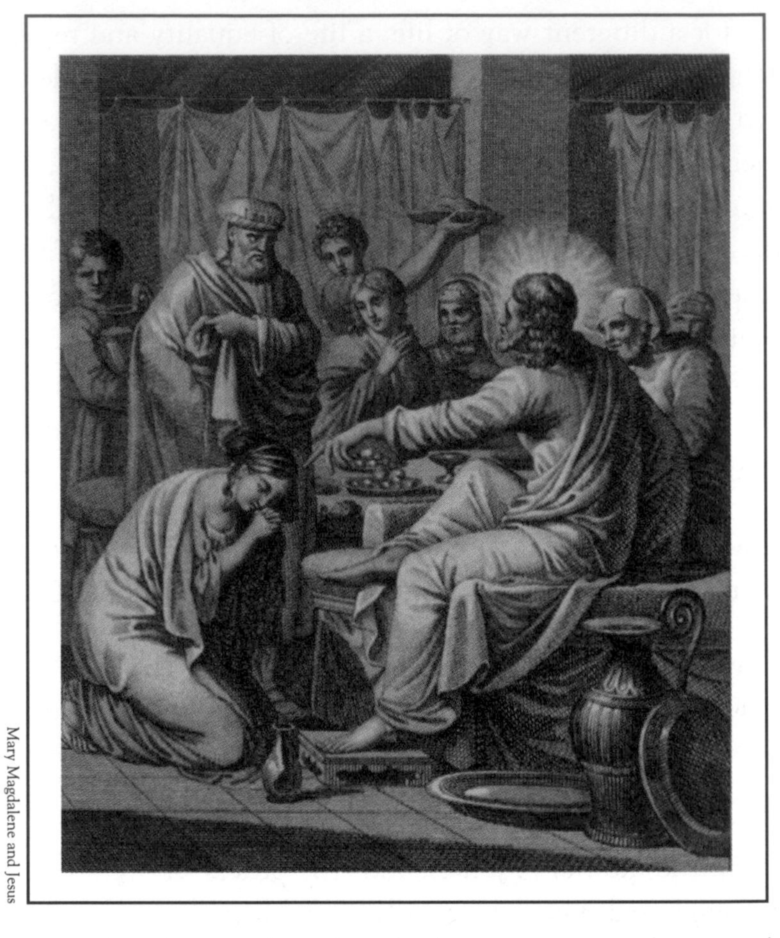

Mary Magdalene and Jesus

It is really a loss to the Church that more is not known about the women of the Gospels. Surely their faith stories and their life experiences would be incredibly inspiring. (Of course it is not only the details regarding women that are overlooked or dismissed within Scripture; just think of how little we know about the childhood of Jesus, for example.) But one very intriguing fact is mentioned repeatedly about Mary Magdalene whenever she is named in the Gospels. That fact is that she was the woman from whom Jesus drove out seven demons.

The idea of demon possession seems very strange to modern minds. It conjures up all sorts of images, usually similar to the ones we might see on television on Halloween or on Friday the 13th. (Even in the twenty-first century, we are fascinated by the unknown or by the imagined. Actually, it is probably our imaginations that can, at times, be the most frightening of all.) In the case of Mary Magdalene, we will never know exactly what was meant by "seven demons." This is just one more of those facts that have been lost through time. We can, however, make some logical assumptions.

In the time of Jesus, not much was really known about the causes of physical illness, let alone about how to cure sickness. Medical care, by today's standards, would have been quite primitive. Also, disease was often considered a punishment from God for disobedience. Diseases such as leprosy, bubonic plague, tuberculosis, and cholera were dreaded, but none would have been more frightening to people of that time than mental illness.

Mental illness, of any sort, would always have been attributed to demons living within the sick person's body. Perhaps Mary Magdalene had been mentally ill, and Jesus healed her. The only way that people of this time would have known to describe this would have been to say that the demons had been driven out of her body. To say that seven demons had been present would have signified a fullness or a completeness, since the number seven had that type of significance in Hebrew culture. This could either, then, have meant that Mary had been extremely mentally ill, or it could mean that she had been fully and completely cured of whatever mental illness or emotional illness once afflicted her.

There is another possibility, however. What if Mary Magdalene's "demon possession" was nothing more than a strong, healthy, and self-assured woman's normal reaction to living within a culture that was "sick" (in the sense of being dysfunctional or difficult for a person who did not cope well with the prevailing level of oppression)? Might Mary Magdalene have been a visionary who was way ahead of her time? Could it be a possibility that her actions and reactions to the limitations that her society placed upon her would have been interpreted as insane behavior? History is silent, and we are left to wonder: Did she fight against the way things were, and might she have been thought of as a little "strange"? It is an intriguing possibility. We will probably never know.

What we do know with some certainty, however, is that Mary Magdalene and other women disciples of Jesus were women whose presence to his ministry and to the development of the early Church was significant, meaningful, and definitely counter-cultural. As we have seen, some of the female desciples, like Mary Magdalene, Salome, and Joanna, were named in the Gospel narrative. Most were not. Seemingly, it was only when a woman's importance to the story could not be denied that we find her actually mentioned by name. This, however, in no way means that women were unimportant to Jesus, for they were. And it was not only his friends who mattered to him, such as the disciples we have already mentioned, and Mary and Martha, the sisters of Lazarus.

Once again, history is silent, and Scripture provides few clues. But it would be logical to assume that, on those rare occasions when Jesus could spare a few moments for himself, he might have spent them at the home of friends like Mary and Martha. The picture is clear. Jesus, the itinerant preacher with no home of his own, being followed by growing crowds of peoples clamoring for miracles, signs, and cures, must have been truly exhausted at times. It is nice to think that he may have found comfort and rest at the home of his dear friends.

Christ in the House of Martha and Mary

The Women Whom Jesus Healed

Mary Magdalene was not the only woman Jesus cured, of course. There is a story in the Gospels of Matthew (9:20–22), Mark (5:25–34), and Luke (8:43–48) that is a wonderful account of Jesus' compassion toward a woman whom society considered unclean. For twelve years this woman had suffered from some type of continuous, vaginal flow of blood. Remember that, according to the Hebrew law concerning blood flow, she was considered ritually unclean. Being ritually unclean meant that she was not allowed to associate with the people of her town. Not only was she thought of as unclean, but anyone or anything that she even touched was considered unclean as well. Just imagine what her life must have been like. For twelve long years she suffered physical pain, isolation from society, and probably, quite understandably, severe mental anguish. She no doubt bought into her culture's belief that God was punishing her. It is understandable, on our part, to believe that she would have felt totally forsaken and alone.

Just picture it: The woman had heard about Jesus and about the wonderful and miraculous healings and cures that he performed. She must have thought of him as her last hope ever to be freed from the prison of her pain and social isolation. This awareness made her brave enough to dare to approach him. And so she did, silently and with great fear, socially conditioned to believe that she had no business being anywhere near him or other good people. She knew that she must not speak to him, for to do so would break Hebraic Law, and this would bring significant consequences for her. But this meant that she could not ask him for a cure, which she so desperately needed. She also knew that even if she silently reached out to him, her touch would be enough to make Jesus unclean. She must have agonized over her decision. It is a sign of her intense desperation that she even dared to try anything. How inventive that she thought to touch the hem of his cloak. Perhaps it was just her desperation, since she also knew that even this touch by her would make Jesus ritually unclean. Still, she took the risk and was probably resigned to face whatever consequences befell her. She probably figured that nothing could be much worse than the anguish she was already living.

Scripture tells us that as Jesus approached, a huge crowd crushed in upon him. Everyone was excited to see him, for he was such a worker of miracles. The people in the crowd probably were there either to ask for healing for themselves or for a loved one. Maybe some of them were casual observers. Not this unnamed, bleeding, and suffering woman, however! As Jesus passed, she took her chance and touched the tassel at the bottom of his cloak. Immediately she felt herself cured. What joy she must have felt at that moment! But almost instantly, Jesus stopped and asked who had touched him. Discovered, the woman cowered in front of him, begging his forgiveness and his understanding. Jesus simply told her that her faith had healed her and that she should "go in peace."

It is pretty easy to understand how this unnamed, long-suffering woman must have felt as she heard the compassion in Jesus' voice rather than his condemnation. And, of course, her miraculous cure must have filled her heart with joy. What was

even more miraculous than her cure, however, was the powerful message that the crowd received concerning the Hebraic Law and the ritual uncleanliness of women. No more were women to be shamed for the natural, God-given cycles of their bodies that allowed them to share in the awesome act of giving life. No longer were they to feel isolated or to have their dignity as humans lessened. It would be nice to say that the people who witnessed Jesus' compassionate presence to this woman instantly understood and changed their attitudes and the laws that reflected their fears concerning the blood taboo. Unfortunately, this did not happen for them, even as it has not yet totally happened today.

The fact that this story was recounted in three of the Gospels, however, gives testimony to it's impact on the followers of Jesus as the developing movement grew and spread to other regions, including areas that were not familiar with the laws of the Hebrews. Not surprisingly, these different cultures had their own taboos, laws, and regulations regarding women, especially regarding women's sexuality and reproductive functions.

Found in the Gospel according to John 8:1–11 is the story of the woman who was caught in the act of adultery. She was brought before Jesus, no doubt to have him condemn her to her fate (which, according to the Hebraic Law, could have been stoning, even to the point of death). The woman must have been terrified. Instead of condemning her, however, Jesus forgave her and told her, "go and from now on do not sin anymore." Here is a perfect example of how Jesus could condemn and name sin for what it was while never condemning or hating the person who had sinned. There is more to this story, however, than what may first be readily apparent.

> *The question must be asked: Where was the man caught in adultery with the woman? Did he run away? Did he hide? So pervasive in Jewish society and in the subsequent centuries was the acceptance of an anti-woman sexual bias that no one has asked this crucial question. (When I recently raised the question of the man's whereabouts to a large group of women, one woman suggested calmly, 'He probably ran outside and picked up a stone.')*
>
> Rachel C. Wahlberg, *Jesus According to a Woman* (New York: Paulist Press, 1986).

This story is an excellent example today of how easy it is to accept concepts or ways of relating to people or to situations that are just not appropriate for where we should be as a modern society. The author quoted above is exactly right. Why has it taken biblical scholars all these centuries to realize what Jesus recognized immediately—that not only was there another person involved in the inappropriate sexual behavior, but that many of the men who brought her forth to be condemned may themselves have committed the same sin or sins just as serious. Jesus wrote something in the sand as the accusers brought forth this woman. Maybe he wrote the names of the women whom some of the men had been with the night before. Or maybe he wrote something from the Torah that shamed them in their prideful arrogance. At any rate, Scripture tells us that the men left Jesus, one by one. It is interesting to note that this is the only record that has ever been recorded of Jesus writing. By the men's reactions, we can assume that whatever he wrote was incredibly powerful.

Scripture contains many references to the care and concern, as well as the respect, that Jesus had for women. But even as these women's names are unknown to us, what also generally happens

is that the woman in the story becomes lost in the details that the male authors provide. In other words, what becomes most important to the story is not the woman as a person or even the solving of her problem or illness. Instead, if a woman is mentioned in Scripture at all, she is generally nameless, and she is used as little more than a backdrop to the issues that the Gospel writers wished to convey. An excellent example of this is the story of the Samaritan woman at the well that is found in John 4:4–42.

In this story, another nameless woman has a life-changing encounter with Jesus. Scripture tells us that she is a Samaritan woman. This factor is important to the story because Jews and Samaritans were at odds over many religious issues, and there was great animosity between the two groups. She was also a woman who had been married five times and who was currently living with a man to whom she was not married. Yet Jesus approached her and asked for a drink of water. During their discussion, he revealed to her that he was the Messiah. She questioned him, responded to him, believed him, and then left to go and tell the good news. And the people believed her! This nameless woman became the very first messenger to the world that Jesus was the long-awaited Messiah.

> *Could it be possible that Jesus saw this woman as one whom people would listen to precisely because she was different? Did he respond to her intelligence with a sense of expectation and confidence? Did he think of women as goers and doers, as articulate communicators? Did Jesus appraise this woman as a dynamic person who would make an impact on others . . . perhaps a woman who already in community eyes had broken with standards of propriety was one who had nothing to lose by being outspoken. . . . Could it be that Jesus had another motive, that he deliberately chose a woman to disperse some of the strictures he saw placed on women?*
>
> Wahlberg.

The Woman of Samaria and Jesus

Whatever his intent, it is certainly reasonable to assume that Jesus' choice of revealing his messiahship to the Samaritan woman was not an accidental one. We are left to speculate, however, on what change, if any, her encounter with Jesus had upon her life. Perhaps she, too, became a follower of Jesus. Or perhaps her "healing" came in knowing that Jesus saw her as a person of dignity and worth. Perhaps because the Messiah could see her this way, she could look at herself in a new way, too.

Even in spite of cultural bias, the love and the respect that Jesus had for women shines through the Gospels. The task for us as modern readers is to hear these stories in a new way and to look deeper into them to discover the richness and fullness that is there. We need to ask ourselves in what way Jesus is speaking to us across the centuries. For example, we never read that Jesus related to women in a way that would make them feel diminished as people. Do we? We never read that Jesus allowed cultural or gender stereotypes to get in the way of his inviting women into the full experience of their humanity. Do we? Jesus was not afraid to confront sin when he saw it and to name it for what it was. Do we? Jesus invited women into his ministry, not as servants, but as partners. He befriended women, he loved them, and he honored them. Jesus saw their femininity as a wonderful thing, not as a lesser thing or an evil thing. When women approached him in their need for physical or emotional healing, he never refused them or shamed them in any way; he simply healed them. Jesus was providing a model for his disciples to follow. If we are to consider ourselves Jesus' modern-day disciples (and we do, by calling ourselves Christian), then we need to listen to his voice today.

Some Thoughts for Your Reflection

1. Do you see any similarities between the culture of first-century Palestine and ours? Do we limit educational opportunities for anyone or take away his or her choices simply because of who he or she is as a person? If so, in what ways does this happen?

2. Does our culture observe any taboos, such as the blood taboo of ancient societies? (Think about some of the television commercials and magazine ads that you have seen recently. You might be surprised!)

3. Explore the concept of arranged marriages. Do you believe that people have to first "fall in love" before they marry, or do you believe that love can and does increase over time, especially if a couple share much in common?

4. Jesus refused to put labels on people. Think about your school, your work, your family, your friends. Without hurting anyone's feelings by identifying them specifically with a label, talk about or make a list of labels you hear and use. Do you feel that these labels help these people or hurt them as individuals or as members of a group? If you were to be given a label, what do you think it would be? If you were to label yourself, what label would you want to have, if any?

5. Make a list of adjectives that describe girls and women. Now make a list of adjectives that describe boys and men? How many of these descriptive words, for either gender, are negative? How many are positive? Do any words appear on both lists?

6. Find in one of the first three Gospels (Matthew, Mark, or Luke) a story that pertains to women, or use one of the stories mentioned in this chapter. Rewrite the story, putting it in the present time and modern language. How is the story different? How is it the same?

7. This chapter talked a lot about the stories of several women of faith. Do you know the faith stories of the women in your life? Spend some time with a woman with whom you are close, such as your mother, grandmother, aunt, friend, sister, or perhaps someone in your church community. Ask this person to tell you her faith stories. With her permission, you may want to record or videotape what she has to say.

Chapter Two

Blessed Are You among Women

Youth of Our Lord

Discovering Mary

If you were raised in the Catholic faith, then you probably already know quite a lot about Mary, the mother of Jesus. At least, this is what many of your friends who are not Catholic might assume, just by virtue of the fact that you are Catholic. Your friends might be surprised. Today, being Catholic is no longer an assurance that you either know a great deal about the Blessed Virgin Mary or even that you feel any spiritual or emotional connection to her. This is certainly understandable, in the sense that it really is hard, if not impossible, to love someone whom you do not know. It was different, however, for Catholics of previous generations. For them, people perhaps like your grandparents, Marian devotion was just a natural and integral part of the experience and expression of their Catholic faith. Praying the Rosary, attending novenas, keeping the First Saturdays, wearing a Marian scapular, all were familiar and well-loved devotions to many. In addition, the liturgical year was liberally sprinkled with solemnities, feast days, and memorial celebrations honoring Mary under different titles and aspects of her important role in the mystery of salvation.

To many Catholics today, especially those who are young, however, devotion to Mary seems almost quaint, a definite part of the past. Often the words and concepts associated with Marian doctrine and practice, such as some of those just mentioned, seem

strange to the point of sounding like an unknown language. And yet, the image of Mary is intricately woven into the fabric of Catholic faith and devotion. Perhaps no other human has ever been so loved and honored. In this chapter, we will look at how this one, young Jewish girl of so long ago, came to have such a profound impact on Catholic and Protestant theology, as well as on world history, art, and literature. It was such a profound effect, in fact, that more than two thousand years after her birth, she is still called "blessed among women."

A good place to begin is to define and briefly explain exactly what the Catholic Church teaches regarding Mary. Many of these teachings are among Catholic *doctrine*, and of these doctrines, two have been declared *dogmas*. The difference between the two levels of teaching is this: A *doctrine* is an official teaching of the Church that is part of and that reflects the teaching of Jesus. Doctrine is also seen as the application of the teaching of Jesus to the life of Christians. These applications can change and develop; they may even sometimes be in error. A *dogma* is a doctrine, a teaching of the Church, that meets three conditions: (1) It is found in Scripture or in the early tradition of the Church and thus is understood to be part of God's revelation. (2) The Church defines it as a revealed object of faith, without error. (3) It is so defined by solemn decree or in the Church's ordinary magisterium (universal teaching). To be defined by solemn decree it must be promulgated by either an ecumenical council of the Church, acting in union with the pope, or by the pope acting alone as head of the Universal Church. Explanations of a doctrine or a dogma may change somewhat as our understanding, with God's grace, increases.

Regarding Mary, the Church teaches four major doctrines, two of which are dogmas. These are:

1. Mary was a virgin before, during, and after the birth of Jesus (doctrine).
2. Mary's pregnancy was of divine origin (doctrine).
3. Because Jesus would receive his humanity from Mary, she was kept from original sin (the Immaculate Conception) (dogma).
4. At the end of her life, Mary was taken, body and soul, to heaven (the Assumption) (dogma).

Within the liturgy of the Church, which is the official prayer of the Church, Mary is honored with three solemnities. The first is the Immaculate Conception, celebrated on December 8. On January 1, the Solemnity of Mary, Mother of God, celebrates the fact that Jesus, while truly human, is also truly divine. Since Mary is the mother of Jesus, she, therefore, can rightly be called the Mother of God. This title—in the original Greek, *Theotokos*, "God bearer"—was first given to Mary at the Council of Ephesus in A.D. 431. The third solemnity, the Assumption of Mary, is celebrated on August 15.

In addition to the solemnities, the Church also honors Mary with two feast days and a number of memorials. The first feast day is the Visitation, celebrated on May 31, when the Church remembers Mary's visit to the home of her cousin Elizabeth after Mary learned that she was going to be the mother of Jesus. The Church celebrates the birthday of Mary on September 8. The memorials in honor of her include celebrations such as Our Lady of the Rosary (October 7) and Our Lady of Guadalupe (December 12).

Solemnities Honoring Mary

- The Immaculate Conception—December 8
- Mary, Mother of God—January 1
- The Assumption of Mary—August 15

Feast Days and Memorials

- Our Lady of Guadalupe—December 12
- Our Lady of Lourdes—February 11
- The Visitation—May 31
- Immaculate Heart—Saturday after Sacred Heart
- Our Lady of Mt. Carmel—July 16
- Dedication of Saint Mary Major—August 5
- Queenship of Mary—August 22
- The Birth of Mary—September 8
- Our Lady of Sorrows—September 15
- Our Lady of the Rosary—October 7
- Presentation of Mary—November 21

A Feast and Solemnity Celebrating Jesus (secondarily honoring Mary)

- The Presentation of the Lord—February 2. This feast commemorates the ceremony at which Jesus, as a baby, was brought to the temple, and Mary observed the purification rights, according to the Torah, that all women had to observe after childbirth.

- The Annunciation of the Lord—March 25. This solemnity recalls and celebrates the incarnation. When Mary responded affirmatively to the angel, "the Word was made flesh."

The Visit Between Mary and Elizabeth

As you can see from even this very brief look at some aspects of the theology of Mary (called *Mariology*), the Blessed Virgin Mary holds a very special and honored place in Catholic theology and practice. In addition, Mary has been an integral part of the private devotions of countless Catholics throughout the history of the Church. (Prayers such as the Rosary fall into this category of a private devotion, as does belief in the apparitions or appearances of Mary. Both of these topics will be discussed in more depth in later chapters). Now having briefly examined an overview of some components of Mariology, it is appropriate to refer to the *Catechism of the Catholic Church* to see what it has to say in regard to Mary.

By her complete adherence to the Father's will, to his Son's redemptive work, and to every prompting of the Holy Spirit, the Virgin Mary is the Church's model of faith and charity. Thus she is a "preeminent and . . . wholly unique member of the Church"; indeed, she is the "exemplary realization" (typus) *[*Lumen Gentium *53; 63]. (#967)*

*Her role in relation to the Church and to all humanity goes still further. "In a wholly singular way she cooperated by her obedience, faith, hope, and burning charity in the Savior's work of restoring supernatural life to souls. For this reason she is a mother to us in the order of grace" [*Lumen Gentium *61]. (#968)*

"All generations will call me blessed": *"The Church's devotion to the Blessed Virgin is intrinsic to Christian worship" [*Luke *1:48; Paul VI,* Marialis Cultus *56]. The Church rightly honors "the Blessed Virgin with special devotion. From the most ancient times the Blessed Virgin has been honored with the title of 'Mother of God,' to whose protection the faithful fly in all their dangers and needs. . . . This very special devotion . . . differs essentially from the adoration which is given to the incarnate Word and equally to the Father and the Holy Spirit, and greatly fosters this adoration" [*Lumen Gentium *66]. The liturgical feasts dedicated to the Mother of God and Marian prayer, such as the rosary, an "epitome of the whole Gospel," express this devotion to the Virgin Mary [cf. Paul VI,* Marialis Cultus *42;* Sacrosanctum Concilium *103]. (#971)*

Catechism of the Catholic Church (Washington, DC: United States Catholic Conference, 1994).

As you can see from the quotations from the Catechism, the Church is very supportive of a rightly formed devotion to Mary—one that does not diminish adoration to God but rather enhances it. In Marian theology, Scripture and the long-standing tradition of the Church are the basis for all Marian doctrine and devotion. Therefore, in order to discover the historical person of Mary, it will be necessary to examine Scripture in some detail. Although there is not a great deal of information about Mary in Scripture, it still serves as our earliest and most reliable source about the mother of Jesus.

Virgin Mary and Christ Child

The Mary of Scripture

Those persons who are looking for a complete and extensive profile of Mary in the New Testament are going to be disappointed. Much of Mary's life and her personal story are lost to us. Also, as was mentioned in the previous chapter, the human authors of the Bible were writing with a specific purpose in mind and to a specific audience. In this focus any woman—even the mother of Jesus—would not have merited an extensive mention. This does not mean, however, that there is no mention of Mary to be found in Scripture. The Bible does provide some clues, beginning with the earliest allusion to Mary that is found in Paul's Letter to the Galatians. (Remember that Scripture was not necessarily written in the order in which we now find it in the Bible. For example, although the Gospel according to Matthew is placed prior to the Gospel according to Mark in the Bible, almost all biblical scholars agree that Mark was composed first. Predating even Mark was Paul's Letter to the Galatians, probably written sometime between A.D. 54 and 57.)

In her book, *Alone of All Her Sex: The Myth and the Cult of the Virgin Mary*, Marina Warner writes about Paul's urgent desire to stress both the fullness of Christ's humanity as well as the fact that he was also the Son of God.

> *To drive his point about Jesus' humanity home, [Paul] tells his readers that Jesus was "made of a woman" (Galatians 4:4). It is the earliest reference to the mother of Christ that has come down to us, and it is a very quiet entrance for the Virgin Mary. . . . Apart from this passing and anonymous mention in Galatians, Paul never refers to Jesus' mother again. Nor is the rest of the New Testament more generous.*
>
> Marina Warner, *Alone of All Her Sex: The Myth and the Cult of the Virgin Mary* (New York: Vintage Books, 1983).

Aside from Mary's name, we really do not know much about her. For example, we do not know what Mary looked like, although we might assume that she would have had the traditional olive complexion, dark hair, and dark eyes of today's Middle Eastern peoples. Her age at the time of the annunciation is not known except that she was young and unmarried; therefore, she was most likely somewhere around the age of fourteen or fifteen, the traditional age at that time for marriage. How old she was at the end of her life is, and probably always will remain, a mystery. In addition, the few biblical references to appearances of Mary are often rather negative, as if the human authors of the Gospels sought to use her as a vehicle to get across a particular point or to reinforce a certain aspect of Christianity. An excellent example of this is found in the Gospel according to Mark, most certainly the earliest Gospel written, probably around the year A.D. 70.

Mary in the Gospel according to Mark

In Mark's narrative, Mary appears only once, and her presence seems to be unwanted. In fact, Mary seems diminished if not totally dismissed by her son (3:31–35). Later, she is referred to once again in the following manner, as the people of Nazareth sought to use his common origin as a reason to reject him: "Is he not the son of Mary . . . ?" (6:3). Digging deeper, however, we may find that there is more to the biblical references found in this Gospel than first seems apparent.

The story goes like this: Jesus had been teaching, preaching, and working many miracles, and, as we might imagine, large crowds had formed around him. Their demands on Jesus and on his disciples were probably great, and the Scripture reflects this: "And the crowd came together again, so that [Jesus and the Twelve] could not even eat" (3:20). Scripture continues to say, "When his family heard it, they went out to restrain him, for people were saying, 'He has gone out of his mind.' And the scribes who came down from Jerusalem said, 'He has Beelzebul, and by the ruler of the demons he casts out demons'" (3:21–22).

Mary and Jesus' family members were outside the house where Jesus is, and they sent word through the crowd that they would like to speak to him. Jesus no doubt realized why they were there, and he seemingly abruptly dismissed their concern (and them) by saying, "Whoever does the will of God is my brother and sister and mother" (3:35). Jesus' words regarding his family

could hardly sound harsher. How out of character it seems for Jesus, the epitome of compassion, charity, and love, to treat in this way his mother and his family who loved him.

This is mere speculation, but it does seem possible that Mary's presence, as cited in this passage of Scripture, was used as an opportunity to convey a significant theological message. In this instance, that message would be that loyalty and love of God and others is more important than earthly family ties or concerns. This seems a logical assumption, but then we also need to remember that it was Mary's trust in God and her willingness to "do the will of God" that made possible Jesus' birth in the first place. Surely he had not forgotten this anymore than Mary would have forgotten the divine mystery that surrounded her baby's birth.

Consideration might also be given to the possibility that perhaps it was not Mary's concern at all that her son had "gone out of his mind" but rather the concern of the scribes who had come down from Jerusalem. They certainly would look for a way to curtail Jesus' ministry and lessen his popularity with the people. But this would not have been Mary's desire. As a mother, it was more likely that Mary, upon learning that Jesus was not even taking time to eat, would want to check on his physical well-being and offer to assist Jesus in whatever he may have needed.

If Jesus was truly frustrated with his family, an assumption could be made that his frustration was similar to that of any person who is passionate and zealous about something. A passionate person focuses on a goal and does not want to be distracted or detoured from achieving that goal. Jesus may have used the occasion of his family's visit as an opportunity not to reject or scold them, but to teach those present about the primacy of place that love of God should have in a person's life. After all, his mother would hardly

need to hear a lecture of that kind. At any rate, the Gospel falls silent after Jesus' discourse about "Whoever does the will of God is my brother and sister and mother." We are left to wonder if Jesus did see his mother and the rest of his family after all.

More problematic for the Church than Jesus' possible attitude toward his mother in this passage from Mark is its reference to other siblings of Jesus: "Then his mother and his brothers came" (3:31). Later in the same Gospel, Mary is mentioned for the second and last time, but again, so are Jesus' siblings: "Is not this the carpenter, the son of Mary and brother of James and Joses and Judas and Simon, and are not his sisters here with us?" (6:3).

This Scripture passage is frequently cited by those who believe that, contrary to the teaching of the Catholic Church, Mary did not remain virginal. At first glance, it would indeed seem that this passage validates such a belief—that after the birth of Jesus, Mary and Joseph assumed a normal marital relationship and had other children. There is, however, a different interpretation that can be made of these two Scripture verses from the Gospel according to Mark. This interpretation, as taught by the Catholic Church, supports the concept of Mary's perpetual virginity.

In the Hebrew language, *brothers* and *sisters* are two words that can be used to describe other familial relationships, such as nephews, nieces, cousins, half-brothers, and half-sisters. In translating from the Aramaic oral traditions to the Greek of the finally written Gospel, clear designations were not made at times. Therefore, when the Gospel according to Mark refers to the brothers or to the brothers and sisters of Jesus, it is possible that Mark was referring to family members other than siblings. (Two English words, although somewhat dated, that would be of comparable translation would be to refer to family members as *brethren* or as *kin*.)

Mary in the Gospel according to John

Just as the Gospel according to Mark was the earliest Gospel written, the Gospel according to John was the last, most likely written somewhere between A.D. 90 and 100. In John, the mother of Jesus makes two appearances, both of which are highly significant to Mariology, even though, ironically, Mary is not mentioned by name in either account. The first appearance of Mary occurs at the wedding feast at Cana. Of special interest is the fact that this account includes a conversation between Jesus and Mary, one of only two recorded in the entire New Testament.

In the Gospel story (John 2:1–12), Mary, Jesus, and the disciples were invited to a wedding at Cana, in Galilee. In all likelihood, it was either the wedding of a family member or of a close friend of Mary and Jesus, although this is not specifically noted in Scripture. When there was not enough wine to go around (which would have been a tremendous embarrassment to the host and a breach of hospitality), Mary sought to intercede with her son. The Gospel records her as simply saying to Jesus, "They have no wine." Jesus replied, "Woman, what concern is that to you and to me? My hour has not yet come." Mary then said to the servers, "Do whatever he tells you" (2:3–5).

Again, as in the Gospel according to Mark, it appears as if Jesus was being very abrupt with his mother. In particular, his use of the title "woman" when addressing her seems incredibly disrespectful to our modern ears. *The Catholic Study Bible* (New York: Oxford University Press, 1990) notes, however, that Jesus' use of the word *woman* to address his mother would have been a normal, polite form of address for that time.

Regardless of his own concerns, however, Jesus complied with his mother's wish, and he asked the servers to fill six, large stone jars with water. Then he told them to dip some out and to take it to the server in charge. Immediately the servers knew what had happened. More importantly, Jesus' "disciples believed in him" (2:11). This was the first miracle Jesus performed, and it was also the only one that was ever recorded as being done to an object rather than to a person.

Since Jesus performed this miracle at the request of his mother, and seemingly against his own judgment or desire, this incident at Cana became the basis for a strong belief, by many, in Mary's role as mediator with Christ. To this day this is an issue of theological discourse, as the Church seeks to define an authentic and balanced Mariology. What happened at Cana is only one small part of an expanding theological debate regarding Mary that we will examine in more detail in chapter 6.

Maurice Hamington states that many theologians and popes have used the Cana story as a biblical foundation for Mary's mediation.

> *Interpreting the story of the feast at Cana, Pope John Paul II in his encyclical* The Mother of the Redeemer *attempted to balance Mariology and Christology. He proclaimed that Mary did indeed intercede at Cana, but the Pope placed this intercession in the context of Jesus' mission: At Cana in Galilee there is shown only one concrete abstract of human need, apparently a small one and of little importance ("They have no wine"). But it has symbolic value: this coming to the aid of human needs means, at the same time, bringing those needs within the radius of Christ's messianic power. Thus there is mediation. . . . At Cana, thanks to the intercession of Mary and the obedience of the servants, Jesus begins "his hour."*
>
> Maurice Hamington, *Hail Mary? The Struggle for Ultimate Womanhood in Catholicism* (New York: Routledge, 1995).

The second appearance of Mary is also in the Gospel according to John, this time at the foot of the cross, as her son hangs dying (John 19:25–30). The account tells us that with Mary is her sister, Mary the wife of Clopas, and Mary of Magdala (Mary Magdalene), and the disciple, John. The Gospel records that, "When Jesus saw his mother and the disciple whom he loved standing beside her, he said to his mother, 'Woman, here is your son.' Then he said to the disciple, 'Here is your mother.' And from that hour the disciple took her into his own home" (19:26–27).

For the Catholic Church, Jesus' words from the cross to John regarding Mary are highly significant on at least two levels. These words support the doctrine that Mary was a virgin before, during, and after the birth of Jesus. Assuming that Mary's husband was dead, why would Jesus need to entrust the care of his mother to John if Jesus had brothers? According to Hebraic law and Jewish custom, Mary would not have been

Weeping Madonna

able to live on her own without being under the care and the legal protection of a man. This care, assuming that her husband was deceased, would normally fall to a male relative, often the eldest son. To ask someone like John to care for her certainly would support the argument that Mary had no other children, thus substantiating the Church's doctrine that Mary was truly "ever virgin."

Of more significance than this, however, is the symbolism present in the action of the "giving" of his mother (who now becomes our spiritual mother) to John (who in this instance represents all of humanity). In other words, Mary's continuing *fiat*, her acceptance of God's will in her life and of Christ's supreme act of atonement for the sins of humanity, unite her in a special way to those actions. Lending further clarity to this important aspect of Mariology, the Church taught in the Second Vatican Council's "Dogmatic Constitution on the Church":

> *Thus, in a wholly singular way she cooperated by her obedience, faith, hope and burning charity in the work of the Savior in restoring supernatural life to souls. For this reason she is a mother to us in the order of grace. This motherhood of Mary in the order of grace continues uninterruptedly from the consent which she loyally gave at the Annunciation and which she sustained without wavering beneath the cross, until the eternal fulfillment of all the elect (#s 61–62).*
>
> "Dogmatic Constitution on the Church," *Vatican Council II: The Conciliar and Post Conciliar Documents*, Austin Flannery, Gen. Ed. (Collegeville, MN: The Liturgical Press, 1975), pp. 418–19.

Mary in the Gospel according to Matthew

John's Gospel, on many levels, is richly symbolic and poetic. So, too, in it's own way, is the Gospel according to Matthew. Its human author, who was writing for a primarily Jewish audience, heavily uses allusions to the Hebrew Scriptures (Old Testament). In this way, Jesus' birth is seen as having been foretold and is, therefore, seen as a fulfillment of prophecy. The Gospels according to Matthew and Luke are the only Gospels to include an infancy narrative. Both Gospels were probably written about eighty years after Christ's birth, so it is understandable how that amount of time would allow for a well-developed linkage to Jewish prophetic fulfillment as seen in this Gospel.

The opening narrative of Matthew begins with an extensive genealogy of Jesus, a descendent from the House of David. Thus Jesus is presented as the true Messiah, the total fulfillment of the Law. This was of paramount importance to Matthew. In the Gospel, Mary, who is central to the narrative, is silent, and the events directly associated with her are often quickly turned toward associations with prophecy. An example of this with which you may be familiar is found in the first chapter of Matthew. Please note that Mary and Joseph's betrothal would have been taken as a very serious and contractual agreement, as all betrothals were. Legally, it would have been considered almost as binding as marriage. For that reason, betrothed couples such as Mary and Joseph were thought of as virtually married. Thus, in the following excerpt, Joseph, while not yet wed to Mary, is nonetheless called her "husband."

Now the birth of Jesus the Messiah took place in this way. When his mother Mary had been engaged to Joseph, but before they lived together, she was found to be with child from the Holy Spirit. Her husband Joseph, being a righteous man and unwilling to expose her to public disgrace, planned to dismiss her quietly. But just when he had resolved to do this, an angel of the Lord appeared to him in a dream and said, "Joseph, son of David, do not be afraid to take Mary as your wife, for the child conceived in her is from the Holy Spirit. She will bear a son, and you are to name him Jesus, for he will save his people from their sins." All this took place to fulfill what had been spoken by the Lord through the prophet: "Look, the virgin shall conceive and bear a son, and they shall name him Emmanuel," which means, "God is with us" (Matthew 1:18–23).

The Annunciation

As you can imagine, Matthew 1:18 is somewhat problematic for the Church in regard to Mary's perpetual virginity when it speaks of the time "before they lived together." Even more difficult, at first glance, is Matthew 1:25: "[Joseph] had no marital relations with her until she had borne a son; and he named him Jesus." Regarding the first passage, Joseph and Mary's betrothal (as all betrothals) would have been considered the first part of a marital union. Usually, after a period of several months, the betrothed couple would then establish a home together. In that sense, it could be said that Joseph and Mary "lived together." Today's modern understanding of the term would not necessarily apply, and we should be careful not to attribute more to the passage than was originally intended. *The Catholic Study Bible* explains this passage in the following manner: "The evangelist (Matthew) is concerned to emphasize that Joseph was not responsible for the conception of Jesus. The Greek word translated "until" does not imply normal marital conduct after Jesus' birth, nor does it exclude it."

Matthew's infancy narrative continues with the visit of the Magi (2:11), where Mary is seen with her child, Jesus. Immediately after their departure, Joseph was warned in a dream to flee Egypt with Jesus and his mother so that Herod could not harm Jesus (2:12–15). After Herod's death, an angel once again interceded, this time to let Joseph know that it was safe to return from Egypt: "Then Joseph got up, took the child and his mother, and went to the land of Israel" (2:21). As you can see from the infancy narrative of Matthew, Mary, although mentioned and obviously central to all that is taking place, becomes somewhat of a passive participant in this Gospel writer's story.

Mary in the Gospel according to Luke

Luke's Gospel was written slightly later than Matthew's and was directed toward a non-Jewish or Gentile audience. His infancy narrative, like Matthew's, brings heaven and earth together through the mystery and majesty of angelic visitors, miracles, and extraordinary phenomena (such as the star that shone over the place of Jesus' birth). Unlike Matthew's Gospel, however, Mary is at the heart of all the action, even being given voice by the author on five occasions, one of which is the *Magnificat*, Mary's psalm of praise (1:46–55). The enigmatic scene where Jesus, as a child of twelve, was "lost" but then found in the temple, astounding the rabbis with his understanding and knowledge (2:41–52) is one of only two times when Jesus and Mary are recorded, in Scripture, as speaking directly to each other. The other occasion when Mary and Jesus speak to each other, as discussed earlier, is the wedding feast at Cana.

Mary Speaks in the Gospel according to Luke

The annunciation	Luke 1:26–38
The visitation (including the *Magnificat*, Luke 1:46–55)	Luke 1:39–56
The nativity	Luke 2:1–20
The presentation of Jesus in the temple	Luke 2:22–38
Jesus is "lost" and found in the temple	Luke 2:41–52

Luke's intent was to reveal to the reader the divinity of Christ. But rather than attempting to parallel or to tap into Old Testament themes in the way that Matthew did, Luke approached the prophetic nature of Christ's life in a somewhat different manner. A connectedness with Old Testament themes is present in Luke, but only in order to establish the fact that the teachings and the actions of Jesus were deeply grounded in a historical faith tradition that formed the basis for the Christian movement. This historical connection to the past, therefore, would have made it a viable form of worship to a Roman world that was used to embracing many different expressions of the divine.

The Gospel according to Luke truly does form the basis—the heart and soul—of so much of Mariology. The Gospel's infancy narrative actually begins with a prologue. The use of a prologue would have been very familiar to the Greek and Roman audience to which Luke was writing. In addition, his testimony to the truth of what he was about to say, as well as his promise to set things out in an orderly and accurate fashion, would certainly have lent a great deal of credibility to his writing. Following the brief prologue, Luke's story begins with the announcement of the upcoming birth of John, who would be a first cousin to Jesus. John's birth, like that of Jesus, contained elements of divine intervention, angelic visits, and answered prayers.

Zechariah and Elizabeth, the future parents of John, were good and holy people whose greatest sadness was that they had never been able to have a child. (Remember, in Jewish society this would was seen as a tremendous burden, even a punishment from God. Their inability to have children, according to Luke, was attributed to the fact that Elizabeth was barren.) An angel of the Lord appeared to Zechariah and promised him that his prayers had been heard and that Elizabeth would have a baby who was to be named John. According to the angel, John would be filled with the Holy Spirit and would be the one who would "make ready a people prepared for the Lord." Naturally, it was difficult for Zechariah to believe all that he heard. He questioned the angel, who then identified himself as Gabriel. Then, when Zechariah doubted that God could do all that the angel had announced, Gabriel took away his ability to speak.

Next, the infancy narrative of Luke switches focus to Mary: "In the sixth month the angel Gabriel was sent by God to a town in Galilee called Nazareth, to a virgin engaged to a man whose name was Joseph, of the house of David. The virgin's name was Mary" (1:26–27). Again the angel announced a miraculous birth, even more miraculous than Elizabeth's pregnancy since Mary had never had a sexual relationship with Joseph or with any man.

Mary, like Zechariah, questioned Gabriel, but she did not doubt God's ability to make this happen. Even in her fear and her confusion, Mary consented to what would now become reality. Then, having learned from the angel that her cousin Elizabeth was also expecting, Mary traveled to see her. Upon Mary's arrival, as Elizabeth heard her voice, Luke tells us that "the child leaped in her womb" (1:41). Elizabeth realized immediately that Mary was pregnant with the Lord. Luke continues with Mary's beautiful canticle of praise to God—the *Magnificat* (1:46–55). Zechariah offered a similar canticle later when, upon the birth of John, his ability to speak was restored (1:67–79).

The infancy narrative continues with the story of the birth of Jesus that is so familiar to all Christians (2:1–7). Once again,

The Adoration of the Shepherds

earth was visited by an angel who announced the birth of Jesus to the shepherds who were in the fields. Choirs of angelic voices joined the angel in praising God. The shepherds, upon the angel's departure, immediately went to the place where they had been told Jesus was born. They told Mary and Joseph what had transpired, and Luke records that "Mary treasured all these words and pondered them in her heart" (2:19).

The Gospel continues with a rather brief mention of the naming of Jesus, which, according to Jewish custom, would have taken place at the time of his circumcision when he was eight days old. This would have been followed by Jesus' presentation and dedication ceremony to God. At the time of Jesus' presentation, there was an encounter with an old man named Simeon, who frequented the temple awaiting the Messiah. Upon seeing Mary and Joseph, Simeon blessed them and said to Mary, "This child is destined for the falling and the rising of many in Israel, and to be a sign that will be opposed so that the inner thoughts of many will be revealed—and a sword will pierce your own soul too" (2:34–35).

The infancy narrative then concludes with a brief mention of Jesus as a child of twelve, who was separated by accident from Mary and Joseph during the Passover celebration. After looking for him for three days, his worried parents finally found him in the temple, astounding the rabbis with his understanding and answers. This incident is the only one from Jesus' youth recounted in Scripture. Aside from its brief mention, the childhood of Jesus remains a scriptural mystery. In a similar manner, however, so, too, does the hidden life of Mary.

Scripture gives us little mention of Mary, and then, as has been noted, often the human authors of the Gospel accounts used Mary's presence to define or to teach a basic belief of the followers of Jesus. This was often at Mary's expense, as she was sometimes portrayed, especially in the Gospel according to Mark, as a person who "just doesn't get it." According to some of the few Marian references that are found in the Bible, one could form a very distorted image of Mary, seeing her as a woman who somehow forgot all the miraculous events that preceded the birth of her son. Seemingly, she just could not comprehend that Jesus truly was the Son of God and the Messiah for whom she, as a Jew, had been waiting. Did she forget the sound of the angel's voices on the night of her son's birth? Did she not notice that Jesus could heal people of their illnesses and raise others from the dead? According to what little we can piece together from Scripture, some persons would be quick to jump to the conclusion that Mary just did not have a clue about the messianic nature of her son. These persons would be wrong.

Isn't it possible that Mary really did understand? Could it be that when we are told in Luke that "Mary treasured all these words and pondered them in her heart," this really happened? What if she never had forgotten the visit of the angel that forever changed her life? What if the sound of the heavenly hosts singing "Glory to God in the highest" upon the birth of her son still echoed in her ears? What if Mary faithfully followed Jesus, as much as she was able, throughout his three-year ministry, even though her presence is seldom mentioned in Scripture? What if her heart really did feel as if it had been pierced by a sword as she watched her son's tortured death upon a cross? And then, what if Mary would have been considered by the early Christian community as a person who was deserving of a place of honor and leadership within that same community?

Mary was present to the first community of the faithful in Jerusalem. The Book of Acts, written by the human author of the Gospel according to Luke, records her presence in this community.

When they had entered the city, they went to the room upstairs where they were staying, Peter, and John, and James, and Andrew, Philip and Thomas, Bartholomew and Matthew, James son of Alphaeus, and Simon the Zealot, and Judas son of James. All these were constantly devoting themselves to prayer, together with certain women, including Mary the mother of Jesus, as well as his brothers (Acts 1:13–14).

In a culture that was accustomed to an oral tradition of storytelling, just think of the stories Mary had to tell! And think of how hungry for those stories the followers of Jesus probably were. Mary was most likely a tremendous comfort to the disciples. And in a very profound sense, Mary was the first and greatest disciple of all.

Some Thoughts for Your Reflection

1. Close your eyes for a few moments. Picture in your mind a memory of a statue, a painting, or a picture of Mary with which you are familiar. What does it look like? What is she doing, or how is she portrayed? Now try to think of an image of Mary as she must have looked when Jesus was a little boy. What is she doing? Can you imagine Mary and Jesus playing childhood games together? Can you imagine Mary laughing? Can you imagine Mary spinning around and around, with her little boy in her arms? Can you feel their joy? Why do you think it is that we never see Mary (or Jesus) portrayed in this way?

2. In some respects, the real, historical Mary has been remade into an image or into images that suit the needs of the Church. Have you ever felt that someone was trying to "remake" you to fit into his or her idea of how you should be? How did you feel? Have you ever tried to change yourself, so as to fit in or to conform to someone else's standards? Have you ever tried to impose your own will, your own ideas about these things, onto someone else? How do you think that person felt?

3. In Scripture, Mary is seldom mentioned. When she was a part of the events unfolding around her son, quite often she was "given no voice" by the authors of the Gospels. Zechariah also lost the ability to speak for months. Try this: At an appropriate time, "lose your own voice." See how it feels not to be able to communicate your thoughts, needs, or feelings to anyone else for a period of time. (No writing, either.) Does what you experience make you more aware of and sensitive to those persons whose ability to speak is limited due to physical disability or a stroke or to those who are new to our country and have not yet learned English?

4. In the infancy narratives of the Gospels, angels and dreams are both important avenues of information. Do you believe in angels? Do you listen to your own dreams and what your dreams may be telling you? What is the most vivid dream that you have ever had?

5. In the Gospels according to Matthew and Luke, heaven and earth meet as angelic messengers, heavenly music, and other miraculous events foretelling the birth of Jesus occur. Do you believe in miracles? If so, do you believe that miracles occur in our world today? Have you ever experienced a miracle? Have you ever thought of yourself as a miracle?

6. Luke's Gospel tells us that after the events surrounding the birth of Jesus, "Mary treasured all these words and pondered them in her heart" (2:19). What memories do you most treasure? What people play a significant role in your memories? If you have a special memory associated with a person still living, tell that person. If the person in your most cherished memory has died, say a prayer of thanksgiving for the gift of his or her life.

Chapter Three

The Role of Women in the Early Church

Saint Thérèse of Lisieux

The Church of the First Three Centuries

One of the difficulties in discovering (or uncovering) women's contributions to history is that women's history is so often "hidden history." It is a quiet, long-overlooked or even forgotten feminine presence that has nonetheless helped shape humanity in immeasurable ways. This is all the more remarkable when we remember that, throughout much of history, women did not have equal access to the educational opportunities, financial resources, or personal freedoms that were available to men. No wonder, then, that the recorders of historical events (who were usually men) tended to record male deeds. Waging war, conquering cities, building empires—these were the kind of events that mattered to male historians. And, of course, these events were history-making. But also of tremendous importance were the contributions of women that were most generally not recorded, if they were even noticed at all. Just as this has been true in the secular world, so it has been true for the Church.

This lack of historical record makes it difficult to piece together the beautiful mosaic that is the history of women within Christianity. It is especially difficult when studying the early history of the Church—the Church of the first few centuries following Jesus' life, death, and resurrection. The lack of historical record does not, however, make it impossible to do so.

In the Bible, it is not uncommon to find only a brief, passing reference to a particular woman, even if what she achieved or saw or did had great significance. An excellent example of this is Luke's Gospel account of the empty tomb (24:1–12). According to Luke, Mary Magdalene, Joanna, and Mary, the mother of James, all saw that the empty tomb of Jesus and believed that he had truly risen from the dead. When they ran to tell the others, the apostles did not believe the women and felt that their "words seemed to them an idle tale." It was not until Peter went himself to the tomb and found it empty that the others believed.

It is important to note that the primary reason for the lack of recorded presence and contributions of women in the Bible is that by the time biblical writings were compiled, cultural and societal attitudes had become increasingly patriarchal. Thus stories that affirmed women's ministry most likely did not make it into print. It seems that by the middle of the second century, Paul's beautiful proclamation from the Book of Galatians had been long since forgotten.

> *As many of you as were baptized into Christ have clothed yourselves with Christ. There is no longer Jew or Greek, there is no longer slave or free, there is no longer male and female; for all of you are one in Christ Jesus (3:27–28).*

In addition to the poverty of reference to women in Scripture, there is another problem for today's reader. That problem is as simple as trying to see with "new eyes" what is written and what may be so familiar. This is not as easy as it sounds. Because we can become so accustomed to reading a familiar story, we may not even truly comprehend what it is that the story is saying (or not saying). Think for a moment about the story of the miracle of the loaves and fishes. So awesome was this miracle to the followers of Jesus that it appears in all four Gospels: Matthew (14:13–21), Mark (6:34–44), Luke (9:10–17),

and John (6:1–14). But it is only in the Gospel of Matthew that women are referred to at all, and then only in a diminishing manner: "And those who ate were about five thousand men, besides women and children" (14:21). Of course, the obvious question that we might ask is: Why not count the women and children?

Contemporary biblical scholarship can help us understand that during this period of time, women and children were hardly ever counted. What if the women and the children had been counted? In an already huge crowd, how many people must there have actually been? Having made an educated estimate in our minds, Jesus' feeding of the multitude with only five loaves of bread and two fish seems all the more miraculous. We might even allow ourselves to wonder about the nature of the miracle. Could it be that the real miracle was not as much in Jesus' feeding of the people but in the fact that the people shared what little they had? The people must have trusted Jesus greatly to be willing to relinquish their meager amounts of food to him, believing that he could accomplish what seemed impossible. As you can see in this example from Scripture, looking at a familiar story in a new way, with "new eyes," can help open our eyes.

Sometimes, however, because of a lack of available information, modern readers of Scripture can do little more than speculate about how something might have been (and we might actually be very close to the truth). But our speculations are merely that—speculations. We simply cannot know for sure because there is not enough information available to us. Sometimes one word or a passing reference may lead us to believe that there is "more to the story." Much of this chapter will deal with this type of speculation. But when what is presented is speculative, you will be told that it is.

Jesus Taken Down from the Cross

One such event from Scripture that leads to this type of speculation begins in an upper room in Jerusalem following the death of Jesus. In the upper room were gathered many of the followers of Jesus, including the apostles, Mary, the mother of Jesus, and some other women. This event sets the stage for the true beginning of the Church at Pentecost, and so it is an appropriate place to begin our examination of the role of women in the Church during the early centuries of Christianity.

Can you imagine how afraid the followers of Jesus must have been immediately after his death? They no doubt questioned everything in which they believed. They saw their dear friend and the person whom they had come to believe was the long-awaited Messiah die the most tortuous of deaths. The person

whom they knew as a worker of miracles was not even able to save himself from his terrible fate. For those who also thought of Jesus as the person who would free their country from Roman occupation, his death was especially bitter.

No one, however, felt the pain of the loss of Jesus as deeply as did his mother, Mary. In the Gospel of John, we are given a brief glimpse of the fear that the disciples felt: "The doors of the house where the disciples had met were locked for fear of the Jews . . ." (20:19). In this environment of suspicion and fear, it's logical to assume that it was Mary to whom the others looked for comfort in their own grief. After all, Mary was able to share with the others the miraculous events that surrounded her baby's birth many years ago. In the strong oral tradition of the Jewish people, Mary probably told these stories over and over again as the disciples hid in the upper room trying to avoid a fate similar to that which Jesus had met. (Remember, too, that just because Scripture relates few stories about Mary and Jesus during his early life and the years of his ministry, it does not mean that there were no stories to tell. It is quite possible that Mary was with her son through the greatest share of his public ministry.) As Mary shared her stories of Jesus, the disciples probably jumped in with stories of their own, finding in each telling the comfort that they so desperately needed.

No doubt, for the followers of Jesus, Mary provided not only a spiritual link to Jesus but a physical one as well. She gave birth to him, gave him nourishment from her own body to sustained him as an infant, loved him, taught him, and believed in him every day of his life. Perhaps, in Mary, the disciples even saw a reflection of their Lord's features, for it was from her that

Jesus received his humanity. They would most likely have felt protective of her, even as they looked to her for solace. All that Scripture tells us, however, is that Mary was with the disciples in the upper room. The fact that she was named as a part of this group gives us our only suggestion of her importance to the group.

> *When they had entered the city, they went to the room upstairs where they were staying, Peter, and John, and James, and Andrew, Philip and Thomas, Bartholomew and Matthew, James son of Alphaeus, and Simon the Zealot, and Judas son of James. All these were constantly devoting themselves to prayer, together with certain women, including Mary the mother of Jesus, as well as his brothers (Acts 1:13–14).*

It was not long, however, before this group was transformed with the joyful knowledge that Jesus had truly overcome the power of death, just as he had foretold. Now, to his followers, everything made perfect sense. With the benefit of hindsight, all that Jesus had tried to help them understand, and all the allusions to the coming of the Messiah that they would have known from the Torah, finally, ultimately, made sense. After Jesus' resurrection, and before his ascension into heaven, Scripture recounts that he appeared many times to his followers.

> *After his suffering [Jesus] presented himself alive to them by many convincing proofs, appearing to them during forty days and speaking about the kingdom of God. While staying with them, he ordered them not to leave Jerusalem, but to wait there for the promise of the Father. "This," he said, "is what you have heard from me; for John baptized with water, but you will be baptized with the Holy Spirit not many days from now" (Acts 1:3–5).*

Pentecost: The Beginning of the Church

By the time of the apostles, the Jewish feast of weeks, or *Shavuoth*, had come to be known as *Pentecost*. In Greek, the word *Pentecost* means "fiftieth." The feast fell on the fiftieth day after Passover, marking the end of the seven-week season for harvesting grain. Pentecost has traditionally been thought of as the true beginning of the Church. But there are two important things we need to remember regarding the beginning of the Church. First, although the Church may have been formed at Pentecost, the community of believers was not. That community was already formed with each experience shared, each story told, each gesture of compassion given. What Pentecost marked was the coming of the Spirit upon the community, blessing and gracing it, in a special way, with the presence of God.

> *When the day of Pentecost had come, they were all together in one place. And suddenly from heaven there came a sound like the rush of a violent wind, and it filled the entire house where they were sitting. Divided tongues, as of fire, appeared among them, and a tongue rested on each of them. All of them were filled with the Holy Spirit and began to speak in other languages, as the Spirit gave them ability (Acts 2:1–4).*

Second, we need to understand that the formation of the Church (as we understand the Church to be today) did not miraculously occur at the moment of Pentecost. It took centuries of interpreting the will of God, guided by the Holy Spirit, before the

Pentecost

Church took the form that is familiar to us today. And the form that is familiar to us today, in all likelihood, may not be the way the Church is patterned and experienced in the future. Of course, those dogmatic beliefs that are central to our faith (such as our belief in the Holy Trinity, for example) will not change. Other things might, however, since the Church is "alive" and responding to the Spirit's guidance.

At that first Pentecost, and as it is today, the Christian community was a Church marked by charisms (special gifts of the Spirit that are meant to build up the community of believers). Those charisms included the gifts of prophecy and evangelization, of leadership and teaching, and the gift of healing, to name a few (see 1 Corinthians 12:1–11).

The Church was marked further by a definite fluidity of ministries. The rather rigid, hierarchical structure that we know today did not exist during this time. In other words, there were no separations or designations, such as pope, bishop, priest, or laity (although the leadership of the apostles was definitely of primary importance). Ministry was instead generally experienced as an action that was common to many rather than limited to a relative few. And, being patterned upon the model and example of Jesus, these ministries were open to both males and females, depending on a person's gifts from the Spirit.

From the Acts of the Apostles, we get a very good idea of how the communal life of the Church in Jerusalem was structured (2:43–47; 4:32–35; 5:12–16). The members devoted themselves to learning about the teachings and the life of Jesus, to prayer, and to the care of the poor. Scripture tells us that many miracles occurred, including numerous healings, and countless conversions took place.

At this point there was still a definite connection to the Jewish temple, but the group would then meet in people's homes where they continued their worship through the "breaking of the bread." It can safely be assumed that many female converts to the faith opened their homes to their fellow believers. In their homes, the "house churches" of the first century were born. From comments of Paul in some of his letters to the faith communities that were expanding into other areas of the Mediterranean, it is clear that many women were active participants in the various ministries of the Church. As deacons, missionaries, prophets, and teachers, they served in some sense as presiders at worship gatherings, assumed leadership roles, and served those in need. A sense of this can be gained from Paul's letter to the Romans, which was most likely written sometime between A.D. 56 and 58.

I commend to you our sister Phoebe, a deacon of the church at Cenchreae, so that you may welcome her in the Lord as is fitting for the saints, and help her in whatever she may require from you, for she has been a benefactor of many and of myself as well (Romans 16:1–2).

Paul goes on to greet Prisca, Mary, Tryphosa, Julia, and other women who are not identified by name but rather through association, such as the mother of Rufus and the sister of Nereus. In his book Paul Bernier mentions this segment of Paul's Letter to the Romans, as well as others.

Paul explicitly includes women among the leaders of local churches. Phoebe is a deacon (Romans 16:1), while Prisca and her husband Aquila are co-workers (16:3), as Paul and Apollos are in 1 Corinthians 3:9; Maria (Romans 16:6) has worked hard for the church. . . . They were not automatically excluded from key roles because of gender.

Close to 150 of these co-workers of Paul are named. Despite that, they cannot be fitted into one neat pattern of church office. Besides their large number, they cut across the traditional religious lines of Jew and Gentile, slave and free, male and female; and they have no official titles.

Paul Bernier, *Ministry in the Church: A Historical and Pastoral Approach* (Mystic, CT: Twenty-Third Publications, 1992).

As we read lists of names of women who lived so very long ago and who were part of a Church that we have never experienced, it might be difficult to see them as more than just names. Remember that what was happening in the Church during this very exciting time was nothing less than amazing. The miracles done in the name of Jesus were real miracles. The people who were healed were truly healed, and because they were, they were able to resume their lives, hopefully living those lives to the fullest. (Imagine your own family, and then allow yourself to realize that those persons who were miraculously healed included someone's mom, someone's little boy, someone's grandfather, and so on.) Real people, who upon receiving Christ's healing presence through the hand of his disciples, went on to become Christianity's strongest converts. No wonder the Church spread rapidly through the region, alive with vitality and the gifts of the Spirit!

Of course, being comprised of fallible humans, the Church was not without conflicts, both external to the group as well as internal. There was, quite understandably, a serious conflict between the followers of The Way (as the Christians were then called) and many of the Jewish religious authorities. It was only a matter of time before the believers in Jesus were no longer welcome in the temple.

As the Church spread into the non-Christian world of the Gentiles, new conflicts arose and almost divided the Church. There was division over whether or not Gentile converts needed to follow the dietary laws that the Jewish converts adhered to and disagreement as to whether or not Gentile followers of Jesus should be circumcised, as all Jewish males were. Eventually these conflicts and others were resolved, in part, through the Council of Jerusalem in A.D. 48. What the council decided was that the Church would be open to everyone, both Jew and Gentile. Non-Jewish male converts would not need to be circumcised, but all Gentile converts, male or female, would need to observe some of the Jewish dietary laws and avoid unlawful marriages.

An even more serious issue faced the Church as the apostles and others who had known Jesus personally began to die. As the apostolic age came to an end, the Church was forced to rethink its understanding of the second coming of Christ (the *parousia*). Until this time, the Christian community believed that Jesus' return was imminent. Because of this belief, there really was little concern for "worldly" matters. In fact, the Church had given little thought to passing down the stories of the faith to future generations. As it became obvious that the followers of Jesus had misunderstood his teaching regarding the coming of the kingdom of God, the Church had to prepare itself for "the duration," so to speak.

Judaism enjoyed many exclusions from Roman religious practices, and, as long as it was seen as a sect of Judaism, so did Christianity. When the temple in Jerusalem was destroyed by Rome in A.D. 70, Jerusalem ceased to be the center of the world's Christian community. By the latter half of the first century, Rome was the hub of Christianity, and in the rather accepting, eclectic secular world, Christians came to be thought of as members of a religion rather than as members of a sect within Judaism. (Of course this acceptance did not last long, as we shall see, for Rome becomes the site of the massacre of thousands of Christians.)

The Period of Martyrdom in the Roman Empire

The hostility that Roman authorities exhibited toward the Christians began with Emperor Nero in A.D. 64, when a fire destroyed much of Rome. Needing scapegoats, Nero ordered the death of a vast number of Christians. The persecution of Christians continued in one place or another for almost two centuries. During this time, there were ten major persecutions or purges, with periods of relative peace in between. This "peace," however, was marked by a pervasive attitude of distrust and prejudice toward members of the Church. When things would go badly for the nation in a battle or during a period of drought, for example, it was the Christians who were often blamed. Many of the persecutions were of a local or regional nature. All of them were deadly.

The reasons for the Romans distrust and hatred were many:

> *The Christian encouragement of celibacy was seen as an attack on Roman family life. The Christian practice of fasting irritated the banquet-loving Romans. The Christian practice of severe restraint in dress and cosmetics offended the fashion-conscious Romans. Such habits set Christians apart from the Roman state, family, and religion. Christians saw Jesus as their real leader. Rome saw them as a* third race *that had to be destroyed.*
>
> Alfred McBride, *The Story of the Church: Peak Moments from Pentecost to the Year 2000* (Cincinnati, OH: Saint Anthony Messenger Press and Franciscan Communications, 1996).

Perhaps the most offensive aspect of Christianity to the Roman people was the Christian belief that theirs was the only true religion and that there was only one God. In rejecting the Roman religions which honored many gods and goddesses, the Christian people became, in essence, enemies of the state. This happened because, in the Roman way of thinking, it was a citizen's duty to honor the gods of the nation, as that would give honor and adoration to the emperor. But, for Christians, giving honor to the Roman gods was a violation of the first commandment: I am the Lord your God; you shall not have strange gods before me. (This honoring of Roman gods usually was not required of the Jews.) Many Christians chose to die rather than deny their faith. You may have heard the saying, "the Church was born from the blood of the martyrs." In a very real sense, this is true. It is hard to imagine the horror of what some early Christians endured.

Perpetua of Carthage was a catechumen, a person in preparation to be baptized. Usually this time of preparation took between two and three years. In Perpetua's case, she did not live long enough to experience the full process of initiation. She was baptized just prior to her death by martyrdom. We know of these events because of a diary Perpetua kept and through the eyewitness account of Tertullian, a Carthaginian lawyer who became an important Christian theologian and historian. In her book *Women in Church History*, Joanne Turpin tells Perpetua's story, excerpts of which are paraphrased here.

Perpetua came from a noble Roman family; she was a dutiful daughter, a good wife, and the mother to an infant son. She also believed in Jesus and wanted, with all of her heart, to be baptized. During Perpetua's time of preparation, the Roman Empire was experiencing threats to its borders and the Christian stance of nonviolence was seen as a direct threat to national security. In order to stop the growing Christian movement, Emperor Septimius Severus issued an edict banning conversions to Christianity and ordering all citizens to prove their loyalty to the state by offering sacrifice to the gods of Rome. The year was 202, and the arrests of the catechumens began. Perpetua was one of them, as was her servant, Felicity. In her diary, Perpetua wrote of her terror at being arrested, of the mystical visions she was granted that gave her some comfort, and of her anguish at seeing what pain her arrest had caused her family. They begged her to recant and offer a sacrifice, which would be as simple as burning incense in public as an offering to the gods. She refused, as did Felicity, Perpetua's brother, who was also a Christian, and others. Her fate and the fate of the others was sealed.

> *On the morning of March 7, 203, the prisoners are marched from the prison to the amphitheater where they will form part of the public's entertainment during festivities marking the emperor's birthday. . . . The men are forced to put on robes worn by priests of Saturn, the god of harvests. When the women are given the dress for priestesses of Ceres, a goddess associated with fertility rites, Perpetua resists. . . . Stripped naked and put into nets, they are brought into the arena (after everyone has first been severely whipped). Perpetua is tossed into the air by a mad animal . . . she sees [Felicity] in a heap on the ground and hurries over to give her a hand, lifting her up. The two stand side by side, a noble matron and her personal slave, facing death as sisters. (Throughout the ordeal, Perpetua offers encouragement to the others.) "You must all stand fast in the faith and love one another, and do not be weakened by what we have gone through." (Wild boars, bears, and leopards are next used against the Christians.) Still the entire group has thus far survived the attacks, which means that they must be put to death by the sword.*

The mob clamors for the prisoners to be brought into the open where they can witness the bloody spectacle. Assembling in full view, the five give each other the ritual kiss of peace before each is executed by the sword. Perpetua's turn comes last. The gladiator assigned to dispatch her nervously takes poor aim. His hand slips and the sword strikes bone. Perpetua emits a brief scream, but "then she took the trembling hand of the young gladiator and guided it to her throat.

Joanne Turpin, *Women in Church History: Twenty Stories for Twenty Centuries* (Cincinnati, OH: Saint Anthony Messenger Press and Franciscan Communications, 1990).

It truly is almost impossible to comprehend the inhumanity that was shown to Perpetua, Felicity, and their fellow Christians. But multiply it by thousands and you will have a sense of the unbelievable persecutions that Christians throughout the Roman Empire experienced. The persecutions did not end, in fact, until Emperor Constantine's Edict of Milan was issued in the year 313. Perpetua's martyrdom, as well as accounts of countless other men and women, such as Cecilia, Agnes, Agatha, and Lucy—who met their death with Christian dignity and even forgiveness, in the memory of Jesus who forgave his executioners—served to strengthen the faithful.

In memory of these brave and holy men and women, the martyrs are mentioned today in the Eucharistic Prayers at Mass and during the Litany of Saints, which is part of the liturgy at Baptism. In addition, the Church celebrates feast days and memorials in their honor; the Roman Martyrology is the official listing of martyrs (and other saints) and their feast days. Churches, shrines, and basilicas are named after many martyrs. Christians everywhere daily pray for their intercession. The following is a prayer the Church prays in honor of Saint Polycarp, bishop of Smyrna and a disciple of the apostles. He was martyred around A.D. 155.

God of all creation,
you gave your bishop Polycarp
the privilege of being counted among the saints
who gave their lives in faithful witness to the gospel.
May his prayers give us the courage
to share with him the cup of suffering
and to rise to eternal glory.
We ask this through our Lord Jesus Christ,
your Son, who lives and reigns with you and the
Holy Spirit, one God, for ever and ever.

> *The Church has painstakingly collected the records of those who persevered to the end in witnessing to their faith. These are the acts of the Martyrs. They form the archives of truth written in letters of blood.*
>
> *Catechism of the Catholic Church* (Washington, DC: United States Catholic Conference, 1994), #2474.

It would be nice to think that martyrdom for the faith is a tragic happening of a long-ago past. Unfortunately, martyrdom did not end in the early years of the Church. It still occurs, even to this day—not in coliseums, but in many modern places. We will examine this issue in more detail in a later chapter. The next time you hear the names of martyrs of the Christian faith, remember this about them: They sacrificed their lives so that we might be inheritors of the faith they loved so dearly.

Before leaving the subject of the martyrs, the issue of mysticism will be addressed, for both Perpetua and Cecilia had mystical

Saint Cecilia

experiences. Perpetua had visions; Cecilia heard the songs of the angels. In our "sophistication," either of these two experiences, had they happened in modern times, would have been instantly attributed to some type of mental disease or dissociative disorder. But Christian mysticism, by definition, is really the prerogative of all the baptized.

Mystic: *a person whose experience of the presence of God is intense, direct, and transforming, but not necessarily accompanied by extraordinary phenomena. Mystics experience a deep communion of love and of knowledge with God and, in God, with other people and all reality.*

Richard P. McBrien, gen. ed., *Encyclopedia of Catholicism* (New York: HarperCollins Publishers, 1995), p. 900.

Usually, when we think of mystics, we image them as persons who have "visions" or who go into periods of ecstatic trances and the like. For some mystics, this has been a part of their religious experience. For most, however, it is not. According to the above definition, everyone, by virtue of their Baptism, should be defined as a mystic because we all are called to be transformed by the Spirit of God.

Changes in the Church

As devastating to the Christian community as the Roman persecutions were, the community not only survived but also thrived. There was, however, through contact with the Greek and Roman world, a definite change that occurred in the way the Church understood its mission and structure.

During the Apostolic Age, when the second coming of Jesus was thought to be imminent, there was an unusual freedom within the Christian community. Jesus' inclusive model of ministry was fresh in the minds of the believers who followed his example. Even though, in many respects, women were an oppressed group within society, this was not the way it was within the Church. (Of course, there were those who were not comfortable with this reality, but the praxis of Jesus prevailed, and women were welcomed as partners.) As has already been noted, women served the community by presiding over house churches, as well as by being missionaries, prophets, and deaconesses. In fact, all the roles of service and leadership that existed in the first several decades of the Church's history were open to women as well as to men. Since it was presumed that Jesus would return soon, there was no need for an organized structure for the community of believers. Through their worship and community sharing, the early Christians more or less set themselves apart from Jewish society, and as the Church expanded, from Greek and Roman society as well. (Why be "engaged" with the world when the world was about to end?)

As time went on, the Church, no longer centered in Jerusalem and still undergoing persecution in some places, sought ways to "fit in" with society without losing its identity. Hence, the Church began to pattern itself after the patriarchal Roman model of family and society. As the Church established itself as a stable entity and its members as respectable members of society, the desire to accommodate the Roman government increased. In spite of the fact that the Christian community knew itself to be "one in Christ," the ambiguity that many members already felt in regard to women in positions of leadership now began to transform into the subordination of women. Pheme Perkins expresses this well.

> *The social model adopted for Church order always considered women inferior to men. Indeed they often had much less education, were much younger than their husbands, and could not assume important roles of public leadership. As leadership in the community was shaped by a patriarchal model, women could not be designated as leaders of the community. Just as they did not teach or exercise authority over men in the larger society, so they were not permitted to do so in the Church (1 Timothy 2:12 and 1 Corinthians 14:33–36).*
>
> Pheme Perkins, *Reading the New Testament: An Introduction* (Mahwah, NJ: Paulist Press, 1988).

Although the issue of gender equality and roles of service and leadership within the Church do not necessarily have to translate into arguments for or against women's ordination, they usually do. This is so because we, as Church, have become so conditioned to seeing leadership and service only in terms

of ordination. But ministry is much more. (We will examine this issue in further detail in chapter 8.) Nonetheless, as the following passage shows, the controversy regarding the equality of the genders has been around for some time.

> *The Apostolic Constitutions, a fourth-century document, describes a ceremony for ordaining deaconesses. When the bishop laid hands on a woman, he was to pray, "Do Thou look down on this Thy servant, who is to be ordained to the office of woman deacon and grant her Thy Holy Spirit." Later councils forbade the practice of ordaining women as deacons. Numerous reasons were given, the final one being "because of the weakness of their sex." The discipleship of equals established by Jesus was overcome by societal and cultural forces of patriarchy.*
>
> McBrien.

The exciting and vibrant ministry of women within the early Church, the Church of the Apostolic Age, is a fact of history. So, too, are the acts of bravery and faith that Christian women exhibited during the Roman persecutions. The increasing marginalization of women in the Church during its second and third centuries is also a historical truth. But nothing that is true can be lost forever. This is especially so regarding the importance of women's roles within the Church, both from a historical perspective and as the Church struggles with the issue today. Hopefully, the argument that women cannot minister within the Church in certain ways because they are inferior to men is an argument that can be relegated to its place in history. The Second Vatican Council spoke to this very issue of equality in "The Church in the Modern World."

> *. . . forms of social or cultural discrimination in basic personal rights on the grounds of sex, race, color, social conditions, language or religion, must be curbed and eradicated as incompatible with God's design.* (#29)
>
> "The Church in the Modern World," *Vatican Council II: The Conciliar and Post Conciliar Documents*, Austin Flannery, gen. ed. (Collegeville, MN: The Liturgical Press, 1975), p. 929.

Perhaps, as we leave this chapter, we should allow the words of Jesus to speak to us across the centuries.

> *This is my commandment, that you love one another as I have loved you. No one has greater love than this, to lay down one's life for one's friends. You are my friends if you do what I command you. I do not call you servants any longer, because the servant does not know what the master is doing; but I have called you friends, because I have made known to you everything that I have heard from my Father. You did not choose me but I chose you. And I appointed you to go and bear fruit, fruit that will last, so that the Father will give you whatever you ask him in my name. I am giving you these commands so that you may love one another (John 15:12–17).*

Some Thoughts for Your Reflection

1. Just as the role of women in the early Church had been, until relatively recently, a "hidden history," so, too, can our personal, family history be lost or forgotten. As a child in school, you may remember tracing your family tree as a class project. Maybe it is time to revisit that project now that you can better understand the richness of your family heritage. Perhaps, with their permission, you might like to videotape or audiotape your parents, grandparents, or other family members as they share with you your family history, stories about the day that you were born, and so forth.

2. After the coming of the Holy Spirit at Pentecost, Scripture records that the followers of Jesus worked many miracles, including countless healings. Is there an area within your life that you feel is in need of healing? Is there someone you know who is in need of God's healing grace? In the quiet of your own heart, ask God for the gift of healing.

3. The names of the martyrs of long ago are often only that to us—names. Pick the name of one of the martyrs mentioned in this chapter, or choose one from the Litany of Saints, and research the life of this person. Then research your own name or the day on which you were born, and find out if you have a connection to the name or the life of a saint.

4. Did you know that when you see a priest wearing red vestments at a weekday Mass it is in memory of a martyr? Find out the meanings of the other liturgical colors.

5. Countless women were martyrs during the first few centuries of Christianity. Can you think of any women in contemporary times whom you would consider to be martyrs?

6. A prophet is a person who, in God's name, calls others to a deeper, more authentic response to God's love. In the history of the Church, many women were prophets. Often, as they prick our conscience and remind us of our failings, prophets quickly become very unpopular people. Can you think of anyone living today whom you would consider to be a prophet?

7. In the history of Christianity, there have been many heroic people. Who is your hero today? Why

Chapter four

Saints and Monastics

Valeria's Story

The following fictional story is based on the historical situation in the Roman Empire in the last years of the third century.

Valeria was born in 284, exactly thirty-five years to the day that marked the anniversary of the death, by torture, of Apollonia and several dozen other Christians. Their crime was disloyalty to the state. Some important people believed that the Christians, through their beliefs and their refusal to sacrifice to the gods, were responsible for the drought and famine that inflicted the entire area. Their punishment was a death sentence; in Apollonia's case, her death by burning her alive followed the torture of having her teeth pulling out.

That was long ago and almost forgotten by everyone. But I, Marcus, remember, for I was there. In fact, I remember it all too well. As a trusted and loyal servant of Valeria's family, I have watched and listened for years to the events that have been happening in Alexandria. Once considered a slave, I am proud to say that I long ago won my freedom, yet I chose to stay. But that is unimportant to the story I have to tell.

Regarding the persecutions: Valeria was not yet alive when the trouble started—trouble that eventually led to Emperor Decius ordering a purge of the Christians.

(Besides, what were Christians to any of us anyway, but a source of constant aggravation?) What mattered to Valeria's parents was the birth of their firstborn child, a beautiful little girl whose sparkling, dark eyes held all the promise of a wonderful future.

And Valeria did have a delightful childhood. She and her younger brother and sister grew up close together in age to become responsible and dutiful members of their family. All three of the children were a joy to their parents, but it must be admitted that Valeria held a special place in her father's heart. That is why the problems that irrupted when Valeria was not quite eighteen hit the family so hard.

Her parents could accept the fact that Valeria now refused to adorn herself in the way that a young woman of her social and economic class should. So what if she refused to wear gold arm bracelets or jeweled combs in her hair? Who would think any worse of her if she did not kohl her eyes or dye her nails orange with henna, as was the custom? After all, it wasn't as if she needed any adornment anyway, not with her natural beauty. No, what had begun to trouble her parents—and trouble them deeply—was Valeria's preoccupation with things of a spiritual nature. It wasn't the normal things that troubled a young person, such as giving sacrifice to the gods, but rather things that appeared to be Christian. This was a cause of great anxiety to her parents, although they really knew very little about those who called themselves *Christians*. What they did know was that being a Christian was very dangerous, for it put a person in direct opposition to the government. And that was a perilous place to be, especially in those times.

The people were getting edgy, and who could blame them? After a long period of peace and prosperity, it looked as if things were about to change. Valeria's parents could almost feel the tension in the air, as could I; it was so palatable, but their words of caution fell on deaf ears. Not only did Valeria refuse to consider the engagement her father had so carefully arranged for her future happiness and security, but she began insisting on entering something called the *catechumenate*. It was really just too much for her parents to bear. Valeria wrote her thoughts in a diary:

I never intended to hurt my parents. My love for them is greater than I could ever express in words. They mean everything to me, and to see the pain that my decisions caused them has wounded my heart as if a lance has pierced my body. But they do not understand my greater love. How could I marry Hadrian when I have come to love another—Christ, the Lord?

I had heard, of course, of the Christians, although I had never met one personally. From all that I had heard, however, it seemed as if I would never desire to meet one either. Their ways sounded too strange and too foreign to me. I especially could not understand their belief in only one God when everyone around me believed in many gods and goddesses. For me, at that time, the power of the rites of Isis, Mithras, and Serapis seemed to be too strong, too true

not to be valid. (I had so much to learn!) My "education" began on that fateful morning, for which I shall forever be grateful, when I first met Claudia.

She had come to minister at the home of a friend of mine whose servant was a new Christian. Claudia must have been about forty-five years of age then, and I later learned that she was what the Christians called a deaconess. *There was something about her that I can only describe as pure goodness and peace. It radiated from her and drew me to her side as if I had no power to resist.*

In her presence, for the first time in my life, I felt ashamed of my appearance, although nothing she said or did should have made me feel that way. In fact, except for a shy smile in our direction, she seemed to be almost unaware of my friend and me in the room. All of her attention was directed to the servant girl who was so ill. Yet I knew that she had to be uncomfortable with us in the room, so we withdrew to the shadows. Even there, I was embarrassed about the gold that adorned my body and the cosmetics that covered my face. I vaguely remembered hearing something about how the Christians shared all of their resources in common so that no one should be in need. As I touched the bracelet that encircled my upper arm, I remember that I wondered how many people could be helped with the money the bracelet would bring. I truly think this was the first time I ever genuinely worried about another person other than myself.

I did not have long to spend in my own thoughts, however, for soon I was enthralled by what was happening before me. Claudia prayed for and with the servant girl, and she anointed the girl with a special oil, not in the way that we used oil—so lavishly and such, as in the public baths—but instead, with reverence and gentleness, she anointed her. Claudia's voice was gentle, too, as she prayed quietly during the anointing. Then, during the prayer, I saw her give the girl a small portion of some type of bread to eat. I did not understand then exactly what was happening, but I knew that what I saw was true, holy, and good. With all of my heart, I longed to be a part of Claudia's world.

As Claudia prepared to leave, I felt compelled to approach her and ask if she had a prayer that she could say for me. I will never forget the surprise on her face that greeted my request! She traced a cross on my forehead and prayed for me. It was as if my eyes were opened for the very first time or as if my heart had finally begun to beat in time with all that was beautiful and good. Suddenly I knew that all I had heard about the Christians had been wrong. They were not at all like I had been told. And more than anything, I wanted to be one of them. My decision was instantaneous, joyous, and complete (although I did my best to keep from showing my elation to my friend and to my family later that day). In fact, I wrapped myself up in my wonderful secret as if it were a beautiful cloak as I waited for an opportunity to speak to Claudia. I did not have too long to wait, for in only two days she was back to see to the spiritual care of my friend's servant (who, by the way, had fully recovered from her illness and resumed her household responsibilities).

When I approached Claudia about my desire to become a Christian, to my great surprise, she did not really seem surprised at all. In fact, she almost seemed as if she had been expecting as much. As she embraced me and called

me "sister," Claudia smiled and said that this was the Lord's way. She said that it was his Spirit alive in the world, drawing all of creation to him. I did not fully understand as yet what she meant, but even in my ignorance, I recognized the truth of what she said. She promised to bring me to a gathering of the community of believers, where I would begin to learn more about Jesus and the reign of God. Soon we did exactly that, and from that very first moment, I felt as if I had "come home" and that everything was finally right in my world.

Valeria may have felt as if everything was right in her world, but the truth of the matter is that her decision to become a Christian was turning her parents' world upside down. Nevertheless, because of their great love for Valeria, they tried to understand. It was difficult, however, for first there was the small matter of her change in appearance followed by her desire to not marry. This was especially hard for Valeria's mother, Pristina, who felt as if her daughter, without the security of marriage (and children who would look after her in her old age), was literally throwing her life away. How could she be so quick to make such a decision? One day she was a normal, outgoing, young girl with a promising future ahead of her, and the next, it was as if she had become a stranger to her own family.

For Valeria's father, Quintus, there was an even deeper sense of foreboding, for he had begun to hear rumors. Just that very morning, at the forum, some of the most respected men of the city of Alexandria had been complaining about the growing Christian movement. It seemed that the men were making connections between the prosperity of the Christians and the recent warfare that had so decimated and drained the economic reserves of the empire. Quintus had never felt that the Christians were a threat to anyone, but he was not so sure of the feelings of Emperor Diocletian.

He remembered hearing the stories of the last great persecution of the Christians in Alexandria only fifty or so years before. It seemed as if history would repeat itself, and although he would not admit it to anyone, he lived in fear. I know that he did, for I saw it in his eyes. If only his daughter would listen to reason! Why rush into that thing that the Christians referred to as the *catechumenate*? She might as well just brand herself as a heretic, for that was exactly how the government would perceive her. Even worse, if things did begin to get out of hand, she could be condemned as a traitor to the empire. Ah, Valeria, what was it about this person called *Jesus the Christ* that was so compelling as to make you risk so much for so little? (Hadn't he been condemned as a criminal and legally crucified? Your own government had said as much. What type of hero was that to command such loyalty?) If only you had come to your senses before it is was too late! You should have known that even your beloved father would not be able to save you when things turned so ugly.

What a blessing the catechumenate was! Under the instruction of the widows and the deaconesses, the other women converts and I grew daily in our knowledge of the Lord and in our love and service for him. Of course, there were things that were still forbidden to us to learn, such as to know the Prayer of the Lord and to participate fully at the table of his sacrifice, receiving his Body and Blood. But I knew that I would learn everything when I was ready. How I looked forward to my initiation, which was expected to be in about two years, when I would be fully received into the Church. On that night, the holiest night of the Christian year, the Church waits in expectation and memory of his resurrection. During the vigil, I would be baptized—literally "dying" to my old self and being reborn in the waters of Baptism. As I anticipated that time, I knew that it would be Claudia, in her role as deaconess, who would assist me through the ritual. And, of course, it would not just be me but the other converts to the faith as well who would be fully initiated at the Easter Vigil. It seemed as if every day the Lord was adding more and more to the number of his faithful. I had even heard through letters from the Church in Rome that some members of the emperor's own family had become Christians! Our community felt great joy at the news.

When Diocletian realized that even his immediate family had been polluted by the spread of Christianity, he vowed to set his empire in order, beginning first of all with his own household. He had no great difficulty dispensing with or dealing with slaves and servants who had become Christians, but his wife and daughter proved to be a greater challenge. Perhaps he thought that if he could destroy the places used for Christian worship and virtually eliminate all of their books and writings, as well as those who taught such things, the Church would simply fade away. It did not happen, and I and the other people of Alexandria watched the developing situation carefully, for experience had shown that the Christians of our area often fared the worst in times of persecution. Normally I would not have wasted much concern on such matters, except that now things had become personal.

When Diocletian's edicts did not work as he had intended, the persecutions began in earnest. Christians, as well as those who were supportive of Christians, were removed from positions of authority. Imprisonment was common if there was even the smallest suspicion that a person might be a believer. The final indignity (and only a Christian would see it as such) was the emperor's edict delivered in 304, which stated that all Christians were to offer sacrifice to the gods. All of us who loved her feared for Valeria's safety. It was the worst time imaginable.

As it became obvious that the persecutions were beginning again, I was grateful that I had already had almost two years of instruction in the faith. My faith was strong, and none of the joy that I had felt at my conversion was lessened by fear of the unknown. I know that this was a true grace from God and not anything of my own doing (just as my conversion had been a grace from God). I was prepared for what might happen, even as I was concerned for the safety of my family. It was not unheard of that entire families would be martyred because of one Christian member. I did not want my family to suffer for even one moment (any more than they had already suffered over my initial decision to become a Christian). I comforted them as best I could, and then I took my leave of them, turning my attentions to those within the community who were faltering in their commitment to the Lord. The stories of the faith of the martyrs sustained us as we waited whatever was to be our fate. Of course we were not idle, as there was much of God's work to do.

It was decided that we would move forward with our Baptisms rather than wait for the Easter Vigil. As I arose from the water and was anointed and clothed in a new, white garment that was a symbol of my dignity as a member of the Body of Christ, I was elated. Of our group of twenty-six, two chose not to be baptized, in fear of the suffering they might endure in the near future. Who among us could blame them? We prayed for them that very night, as the baptismal liturgy continued at the Lord's Table. What a privilege it was to receive Jesus in the sacred Bread and Wine for the first time! How I had longed for that moment! Never have I felt more complete. I was ready, strong in my faith. Why the Lord sought to deny me the glory of martyrdom, I shall never know. Perhaps it was because I was not worthy of dying for him. Perhaps it was my sin of pride, that I should even consider myself worthy. Perhaps there was still something I was meant to do for the Lord and the faithful. At any rate, my life was spared—but Claudia's was not.

Before she was taken to be burned, Claudia said that I should give thanks to God that it was so. She felt that I had been chosen to continue the work of the Lord here on earth, even as she had been chosen to glorify him through her death. She, who was so serene and filled with faith, asked me to pray with her and also for her. I shall always remember that her greatest concern was for the others and for the Church that she was leaving behind. She knew that the persecutions would ravage the community of believers and that they would need to rely on those who were strong in the faith to help them and to minister to them. Claudia confided to me that, in a dream, she had seen me in the role of deaconess. She felt that she had to tell me this before she died. I wept for my fear of what was to come—not for myself, but for my dear friend. Before I had to leave her, we embraced, and, just she had done long ago, Claudia traced the sign of the cross on my forehead as a reminder that I was to do everything in Jesus' name. Then she blessed me and called me "her dear sister in Christ." I never felt so blessed.

Eventually the persecutions ended. "A reign of terror" is what Pristina called them. The Christians said that 144,000 believers chose to give up their lives rather than deny their faith. I'm not sure of the accuracy of that number, because, for Christians, there seems to be a symbolic meaning in the number 144,000. Thank the gods that Valeria's life was spared. It seems that I am one of the few remaining persons who would actually "thank the gods" for anything. With Emperor Constantine's edict of tolerance, issued last year in 313, people all over the empire are becoming Christian.

I know that Quintus never recovered from the stress of it all. It won't be long now before he leaves this world. Until then, as his faithful servant and friend, I shall remain by his side. Of course Pristina is there as well. All these years she has been a wonderful wife to him and his closest friend and confidant. I know that she is secretly hoping that he will convert to Christianity, as she did several years ago. Her faith gives her much comfort, and I truly think that Quintus will convert, if for no other reason than the beautiful example that Valeria and the rest of his family gave him. No doubt, when her beloved husband dies, Pristina will follow her children into the desert to live in solitude there. As in everything else, it has been Valeria who has set the example for her family and for so many others.

Claudia was right; I did eventually become a deaconess, and it was my greatest pleasure to minister to the needs of the faithful in Alexandria for over a dozen years. My joy was truly complete when my sister Augusta, my brother Philip, and my dear mother were received into the Church. How my heart looks forward to the time when my beloved father may know the love and peace of Christ. I pray for him daily and for all those who are in need of God's grace. Most of all, however, I pray for myself—not in a selfish way, but rather in the way that Claudia taught me so long ago. I pray that I may know God's will and that I may have the courage and the grace to act on what I know to be true.

Thus ends my story—or, perhaps, it has only just begun. But this is how I found myself in the desert, for this is where God's Spirit has called me. I am not exactly sure why, but all that I really need to know is that this is where I am meant to be. Here in this wilderness, my whole being feels at one with the Lord. The distractions of the city are far removed from me, and I can truly pray for the needs of the Church and of the world in a way that I have never been able to do before now. Never have I felt so close to God. I remember the words of Holy Scripture from the Book of Isaiah; they speak to me: "In the wilderness prepare the way of the Lord, make straight in the desert a highway for our God. Then the glory of the Lord shall be revealed, and all people shall see it together, for the mouth of the Lord has spoken" (40:3, 5). How honored I am to be a pathmaker.

Thus ends the fictional story of Valeria, a story similar to that of many new Christians at the time of transition between a hostile empire and a tolerant one. As we saw in the previous

chapter, the structure of the early Church—the community of believers—was "unstructured" for some time, although the Church was obviously benefiting from the guidance and leadership of the apostles, Paul, and other men such as Barnabas, Silas, and Timothy. The somewhat unstructured early Church was alive with a vibrancy of different ministries that often overlapped. Ministries were also based much more on the needs of the community and on the particular giftedness of the minister than on whether a person happened to be male or female; some of the women who assumed leadership roles were listed in the previous chapter.

This was the way things were until the Church gradually came to the realization that Christ's second coming was not imminent. The Church, as a result, slowly sought to accommodate itself to the world around it, and the most logical and normative way to organize was to pattern itself after the structure of the Roman household. Over time house churches were replaced by larger churches led by male overseers or bishops assisted by men and women; eventually even the gift of prophesy came to be seen as the prerogative of the bishops. The resulting "stability" helped the Church coexist with the Roman government, despite sporadic and localized persecutions.

With Emperor Constantine's Edict of Milan in 313, the Church achieved legitimacy. With legitimacy, however, came a trade-off, and that was a Church that grew more hierarchical and male-dominated. Although women had long served the Church through a variety of ministries, including presiders of house churches, missionaries, deaconesses, the Order of Widows, prophets, teachers, and so forth, eventually there was little opportunity for the pastoral presence and leadership of women. The Church was well on its way to a male-only clericalism while priesthood was still in the process of formation and self-definition. As the Church hierarchy began to exclude them from ministering in any "official" capacity, many women chose a life of prayer in the desert as a way to serve the Lord. As the number of hermits, both men and women, increased, monasticism (communities of men and communities of women devoted to prayer) developed.

From the Desert to the Monastery

The experience of retreating to the wilderness of the desert for spiritual renewal and ministry was not unfamiliar to the early followers of Christ. In fact, Jesus himself gave a powerful example when he retreated to the desert immediately after his baptism (Matthew 4:1–11). It was there that he was "tempted by the devil," either literally, as Scripture records, or perhaps symbolically. He retreated from all of the distractions of the world so that he could focus on his mission. Jesus and the community of believers also witnessed the example of the Essenes, a religious sect whose members sought spiritual purity by living in desert communities. (It is speculated that Jesus' own cousin, John, was an Essene.) The Christian community was also familiar with Paul's retreat into the wilderness after his conversion to Christianity.

The desire to live austere lives, dedicated in service to the Lord and away from the influence of worldly things, actually had a direct connection to Constantine's edict of tolerance. It was not long before Christianity became the new state religion, and, with the state's acceptance of—and later, insistence on—conversion, it was now the norm for entire families, young and old, to become Christian. This lessened the need for deaconesses who, until this time, had played an integral part

in the preparation of women catechumens. Now countless people of all ages were choosing to be Christian, and the time of preparation was considerably shorter than it had been before Constantine's edict. The reduced need for deaconesses, as well as the developing sense of a male-only priesthood, eventually led to the discontinuation of a female diaconate.

Once Christianity became the state religion, much of the sense of religious purity and of being "set apart" was lost. Those who converted for political reasons, under pressure or out of some other necessity, quite understandably often had little or no true commitment to the faith. Hence, there was a "worldliness" creeping into Christianity that was very hard for true followers of Christ to endure. It was not long before the wilderness of the desert began to beckon to many men and women as a way to oppose that worldliness.

The desert experience of Christianity appealed to so many people that by the middle of the fourth century, monasticism was firmly established throughout the entire area of northern Africa. The monasteries were of lay origin, meaning they were started by people who were not ordained (in other words, not officially ministering within the Church). Although the word *monasticism* is of Greek origin and means "alone," not every early monastic lived as a hermit. Some did lead a solitary life, generally living in caves or very simple dwellings, while others lived in communities with common buildings.

Monastic life, most generally, included aspects of prayer, fasting, the study of Scripture, and, perhaps, other purifications that a person felt might help him or her on the journey toward

spiritual perfection. The goal, of course, was to design one's life so that it was in harmony with God's will; thus all that was accomplished, whether it was work or prayer, would glorify God. Personal sanctification was one reward of such a life, but it was not the primary goal. That goal was the sanctification of the Church and of the world.

Christian monasticism, by origin, grew out of the experience of the Church in Egypt. It is generally believed that it was a man who came to be known as Saint Antony of Egypt and the father of monasticism. Probably sometime around the year 285, he went to live in the desert. Honored and sought out by many, it was not long before others followed. So many followed Antony, in fact, that by the time of his death in the middle of the fourth century, there were already eleven monasteries in northern Africa, two of which were exclusively for women.

See Alfred McBride, *The Story of the Church: Peak Moments from Pentecost to the Year 2000* (Cincinnati, OH: Saint Anthony Messenger Press and Franciscan Communications, 1996).

Although Antony may have been officially recognized as the first male monastic, consecrated life for women actually began in apostolic times with the Order of Widows (1 Timothy 5:3–16). The Order of Widows consisted of women who were over the age of sixty and without family members to care for them. They vowed themselves to live lives of chastity and spiritual purity and to give service to the Church, as well as to offer intercessory prayer. In return, those in the Order of Widows were supported through the charity of their faith community. As time went on, some of the more physically challenging work was delegated to the younger female deaconesses. Eventually, after Constantine's edict, the Order of Widows (as a consecrated ministry within the Church) and the ministry of the deaconesses both came to an end.

This did not mean, however, that women no longer lived in community or that they had no options available to them to serve the Church. They had such options because they chose to develop systems that suited their needs, which were eventually recognized by Church authorities. In society at large, there were very few options for women regarding how they lived their lives. Women were expected to marry at a rather young age and have children. If they were widowed, they either remarried (if widowed at a young age) or lived off the charity of their children. If a woman's children were not willing to assist her, she probably lived her later years in poverty and misery. For some women, this future was just too bleak to be considered. These women often envisioned a different way of living that would offer them the chance to serve the Church, using the gifts that God had given them, while also allowing them some element of freedom from traditional roles and responsibilities. To achieve their goals, many young women chose to consecrate themselves to virginity.

> *Various ways of living out the radical commitment [to virginity] developed: Some remained "in the world" but wore black or gray to set them apart from other unmarried women. Consecration might consist of a church ceremony in which the bishop bestowed a blessed veil, or be made publicly visible when the hair—a woman's "glory"—was shorn as an act of renunciation. Whether living at home or with a small group of other consecrated virgins, the women would fast, pray, and labor—much like contemplative nuns today.*
>
> Joanne Turpin, *Women in Church History: Twenty Stories for Twenty Centuries* (Cincinnati, OH: Saint Anthony Messenger Press and Franciscan Communications, 1990).

The monastic life in northern Africa tended to be contemplative, with nuns and monks living either singly or with their community, away from the world. As monasticism grew in popularity and spread to other parts of the empire, different styles of monastic life emerged. Some, rather than retreating from the world to find Christ, found him to be present inside and outside their community. For communities of this type, charitable works, coupled with prayer, formed the basis of monastic life. Quite frequently, religious communities of this type were a lifesaver to ill women who had been left destitute and without family. Often, after spending time in the monastic environment recovering from their illnesses, these women chose to stay.

In the monastery, women found that their talents were utilized and their productivity appreciated. Perhaps best of all, they had an opportunity for personal growth, education, and self-improvement. Whether the "desert experience" of monasticism took place in an actual desert in Egypt or in a busy part of Rome, whether it was experienced in isolation or in community, whether it was lived in a monastery as a female-vowed religious (nun) or as a male-vowed religious (monk), monasticism quite literally changed the face of the Church and of the world.

Behind the monastery walls, sacred Scripture was studied; one monastic community in Rome, led by Marcella, studied Scripture with Saint Jerome—in Hebrew, Greek, and Latin. Scripture was also meticulously copied and illustrated so that it would be preserved for posterity. (Remember that there was no printing press at this time in history; that invention was still centuries away.) Without the dedication of the monastic communities, it is quite possible that we would have neither the Bible nor countless other writings from antiquity. This preservation was especially important after the fall of Rome in 410. In addition to the written word, the arts flourished in the monasteries, as numerous religious paintings, statues, sculptures, and musical compositions were created by monastics. And the fields of medicine and agriculture advanced greatly from techniques that were developed from discoveries made by monastics.

In the sixth century, monasticism in the West reached a new benchmark with Saint Benedict and his sister Saint Scholastica. Benedict's rule, drawn from the best of previous rules, brought unity and order to the diverse monastic movement in Europe. In a short time the Rule of Benedict was adopted by monasteries for men and monasteries for women all over Europe; over time they facilitated the development of many towns and cities.

Saint Hilda of Whitby

Hilda was born in 614, the great-niece of the king of Northumberland in the north of present-day England. Saint Paulinus, a missionary from Rome, converted King Edwin and all his people. Along with the king, Hilda and many others were baptized in the tiny cathedral in 627. Hilda had been raised at court and remained in the area when the king was overthrown by a non-Christian. This king, in turn, was replaced by King Oswald, a Christian, who brought Irish monks to the realm to solidify the conversion of the people.

Hilda eventually entered the monastic life and in 649 became the abbess of the double monastery (adjoining quarters for women and men) at Harttepool, where she was also the tutor of King Oswiu's daughter.

Some ten years or so later, the king gave Hilda land at Streaneshalch on which to establish another double monastery, later known as Whitby. Under her rule, the monks and nuns studied Scripture and other disciplines as they developed their spiritual lives according to the approach of the Celtic Church. There was no class distinction, and all things were held in common. The monks and nuns copied, translated, and illustrated Bibles and manuscripts of all kinds, gradually creating one of the best libraries in England. In the abbey complex Hilda had built housing for the sick and a school where music was one of the important subjects.

Hilda insisted on good preparation for the priesthood, and over time five of the monks were named bishops; two of those became saints. England's first religious poet, Caedmon, was also a member of the monastery. Royalty, monks, and ordinary people from far and near came to Hilda for advice, which Hilda managed to impart while still participating in community life and prayer.

Hilda presided at a synod for all England, which was held in Northumberland in 664 to determine the Church calendar. The Church in the south followed the Roman calendar regarding the date of Easter, while the Church in the north, heavily influenced by the Irish missionary effort, continued with the Celtic custom. Hilda was a great supporter of Celtic customs, but she was unable to sway the synod to that direction. When the Roman calendar was adopted, Hilda gracefully accepted the decision. Thus she was highly influential in the movement toward unity in the Church in England.

For the last seven years before she did in 680, Hilda suffered from a fever and thus ill health, but she continued her work for the community to the end. It was said that "all who knew her called her Mother, such were her wonderful godliness and grace." Hilda was soon honored as a saint, and over a dozen churches along the northeast cost of England were dedicated to her. She is most often pictured holding the Abbey of Whitby in her hands and with a crown on her head or at her feet. Her feast day is November 17.

It is important to realize that monasticism is not a quaint part of the Church's experience that can now be consigned to the past. Actually, monasticism continues to influence the Church and to shape our world in ways that we may not even realize. The most obvious way is probably through the gift of its witness. In our extremely fast-paced world, perhaps it does us good to pause for a moment and realize that there is another way to experience life. We may be caught up in the hectic pace of our own lives, but others have willingly embraced lives of silence, prayer, charity, and sacrifice. No wonder that through the experience of monasticism, so many persons in the history of the Church have become saints and influenced the direction of the entire Church.

The Experience of Sainthood

Holy cards, statues, stained-glass windows, brightly colored pictures in a book—these are just some of the mental images we have when we think of saints. We may also have the tendency to think of saints as somehow "super-human," having achieved a sanctity and a level of spirituality that is virtually impossible for 99.9 percent of humanity. Often people attribute a hierarchical order to the communion of saints, with some saints (the favorite and the well-known) being honored more than others. For example, who has not heard of Saint Francis of Assisi, Saint Teresa of Ávila, or Saint Jude? But have you heard of Saint Protase, Saint Anastasia, or Saint Gervase?

This type of understanding of sainthood does a disservice to what the communion of saints actually is. It may be helpful to begin our brief examination of the topic of sainthood by looking to the *Catechism of the Catholic Church* for an explanation of how all Christians are called to holiness and then for definitions of the communion of saints and the intercession of saints.

> *"All Christians in any state or walk of life are called to the fullness of Christian life and to the perfection of charity"* [LG *40§2]. All are called to holiness: "Be perfect, as your heavenly Father is perfect"* [Mt *5:48].*
>
> *In order to reach this perfection the faithful should use the strength dealt out to them by Christ's gift, so that . . . doing the will of the Father in everything, they may wholeheartedly devote*

> *themselves to the glory of God and to the service of their neighbor. Thus the holiness of the People of God will grow in fruitful abundance, as is clearly shown in the history of the Church through the lives of so many saints [LG 40§2].*
>
> *Catechism of the Catholic Church* (Washington, DC: United States Catholic Conference, 1994), #2013.

In the Bible, Paul used the word saint on more than one occasion when he referred to all of the Christian faithful (2 Corinthians 13:12; Ephesians 1:1; Philippians 4:21, for example). In the sense that "all are called to holiness," all Christians might be called saints, saintly, or even saints on earth.

But the type of sainthood that we are concerned with here is more specific, dealing with those people who had lived holy lives, who have died, who are now believed to be experiencing the presence of God, and who have been canonized by the Church. It should be noted that in recognition of the fact that all Christians are called to live holy lives—and countless Christians throughout the ages have done so and continue to do so—there are many more saints in heaven than have ever been canonized by the Church. Anyone who has lived a good life, to the best of their ability, could be presumed to be in heaven and thus can be called a saint.

Canonization is the official process of recognition that declares that a person is in heaven and is worthy of veneration, or honor. In the early Church, martyrs were rather automatically considered saints. Later other holy people were often popularly acclaimed by the people of a local church; Hilda is an example of such a saint. Because of abuses, the declaration of sainthood later became the prerogative of the bishop and eventually of the

pope. The first official canonization by the pope took place in 993, but it wasn't until 1234 that only papal canonizations were recognized as legitimate.

The present lengthy and thorough process of canonization involves intense research. The cannonization process usually begins locally, with the bishop of a diocese assigning an expert to conduct an investigation into the life of the person suggested for sainthood. Witnesses, if available, are asked to give testimony on behalf of the candidate. Miracles attributed to the candidate's intercession are thoroughly investigated. When finished, the expert prepares a written report on his or her findings. If the bishop finds that there is reason to believe that the cause is valid, all the research findings, the written testimonies, and a detailed biography of the person is sent to Rome for further study by the Congregation for the Causes of Saints. At this time, the person may be named *Venerable*.

If found to be worthy, the candidate for sainthood is beatified with a formal declaration of a person's holiness and named *Blessed*; this is the second step toward canonization. If additional information and miracles are discovered after a candidate has been beatified, then further investigation takes place. If the candidate's cause if found to be true and can be authenticated, then the pope declares the person to be a saint and worthy of veneration by the universal Church. This process generally takes years of extremely thorough investigation before canonization occurs. Unfortunately, this careful, thorough, and detailed process of canonization is not without its flaws.

> Latin American liberation theologians *have been critical of the present list of canonized saints, most of whom are white, European, and upper- and middle-class. The poor and the oppressed are not represented. . . .* Feminist theology, *too*, *calls*

> *for a reexamination of the theology of the saints, pointing out that over 70 percent of the saints on the liturgical calendar are men and that, of the saints canonized in this century to the end of Paul VI's pontificate (1978), 79 percent are clergy, 21 percent lay, and a smaller percentage, women.*
>
> Richard P. McBrien, *Catholicism* (San Francisco: Harper SanFrancisco, 1994).

Pope John Paul II did considerably better in regard to these two concerns, but there is still much room for improvement. He canonized more saints than did all the other popes of the last four centuries. Many of the people he beatified and canonized were lay people and martyrs from a multitude of countries around the world.

Further clarification of the term *veneration of the saints* is needed. First of all, veneration is not adoration. Adoration belongs only to God, and there is no human person to whom the Church would give adoration, not even Mary, the mother of Jesus. Catholics pray only to God and recognize that God is the origin of any blessings received and that God's grace is freely given. Catholics also do not pray to the saints in the belief that they provide blessings, healings, or other miracles. However, we can ask the saints in heaven to intercede with God on our behalf; these are prayers of intercession.

Veneration of the saints, properly understood, is honor that is given to God, since all holiness and goodness originates with God and is impossible without God's grace. Therefore, if a person feels a connectedness, a love or a devotion to a particular saint—and if through prayer he or she asks that saint to intercede with God on his or her behalf—then those emotions and prayers are ultimately directed to God alone. The Second Vatican Council stated this well in "Dogmatic Constitution of the Church."

Every authentic witness of love, indeed, offered by us to those who are in heaven tends to and terminates in Christ, "the crown of all the saints" [Roman Breviary, Invitatory for the feast of All Saints], *and through him in God who is wonderful in his saints and is glorified in them (cf. v.g. 2 Th 1:10).*

"Dogmatic Constitution on the Church," *Vatican Council II: The Conciliar and Post Conciliar Documents*, Austin Flannery, gen. ed. (Collegeville, MN: The Liturgical Press, 1975), #50.

The spiritual connection that a person may feel in relation to a particular saint or saints is an excellent example, in part, of what the Church means by the term the *communion of saints*. The Church teaches that death neither ends our connectedness to each other nor does it overcome love. The communion of saints, therefore, is the belief that the faithful on earth, and those who have died, are truly formed by God's Spirit into one body. We can and should pray for our loved ones who have died. Also, we can turn to the saints in heaven and ask for their intercession, both for our needs as well as for the sake of our deceased loved ones. The scriptural basis for belief in the communion of saints is found in 1 Corinthians 12:12–13:

For just as the body is one and has many members, and all the members of the body, though many, are one body, so it is with Christ. For in the one Spirit we were all baptized into one body—Jews or Greeks, slaves or free—and we were all made to drink of one Spirit.

Belief in the communion of saints is clearly stated in the Apostles' Creed as an integral belief of the Christian faith: "We believe in the Holy Spirit, the holy catholic Church, the communion of saints. . . ."

The Communion of Saints

Although it seems too obvious a fact to overlook, it should be noted that it was Jesus' own resurrection that formed the early development of the concept of sainthood. Certain religious groups or sects during the time of Jesus were bitterly divided on the issue of an afterlife. For the Sadducees, it seemed an unbelievable possibility, while the Pharisees argued that there must be some form of life after death. Throughout much of the history of Judaism, death was believed to be the end of all relationships, both to other people and to God.

Pheme Perkins notes that it was about two hundred years before Jesus when the possibility of life after death first began to be explored in Judaism. This was due, in part, to a highly developed Jewish concept of justice. Increasingly God was seen as a God whose power to save and whose concern that justice be done would simply have to extend beyond this life. In that way, the good would be rewarded (even if they had suffered in this life) and those who did evil would be punished (even if they seemed to have escaped punishment in this life).

> *. . . resurrection was described as coming out of the tomb or the earth. The righteous would either become like angels or have new "eternal, glorious garments" to put on. No one thought that the resurrection would simply mean the physical body coming back to life.*
>
> Pheme Perkins, *Reading the New Testament: An Introduction* (Mahwah, NJ: Paulist Press, 1988).

All of this is important to our understanding of the development of a theology that was inclusive of sainthood. The resurrection proved life after death to be a reality, even as Jesus' acceptance of his own death served as an example and a source of strength for the Christian martyrs who were to follow.

> *Veneration of the burial sites, pilgrimages to places where the martyrs had lived or died, adoption of a saint as a patron of a church or town, belief in the power of the saints to perform miracles on behalf of the living—all of these practices developed very early in the Church's history.*
>
> McBrien.

As the persecutions escalated and more Christians were martyred, the Christians took courage from the example of Jesus as he faced his own death. Their strong faith comforted them during this perilous time, as they believed that their own death would assure an immediate passage to heaven and "sainthood."

Once the persecutions of the early centuries ended, it was not martyrdom but rather asceticism that came to be seen as the ultimate sacrifice of giving up one's life. The monastics who practiced self-denial through a simple lifestyle, structured prayer, fasting, virginity, and celibacy modeled a holiness that often led to sainthood. Most did not seek to be known as saints, but rather chose to do their good works out of true charity and recognized that holiness is a gift from God and a response to the action of the Holy Spirit. Their lives were (and continue to be) powerful examples of what it means to make a total commitment of self to God.

Many canonized saints, including those who achieved sainthood through asceticism, arrived at sanctity through a lifelong dedication to prayer, virtuous living, and good works. The gospel's call to service, if balanced with a realistic understanding of human limitations, has been a well-traveled path for many saints through the years. Their lives have taught us that charity and service (given out of love of God and love of one's neighbor) is at the core of Christianity.

Sainthood or holiness is still the Christian ideal, whether achieved through martyrdom (still too frequently a reality in our time) or through the practice of prayer and service to others. But sainthood is not an end in itself, for the saints serve only as models who point toward the greater reality that is God.

Perhaps the Church of the third millennium will increasingly recognize that there are many ways of looking at what is holy, and perhaps this will result in a corresponding shift in attitudes regarding sainthood. For example, why do we not more readily acknowledge the sanctity that is possible within the bond of

marriage? Surely there are countless couples who have lived out the Sacrament of Matrimony in such a way as to give a beautiful witness to the holiness that can be attained through marriage.

> *They are to love one another as Christ loved the Church, with a love that is sacrificial, forgiving, service-oriented and faithful unto death. In fact, over the centuries there have been many husband and wife saints. They have come from all strata of society. At the head of the list stand Mary and Joseph, who came from the surroundings of a wood-worker's shop. Priscilla and Aquila, both regarded as saints, earned their living as tent-makers. Justinian and Theodora, saints in the Orthodox tradition, were emperor and empress. St. Stephen and Blessed Gisela (eleventh century) were the first king and queen of Hungary. Isidore of Madrid and Maria de la Cabeza were farmers.*
>
> Robert P. Maloney, "Models of Being Holy," *America* (15 February 1997): 17.

In officially recognizing the saintliness of a person or persons, we do them a grave injustice if we deny them their humanity. The saints are like us; they have unique personal faults and attributes. While some are so far removed from our own experience that we feel little connection to them, others may be so close to us in attitude or personality that we feel a deep, spiritual connection with them. The saints offer us a fascinating glimpse at holiness. Made in God's image, we all have been created for goodness; deep within the heart of every Christian is the desire to be holy and to return to that which is holy. How blessed we are to have the saints as our companions along the way, for they draw us ever closer to our goal.

Some Thoughts for Your Reflection

1. In "Valeria's Story" we met a young woman who was perfectly content with her lifestyle—including her worship of gods and goddesses—until she met the Christian deaconess Claudia. It was that event, their chance meeting, that caused Valeria to see her own life as it appeared through another's eyes. Have you ever had a similar moment, when you could "step outside your own perceptions" to see things in a different way? Who was it that helped you do so? Was the experience a positive one? A necessary one? Was it an agent for change in your life?

2. Just as Valeria worshiped non-Christian deities without much reflection about what she was doing (because it was what everyone did), it is not too difficult for us to do the same. In today's fastpaced world, we often allow a person or things to become our "god." What, if anything, in your life has a priority that it should not have or that is robbing you of serenity? Pray about it, asking God for the strength and the grace so that balance may be restored in your life.

3. In "Valeria's Story" we meet persons who are willing to die for what they believe in and love so deeply. Can you understand the martyr's choice? Had you lived in that time, do you think that your love of God would have been sufficient to allow you to give up your life rather than recant your faith? Spend some time thinking about this, and then ask yourself the following questions: Whom or what in my life would I be willing to die for? Is there anyone in my life who loves me enough to make such a sacrifice on my behalf? If so, thank God for their presence in your life.

4. Would the monasticism of Hilda work today? Why or why not? Why do you think monasticism still appeals to many people? Could you see yourself living such a lifestyle? Many monasteries, convents, and spirituality and retreat centers are available for the public's benefit upon request. They welcome others to share in some of the rhythm and flow of their way of life. If this sounds interesting to you, call a monastery or religious community near you, and see what might be available.

5. In this chapter we are reminded that "all are called to holiness" and that we are all saintly. Do you see yourself as saintly? Do you think anyone close to you would use this word to describe you? Why or why not?

6. Since today's world is often focused on materialism and consumerism, Christians can make a powerful witness by practicing, like many of the saints, a life of simplicity. Does the idea of living a more simple and basic lifestyle appeal to you? What things in your life are you ready to give up so that you can be more spiritually free?

Chapter five

Mystics, Ecologists, Poets, and Artists

Saint Catherine and Saint Marguerite

The Church of the Middle Ages

In order to understand the tremendous contributions that women made to the Church during the centuries known as the Middle Ages—the fifth century to the sixteenth century—it is necessary to first understand this period of time. Of particular importance is an appreciation of the Church in the Middle Ages, for in many respects it was the Church's influence that quite literally held the Western world together as civilization went through its most major transition. A look back into history is helpful and provides a background for our study of some of this period's most influential women.

The Middle Ages began as the western part of the Roman Empire collapsed. (The eastern portion of the empire, however, held together for a considerable period of time). But in the West, this transition took place over a span of approximately three hundred years, which makes dating the exact beginning of the Middle Ages difficult. What is more important, however, is to understand how volatile and unstable the Western world had become. The time was characterized by warfare, societal destruction, religious turmoil, and hardships of almost every kind. Life was hard. Hence, the average life expectancy was somewhere between 30 and 40 years.

For more than 1,200 years, people of Germanic origin moved from Scandinavia southward into central Europe. Most of these tribal peoples eventually adopted the customs of their new surroundings, learned about the agriculture of the areas,

entered into trade with their neighbors, and became Christian, abandoning their worship of the Scandinavian gods Odin and Thor. By the early fifth century, however, this peaceful acclimation into Roman society began to change as the empire's northern borders were invaded by increasing numbers of Germanic tribes who did not have farming and trading on their minds. In Spain, it was the Visigoths; in Gaul (France), it was the Franks; in Britain, it was the Anglos and the Saxons.

The already over-extended and weakened Roman army was not able to adequately defend its frontiers, and the once-great western portion of the Roman Empire was eventually divided into kingdoms ruled by tribal chiefs. Naturally, each tribe was loyal to its king. The ordered and structured pattern of Roman life quickly disintegrated, except, that is, where the Church was well established.

As the empire fell, the Church stepped in, to assume many of the societal responsibilities that should have belonged to the government. The Church attempted to fill, at least to some degree, the necessary "order out of chaos" for society. But the Church sacrificed some of its sense of community for the sake of increased structure and stability. In essence, the Church, in its attempt to hold things together, became more "Romanized," patterning itself after the very government that was falling apart.

Although the Church could not possibly compensate for all that society had lost due to invasions, battles, and strife, it was, however, doing its best to be a constant and stable element in this new and chaotic world. Filling the void left by the government, the Church maintained courts of law so that criminals would be punished, society protected, and the Roman ideals of justice and law, integrated with Christian principles, upheld. The Church also collected taxes to ensure that other territories ruled by the shrinking empire could function, at least nominally. And the Church was quick to reach out to the invading peoples as well, seeing a fertile opportunity to spread Christianity.

It was the Christian missionaries, both men and women, who made great strides in the conversion of the non-Christian invaders. As many of the chieftan-kings converted, they brought (or, as was common practice at the time, forced) their subjects into the Church as well. Consequently, the Church experienced great growth, although there was legitimate concern over the sincerity and depth of belief of the new converts. Nonetheless, even though the people of the former Roman Empire had lost a unified government with all of its advantages, they were gradually, through the spread of Christianity, coming to worship one God and to follow the teachings of Jesus.

Perhaps most significant of all the Church's accomplishments during this time was the establishment of many monasteries in Europe. The monasteries kept education alive through the copying (by hand) of ancient manuscripts, the establishment of places of learning, and the use of Latin as a unifying language for peoples of many different languages and dialects. Monasteries truly were bastions of knowledge in a world that was chaotic.

Woman monastics were as historically significant to the Church and to Europe as were men monastics. Joan Ohanneson summarizes this fact very succinctly as she stresses that we deserve to know the contributions women made to this period of history. (The meaning of ordination of abbesses is still much debated today.)

> *The remarkable women abbesses of the Middle Ages exercised quasi-episcopal jurisdiction, both temporal and spiritual, and*

answered directly to Rome. . . . The Abbess Jeanne Baptiste de Bourbon of the Abbey of Fontevrault was responsible for the nomination of her clergy, for the payment of benefices for their forty rectories, chapels, and churches, and for the nomination of the one hundred prioresses who were dependent on the centralized government of the abbey. The abbesses (not the bishops or priests) personally selected their priors, empowering them with the necessary license to preach, to confess, and to serve women's houses. In addition, they authorized confessors to absolve cases normally reserved to bishops. . . . In these historical settings, priests and monks, together with the nuns, took vows of obedience to the abbess, in imitation of the obedience of Jesus to his mother, while the abbesses, in imitation of Mary, served the community devotedly in an administrative capacity. . . . Abbesses were, in fact, once ordained, replete with the symbols of episcopal office. They received and wore the miter, crosier, ring, stole, alb, gloves, and pectoral cross. . . . In the twelfth century, women not only convoked and presided at Church synods but also emerged as the main leaders in discussions and as outstanding promoters of liturgical reform. In the tenth and eleventh centuries the power of the abbesses of the chief houses in Germany, those of Quedlinburg and Gandershein, were able, under Otto I, to strike their own coins bearing their portraits. . . . The Abbess of Quedlinburg had both a seat and a vote on the Imperial Diet, while the English abbesses were called to Parliament during the twelfth century. . . . And once canonnesses walked in front of clergy carrying the pastoral cross. They lived and breathed, these women, exercising incalculable influence, touching lives, healing souls, and making decisions.

Joan Ohanneson, *Woman: Survivor in the Church* (San Francisco: HarperSanFrancisco, 1983).

Perhaps one of the greatest challenges contemporary Christians face in understanding our collective faith history is that it is not dry, disconnected information about events and people of long ago but rather a heritage—a beautiful inheritance that has been left to us. But as is often true in the case of women's "hidden" history, such as the examples just cited, we may not have known that it was ours to find.

Life was not easy for anyone who lived during the Middle Ages, especially not for women. It is no wonder that so many women chose to live in monasteries, seeing in them an opportunity to be allowed some sense of personal autonomy, to be educated, and to serve God through the use of their natural gifts and talents. Outside of a monastic environment, women generally had few opportunities for personal growth and development. Oddly enough, even with the often-strict Rule that governed monasteries and abbeys, life inside the walls was much more life-giving and free than it was on the outside.

In the early Middle Ages especially, but in fact throughout the entire Middle Ages, superstition abounded. Poverty and disease were rampant, even before the plagues swept through Europe. Generally uneducated and with virtually no hope of ever improving their lives, people of this time often despaired. Hope of heaven was about the only hope they had of ever experiencing anything better.

Understandably, people saw God as a distant but powerful shaper of their destiny. Things were as they were because God made them so. For example, during this time, there was no concept of a "natural" disaster. If droughts or floods occurred, it was not only God's will but also perhaps God's punishment for those who had sinned in some way. This was the rationale even when a mother, her infant, or both died during child-birth, since the people lacked knowledge of the need for

adequate medical care or sanitation. Thus tragedies of this sort were faced by believing that God's will was inscrutable and often harsh.

In the minds of many, God was similar to the distant kings that ruled the divided lands, far removed from the people and their lives. This concept of a distant Creator who was quick to punish was clearly entrenched in the common theology of the time. Obviously some type of mediator was necessary between heaven and earth, and that mediation was found in the Church. Devotion to Mary and the saints played an important role in the people's religious expression.

As Europe entered the feudal period, from the ninth century to the thirteenth century, the overall conditions of the populace worsened. Under feudalism, people who worked the land for the lord of the estate were often reduced to indenturing themselves in order to save their families from starvation. This period of indenture could last for many years, even a lifetime.

The relatively small manors (ruled by the lords and worked by the vassals) were no match for the next threat that faced the West—the invasions of the Vikings. Once again, it was the Christian missionaries—this time primarily the Irish monastics, both men and woman—who were largely responsible for holding together the Christian faith throughout Europe. Considering the large geographic area involved, the difficulty in travel, and the resultant lack of communication, as well as the different ethnic backgrounds of the people, this was quite an accomplishment. While these factors contributed to a significant religious diversity during this time, most people remained Christian, and the Church was once again seen as a fortress of stability against the invasions that plagued Europe.

Nor were the times easy for the Church of the East, which was virtually surrounded by invading Muslims and cut off from the Church of Rome. In this isolation, the long-standing cultural and religious differences between the East and the West became even more pronounced. This physical division was a significant factor, but not the only one, that helped prime conditions for the time in the eleventh century when the Church would separate into East and West.

During the time that is frequently referred to as the High Middle Ages (approximately from 1000 to about 1300), feudalism lost its hold as relative stability returned to Europe. Economically, things were only slightly better, but at least social structures had stabilized. Towns were once again being established, and trade connections with other parts of the world were redeveloping. As an expression of faith and optimism, cathedrals were built, cathedrals whose beauty and majesty have lasted to this day. Universities were begun, often in association with the cathedrals. Education flourished, particularly theological study, along with other disciplines in science and the arts. The Church was the driving force behind all these changes.

Of course, this period of Church history also had its darker side. For example, the end of the eleventh century brought the Crusades, with their goal to free the Holy Land from the Muslims. This periodic invasion by the Christians lasted for about 150 years. Although there were eight "major" Crusades, the movement included countless lesser campaigns. These expeditions often had more to do with religious pilgrimages, trading, and useful work for second and third sons who would not inherit family lands than they did with military action.

Overall, from a military standpoint, the Crusades were disastrous, especially the fourth crusade. During that campaign, the

Christian crusaders acted more like invaders than as allies to the Eastern Church. They vandalized the Christian city of Constantinople, including its beautiful churches, and even went so far as to vandalize and desecrate the Hagia Sophia Cathedral. This was an especially bitter blow to the Eastern Christians and one that they could not excuse. Thus the actions of this group of crusaders helped seal the growing divisions in the Christian Church.

The Crusades did increase Europe's contact with the rest of the world, leading to increased trade, as well as to advancements in other areas. Through contact with the Muslim world, Europe dramatically advanced in philosophy, science, literature, and mathematics. The new understanding helped establish a new way of looking at the world, which helped create a fertile environment for the Renaissance that was to come. At least in this sense, the Crusades provided some positive benefit to the West—but at a terrible cost.

As always in Church history, persons of great vision and faith arose at some of the very darkest of times. During this time of turmoil and strife in Europe and between the Church in the East and in the West, the Dominican Order, also known as the Order of Preachers, and the Franciscans, the Order of Friars Minor, were formed. These two religious orders were significantly different from religious communities of the past. Their ministry took them beyond the monastery walls and into the streets where they were, at least in the beginning, literally dependent upon the generosity of others for their basic needs. Because of this, they came to be known as mendicant orders; the word *mendicant* means "begging." Their approach to vowed religious life was radical, and it quickly attracted scores of followers, including many women.

Dominic de Guzman (1170–1221), who is more familiar to us under the name Saint Dominic, was the founder of the Order of Preachers. The Dominican influence upon the Church of the Middle Ages was profound. In an age when so many of the common people had little or no access to education, Dominic believed that the gospel message and faith of the Church would best be spread through preaching and teaching. Working with this mission, the Dominicans founded and taught at universities all across Europe and produced some of the greatest theologians who have ever graced the Church. Catherine of Siena was a student of the Dominicans; we will explore her fascinating life later in this chapter.

Francis di Bernardone (1179–1226), the founder of the Franciscans, is better known to Christians of all denominations as Saint Francis of Assisi. Born into wealth, he nonetheless felt increasingly drawn to a life of service to those who were poor, of prayer, and of penance. In 1208 Francis founded the Friars Minor, or "Lesser Brothers," the early beginnings of the community that would come to be known as the Franciscans. The lifestyle of Francis was compelling, and it did not take long before young men and women were seeking to follow a similar spiritual path. One such woman was Clare di Favarone, better known as Saint Clare of Assisi.

As we will see, Clare did not live in the shadow of Francis, but rather became known for the depth of her own spirituality—so much so, that she became a consultant to bishops, popes, and royalty. She was the foundress of an order now called the Poor Clares, and her spirit is still evident in religious communities of Franciscan women who keep alive the ideals of service to those who are poor and in need, prayer, and constant reliance on God's mercy and goodness. Clare was eighteen years old when she left her privileged life to follow the way of Francis.

Saint Clare of Assisi

Late at night on Palm Sunday Clare let herself out of her house by the little "door of death"—the side door that in many homes was opened only to carry out the dead—and headed for the Portiuncula [church]. She had dressed herself like a bride, complete to veil and all her jewels, a romantic Italianate touch both saints had evidently planned in advance as a symbolic flourish. Francis met her at the chapel, took off the bridal clothes, cut her hair, and dressed her in the same sort of rough, undyed cloak he himself wore . . . [Eventually] she found her final haven at [the church of] San Damiano, not far from Francis's house, and Clare was never to leave it again except to visit the Portiuncula from time to time. . . .

Clare had imagined herself wandering about the country, free as Francis, to do good deeds and speak ecstatic words. Such an ideal in the twelfth century was about as capable of coming true as was Francis's dream of converting the Sultan in one interview. So she stayed enclosed like other nuns of her era. But the two friends were faithful to the end . . . and between them they invigorated not only Italy but also Christian Europe.

Phyllis McGinley, "Francis and Clare: The Good Companions," *The Francis Book: 800 Years with the Saint from Assisi*, edited by Roy M. Gasnick OFM (New York: Macmillan Publishing Company, 1980), 72–73.

In the forty-two years that Clare lived as a cloistered nun and the abbess of her community, she never once compromised her belief that it was only through absolute poverty that a Christian could learn to depend on God in everything. Clare believed that through this total act of dependence that lives of prayer and service to those in need could be truly embraced. To a medieval world that was becoming increasingly divided between those who were wealthy and those who were poor, this model of Christianity was extremely powerful. We might assume that lay people (who were primarily the peasant class) welcomed the Poor Clares and the ideals of Franciscan Christianity, while the wealthy were quite uncomfortable. No doubt Clare would have been very pleased to know that, through her desire to live a life of Christian simplicity and purity, she left a legacy to the world that includes more than a thousand monasteries that bear her name and house women who strive to follow her example. Obviously Clare's life gave a powerful witness to the world then, as it does today.

The end of the Middle Ages is often called the Late Middle Ages, a time that spanned about 200 years, from 1300 to 1500. It was during this period that Medieval Europe gave way to modern Europe. This was not, however, an easy transition, as Europe witnessed wars, peasant revolts, natural disasters such as droughts and floods, religious turmoil, and the bubonic plague—the Black Death. By the time the waves of plagues had diminished, almost one-third of the European population was dead and the entire region was in economic chaos once again. Especially hard-hit was the Catholic clergy, as countless priests died after being infected with the plague as they ministered to those who were ill. In the devastation many who took their place were often uneducated and motivated by factors other than a desire to serve the Lord. This would become incredibly significant in the times to come, as clergy abuses were one of the factors that eventually led to the Reformation.

Throughout the Middle Ages, during the times of invasions, natural and economic disasters, religious strife, as well as the times of hope and optimism, it was always the Church to which the people turned. Although the Church during this time often failed to live up to its mission, it did provide stability in the midst of great turmoil. It was the Church that gave spiritual sustenance as well as financial assistance to those who were poor.

In return, it was often the common people who kept alive the faith on which the Church had been founded. These people included, as previously mentioned, the powerful abbesses who provided sanctuary to women who sought to follow their call to a deeper spirituality by entering consecrated, religious life. Their monasteries were also bastions of education in a medieval world that was often ruled by superstition and ignorance.

The missionaries who helped spread Christianity to Europe—and then sought to keep Europe Christian in the face of wave after wave of invasions—were female as well as male. Their

anonymity of name does nothing to lessen their tremendous gift to the Church. Just as important were the women who birthed their children, saw to their Baptisms, raised them in the faith, and, all too frequently, grieved their deaths as pneumonia, influenza, measles, and the plague took their young lives. These women were nothing less than heroic, and perhaps it was their deep faith (and the conveyance of that faith to their surviving children) that allowed the Church to remain so central to the lives of medieval people.

But there were other women, too (many of them abbesses), whose contributions to the Church during the Middle Ages were invaluable. For the most part, however, the contemporary Catholic has not heard of their existence, and for that reason, their contributions to the Church are only recently being reclaimed. These women were the mystics of the Middle Ages.

The Medieval Mystics

Hildegard of Bingen, Mechthild of Magdeburg, Julian of Norwich, Catherine of Siena—some of their names may not be familiar, but at one time they were known throughout Europe as women of great wisdom and authority. Many pontiffs even sought their counsel. They were visionaries, authors, scientists, ecologists, physicians, artists, musicians, and more. At a time when the West was overwhelmed by chaos and division, these women, each in her own way, brought order, peace, and unity to their world. The special gift that they give to the Church, even centuries after their deaths, is that through their writings, discoveries, compositions, and art, they continue to grace our world. Perhaps, now more than ever, there is great benefit in seeking their wisdom. As companions to our modern spiritual journey, the stories of these women inspire and teach us to see the beauty and the value in all of God's creation and the interconnectedness of every living thing. Even more, these long ago mystics can teach us today to honor the tremendous gift that is our own story and our own experience. We can almost hear them whispering to us across the centuries, gently reminding us, in the words of Julian of Norwich, that "all will be well."

Hildegard of Bingen

Saint Hildegard of Bingen was surely not the first woman to be a Christian mystic, for mysticism has permeated Christianity from its very beginning. She is, however, often referred to as the *Mother of the Rhineland mystic movement*. Her prophetic grasp of

Hildegard of Bingen

humanity's responsibility to creation and her achievements as a theologian, writer, artist, scientist, and musician provided a path for other women to follow. One can only wonder if any of the other women mystics of that time would have dared to explore so deeply their new paths into truth and experience had Hildegard not preceded them. Truly, she was an incredibly gifted woman, whose courage in calling the Church to accountability served as a reminder that all creation is made in the image of God and is to be treasured. She was a remarkable woman who was not afraid to challenge and push the established gender boundaries of medieval society.

Born in 1098 in Germany, Hildegard was witness to a world that was struggling to create beauty, knowledge, and harmony out of medieval chaos. Even as the cathedrals were being built to glorify God and as testimonies to the people's faith, a different type of faith was also being born—the faith that sought to reclaim the Holy Land, which drove the ill-fated Crusades. Even as universities came into existence and scholarship began to flourish, the reckless power of the Inquisition labeled as a "heretic" anyone who seemed to stray beyond established Church teaching. While Christians of the western Church saw the Church as based in Rome, the Church itself struggled against the alliances and power of the emerging nations and kings. This struggle helped set the stage for the time when the popes and anti-popes would battle for control of the Church.

If Hildegard's life had taken a more customary path, perhaps she never would have risen to the greatness that she achieved, though never desired. A rather shy child, Hildegard most likely would have lived out her life in relative obscurity had it not been for the mentoring of another person, montoring that changed Hildegard's life in a very dramatic way. That person was a woman known as Jutta of Sponheim.

Jutta was a significant woman in her own right. Self-educated and considered a woman of holiness and vision, she chose to live her life within the shadow of a church that was attached to a Benedictine monastery in the town of Disibodenberg. Jutta's lifestyle was not too unusual, for, as we have seen, women's choices during this time were generally limited to either marriage or to a religious vocation. But what was out of the ordinary was Jutta's wisdom and holiness, to the extent that women were drawn to her and to the lifestyle that she led. Eventually, her tiny, two-room hermitage grew into a monastery in its own right, where a dozen women followed the Benedictine Rule.

It was to Jutta that Hildegard's parents came when they desired to "give her to the Lord." (The practice of giving away a child in this manner was not unusual in medieval times. Families were usually quite large, and it was often a struggle for parents to adequately feed and clothe their many children.) So Hildegard was turned over to Jutta's care when she was eight years old; at the age of fifteen, Hildegard made her vows as a nun at Jutta's monastery.

For the next twenty-three years, Hildegard learned from Jutta all that she could, and her education was extensive for the time. She studied Scripture, Latin, philosophy, science, herbal medicine, and music, and she learned all the necessary skills required to keep a monastery running smoothly. Upon the death of Jutta in 1136, Hildegard was chosen as prioress. It was probably difficult for Hildegard to accept such a responsibility, considering her basically reticent nature, but Jutta's influence through the years had no doubt also had its effect. Hildegard accepted the position, seeing it as an opportunity to serve her dear sisters and to continue the ministry that Jutta had long ago began—to make of the monastery a place of harmony in a medieval world that seemingly had sunk into chaos.

Hildegard's skill in administration and her reputation for holiness soon drew to the monastery others who desired to live a similar lifestyle. So many women came to Disibodenberg, in fact, that it became necessary to found a new abbey. In 1148, Hildegard did exactly that near the town of Rupertsberg. Understandably, the Benedictine monks of Disibodenberg were not too happy to see Hildegard and eighteen of the sisters leave, as Hildegard's reputation for holiness and wisdom had become quite a windfall for the monks. (People had begun making pilgrimages to the monastery, and with them, they brought donations of money.) However, even with the abbot's disapproval, Hildegard prevailed and founded her new monastery.

By 1165, however, it became necessary to once again expand; hence, a new abbey opened near Eibengen. In a monastic world that saw physical penance as a necessity for holiness, Hildegard's communities were certainly unique. Rather than espousing severe deprivations for the body, Hildegard believed that care of the total person was more in harmony with God's intent. In other words, her sisters strove to achieve a balanced life of prayer, work, recreation, and rest. The description on the following page is an example of what life at the monastery, under Hildegard's care, was like.

> *To understand Hildegard requires some understanding of the Benedictine way of life. As Hildegard's biographers indicate, life on Mount Saint Rupert maintained a quiet harmony. The monastic discipline made life well-ordered and secure, a balanced rhythm of prayer, work, and study. Seven periods divided the day. The first began at 2:00 A.M. with the chanting of nocturns. After returning to sleep for a short while, the sisters rose again before 6 A.M. to chant lauds. After this, they spent some time in private reading or meditation in their cell, then returned to chapel to recite prime. A simple breakfast followed, and then a brief period of morning work in the laundry, in the kitchen, or at housekeeping chores. The sisters gathered in the chapel again to recite terce and participate in the eucharistic liturgy, usually sung by the entire community. After liturgy, the sisters did manual labor in the herb garden, the vineyards, or the vestry. Before noon, they chanted sext, and then ate lunch. After the midday*

meal, the sisters rested briefly. Then, at around 3:00 P.M., they gathered to sing none, following which they worked again at various jobs. After a light supper and the chanting of vespers, the nuns read, studied, and meditated before ending their day by chanting compline together. By day's end, Hildegard and her sisters had worked about six hours, slept eight hours, and prayed together three or four hours. The rest of the day had been spent in spiritual reading, study, and meditation. All in all, the sisters aspired to live in harmony with God, humankind, and themselves.

Gloria Durka, *Praying with Hildegard of Bingen* (Winona, MN: Saint Mary's Press, 1991).

The desire to live in harmony with all creation and to live out one's life through actions of justice and compassion was truly the hallmarks of Hildegard's existence. She saw to the comfort and care of not only the sisters of her community, but also of anyone who came to the abbey seeking help. Those who were sick and aged were always given a caring and compassionate welcome. The herbs that Hildegard grew in the gardens were shared (as was her medical expertise) with anyone who had need. Elderly women and all who found themselves alone or destitute only had to come to the abbey's door in order to find themselves welcomed home.

In addition to all of her daily responsibilities, Hildegard somehow also found the time to write, prolifically, and to compose the music that she so loved. In addition, she corresponded with some of the greatest leaders of her time—royalty, popes, and other well-known people—sometimes, if Hildegard felt that they were in the wrong, even writing scathing letters that called them to accountability. All of this was probably, at times, exceedingly difficult for a woman who suffered from physical pain and illnesses. Sometimes Hildegard's health was so fragile that she was bed-ridden for weeks at a time. Still, neither the hard work nor her own frail health kept her from being true to what she saw as her vocation to minister to the world, nor did it weaken her incredible spirit. A beautiful example of this spirit is given by Joanne Turpin, who relates a story that occurred near the end of Hildegard's life.

There was a young man who lived near the monastery, and who had been excommunicated by the archbishop. (Such excommunication meant that the man was "outside" of the Church and was not even allowed a Christian burial upon his death.) However, when the young man died, Hildegard allowed him to be buried in the Rupertsberg cemetery because she knew that, prior to his death, he had repented of his sins and had received sacramental forgiveness.

> *Nevertheless, ecclesiastical officials order her to remove the body from sacred ground. When she refuses, her convent is threatened with interdict: No Masses will be said, no sacraments given to her community, no liturgical music sung—and she loves her music. Even the church bells cannot be rung.*
>
> *Eighty-year-old Hildegard goes out to the cemetery and with her walking staff erases the lines around the young man's grave so that his burial place cannot be detected. A furious archbishop gets the pope to agree to the interdict.*
>
> *The impasse drags on for a year, causing Hildegard immense sorrow, but she remains resolute. Only after protracted negotiations and the intercession of influential friends is the ban withdrawn. Hildegard dies just a few months later, in September 1179.*
>
> Joanne Turpin, *Women in Church History: 20 Stories for 20 Centuries* (Cincinnati, OH: Saint Anthony Messenger Press and Franciscan Communications, 1990), 98.

No look at Hildegard's life would be complete without mentioning the visions she frequently experienced—visions that began when she was a child. She described the visions as a reflection of "living light," warm and dazzling, and usually encompassing human forms or intricate designs. A voice that Hildegard knew as coming from heaven helped her interpret each vision. However, it was only when Hildegard was in her forties, and only after being instructed by the voice to record what she saw, that she began to write and to speak publicly about her visions. Of course, her friend Jutta knew about the visions, and Hildegard also confided in an abbot and in the archbishop of Mainz, who spoke of her visions to the pope. Eventually Hildegard received papal approval and encouragement, but she always remained humble regarding what others saw as a great grace that had been given to her.

Perhaps one of Hildegard's greatest gifts to the world was her spirituality, which embraced all of God's creation and saw everything that existed as intimately connected, one to the other. Her spirituality and her teachings were truly creation-centered, so much it seems as if Hildegard belongs in today's world more than she does in the medieval world. Truly, she was a woman who was centuries ahead of her time. One can only wonder what changes might have occurred in our world if Hildegard's voice had not only been listened to, but her words heeded. Listen to her speaking to us across the centuries:

> *Now in the people that were meant to be green, there is no more life of any kind. There is only shriveled barrenness. The winds are burdened by the utterly awful stink of evil, selfish goings-on. Thunderstorms menace. The air belches out the filthy uncleanliness of the peoples. There pours forth an unnatural, a*

loathsome darkness that withers the green, and wizens the fruit that was to serve as food for the people. Sometimes this layer of air is full, full of a fog that is the source of many destructive and barren creatures that destroy and damage the earth, rendering it incapable of sustaining humanity.

Gabriele Uhlein, *Meditations with Hildegard of Bingen* (Santa Fe, NM: Bear & Company, 1983).

As previously noted, Hildegard could be considered the "mother" of mysticism and of the creation-centered type of spirituality that flowed from this region of Europe during the twelfth through the fourteenth centuries. She created a path for others to follow—and follow they did—each woman being true to her own unique call. One such person was Mechthild of Magdeburg, an inheritor of Hildegard's spirituality but a great mystic in her own right.

Mechthild of Magdeburg

Mechthild was born early in the thirteenth century, probably around the year 1212. Like Hildegard, Mechthild was a nun and a mystic, but her religious life began first as a Beguine. Beguines were groups of women (or men, known as the Beghards) who chose to live in community, dedicating themselves to Christian charity and service to those who were poor and others in need. Prayer was a great part of the life of a Beguine, as was hard work. Beguines took no formal vows and were not affiliated with any particular religious order. Generally they supported themselves through whatever skilled labor they could provide to others, such as teaching, weaving, sewing, dying fabrics, and so on. They requested no charity and did not accept alms, but, upon entering a beguinage, a woman did not have to renounce her property.

Therefore, if a woman decided to leave the community and return to society to marry, she would not return with nothing.

During times of epidemics and the plagues that ultimately ravaged Europe, the Beguines were of great service to their surrounding communities as they cared for the dying and ministered to the needs of those who were ill. This movement was so popular during the Middle Ages (and still exists to this day) that, by the end of the thirteenth century, almost every town had at least one community of Beguines.

> *Several, like the Great Beguinage at Ghent, numbered their inhabitants by the thousands. As centers of mysticism, they greatly influenced the religious life of the people, superseding the monks and the secular clergy in molding the thought of the urban population. The Great Beguinage at Ghent, surrounded by its walls and moats, contained at the beginning of the fourteenth century two churches, eighteen convents, over one hundred houses, a brewery, and an infirmary. The beguinage, described as an attempt to harmonize the individual and the communal in the Middle Ages, was actually a town on a miniature scale with the church as the hub.*
>
> Ohanneson.

After Mechthild left the beguinage, she took her vows as a professed nun at the convent of Helfta and wrote of her many visions and of her understanding of the spiritual life. Her *Flowering Light of the Divinity* was one of the earliest books known to have been written in the vernacular (in Mechthild's case, in Low German). Later, her work was translated into High German and Latin. Like Bridget of Sweden, Mechthild of Magdeburg was a major religious figure of the Middle Ages.

Bridget of Sweden

Bridget of Sweden

Bridget of Sweden was raised as nobility. Widowed and left with eight children to care for, Bridget founded a religious order of women and men called the Order of the Brigittines. Members of this community lived in double monasteries (such as we saw in the early desert monastic experience). A mystic like Mechthild, Bridget recorded her visions and spiritual experiences in a book titled *Revelations*. Like her contemporary, Catherine of Siena, Bridget advocated for the return of the papacy to Rome from Avignon, France, where it had moved in 1308. Bridget, who was held in high esteem by both the nobility as well as the pope, was nonetheless unable to procure the move. She died in Rome and was canonized in 1391.

Saint Catherine of Siena

Catherine of Siena

Catherine of Siena is probably a familiar name to many. She was also a mystic and a stigmatic (a person who bears the marks of Christ's passion on his or her body). In 1970 Catherine was declared a Doctor of the Church, an honor that is generally bestowed by the papacy but may be given by ecumenical councils of the Church. Doctors of the Church are those persons whose teachings have been found to be of special quality and significance in the understanding and in the development of theology. She is one of only thirty-three saints who thus far have received such an honor. Of the thirty-three, only two others are women: Teresa of Ávila and St. Thérèse of Lisieux.

Catherine led a fascinating life. She was born in 1347, the same year that the Black Plague first appeared. By the time she died, at age thirty-three, she was the most powerful woman in Europe, although, no doubt, Catherine would not have seen herself as such. The youngest child of twenty-five born to Jacopo and Monna Lapa Benincassa, Catherine, like Hildegard before her, knew at an early age that she was drawn to a religious life. In fact, by the age of seven, Catherine pledged herself to virginity, a desire that, in a few years, was in direct opposition to her parents' plan for her life.

During this time, women married around the age of thirteen. When Catherine reached this age, her father arranged a marriage for her; not surprisingly, Catherine refused the engagement. Seeing her refusal as stubbornness and sheer disrespect, her parents put her to work doing menial household chores within the family home. No doubt, their plan was to keep Catherine so busy that she would have little time for the prayer she seemed to desire so greatly and thus reconsider the positive aspects of a marriage that would get her out of such a predicament. Her parents' plan failed, however.

By the time Catherine was sixteen years old, her parents abandoned all hope that their beloved daughter would ever marry, and Catherine was allowed to join a Dominican Third Order. This type of order was usually reserved for widows—older women who would remain in their own homes, dedicating themselves to working within the community with those who were in need. For the next three years, Catherine did exactly that, until she felt that God was calling her to a different ministry. Gifted as a diplomat with an ability to reconcile groups, Catherine soon found herself immersed in helping settle both political and papal feuds. Her desire was to see the papacy returned to Rome, and to that end, she worked unceasingly.

In between her diplomatic endeavors, Catherine's works of charity drew to her a large following of disciples. She ministered to the sick at La Scala Hospital and worked within the prisons, especially with those persons who were condemned to die. Catherine saw such a sentence as contrary to God's will, and she often accompanied the condemned to the gallows, doing her best to give them courage and to strengthen their faith. As a second wave of the Black Plague descended upon the area in 1374, she turned her attentions to helping the victims of a disease that no one understood and that everyone feared. Before the plague was over, she had lost two brothers, one sister, and eleven nieces and nephews to it.

Always in somewhat fragile health herself, Catherine's life, nonetheless, was one of constant service to others, of prayer, and of personal penance. She was gifted with divine visions, and while experiencing them, she would enter a trance-like state, often while lying prostrate on the floor. During such trances, Catherine was oblivious to her surroundings. During a campaign across Italy that was designed to help move the entire nation to a renewed sense of the need for reconciliation, forgiveness, and penance, Catherine stopped by the Church of Saint Christina. While she was kneeling in prayer before the crucifix, Catherine received the stigmata. The year was 1375, five years before her untimely death.

In November 1378, Pope Urban VI summoned Catherine to Rome in the hope that her great skills as a negotiator might finally resolve the issue of the dual papacy in Avignon and Rome. This issue was increasing dividing the Church. Catherine traveled to Rome with some of her disciples as companions, as requested, and spent the last months of her life trying to negotiate an end to what she had frequently referred to as the "Babylonian Exile." Catherine virtually flooded the nobility and the prelates involved in the schism with letter upon letter, arguing for a return of the pope to Rome. In her campaign, Catherine scolded, pleaded, and bartered. She even addressed the College of Cardinals.

Eventually her efforts were successful, but Catherine was so weakened by the journey to Rome and by all that was asked of her there that she suffered at least two strokes. The strokes ultimately ended her life, and, sadly, she died thinking she was a failure. Truly, however, Catherine acted as the conscience of the Church at a time when it desperately needed a reminder of its call to holiness. And her dedication to living out her own call to holiness literally changed the course of history.

Julian of Norwich

Julian of Norwich was a contemporary of Catherine. But unlike Catherine, Julian lived in the relative solitude and peace of an English hermitage, not drawn into the world of political and ecclesiastical disputes. Julian was also a mystic, whose reputation for holiness brought people from all over Europe to visit her humble monastic cell.

Called "Blessed" by popular consent, Julian has not been officially declared Blessed by the Church. Nonetheless, her life of sanctity, her mysticism, and her historical importance are certainly significant in the history of the Church. Julian wrote one book in her lifetime, titled *The Book of Showings*, which explained her mystic revelations. The theological insights and concepts and rich symbolism of her book have won for Julian a reputation as a brilliant theologian and a skilled author. Julian was also the first English woman to write in the vernacular, which for Julian, was Middle English.

It is ironic that a woman who was so well known and loved during her lifetime, and whose spirituality has had such an influence on modern theology, is known to us only by virtue of the place where she lived. Details about Julian's life are scarce, but what we do know is fascinating because, even by medieval standards, she lived a life that was out of the ordinary during a complex period.

During Julian's lifetime, the dual papacy disrupted the Church, the Hundred Years War between England and France was fought, the plague ravaged Europe, Julian's home country of England saw the reign of three different kings, and the peasant-class fought against the injustices that oppressed those who were poor. Julian, through the tiny window of her cell, learned of all these things from the hundreds of people that came to her in pilgrimage. Her isolation from the world was in the physical sense only, because through her prayer for the people, for the Church, and for her country, she kept herself intimately connected to all that was happening.

The monastic cell that Julian chose for her life of prayer and meditation was attached to the Church of Saint Edmund and Saint Julian in the city of Norwich, England. From the church's name, Julian took hers. If a visitor were to go there today, he or she would find that much of the architecture and the atmosphere of medieval times is still evident.

While it is true that we cannot know many of the details regarding Julian's life, we can make some educated deductions from the few clues that time has not erased. For example, Julian's style of writing is that of a well-educated person, and so it would be logical to assume that she either received her education at home from educated parents or tutors, or, in all

likelihood, that she attended the Benedictine convent school near her home. The fact that she received an education at all indicates that her parents were either nobility (sometimes she is referred to as "Lady" Norwich) or part of the upper-class of professional people and merchants of Norwich. Whether she was of the nobility or from the upper-class, Julian probably spoke at least one language in addition to English. That language was most likely French, but it is possible that she knew some Latin as well.

Again, it cannot be known with certainty, but it is possible that Julian was a Benedictine nun prior to her vocation to the life of a hermit. Saint Julian's church was the property of the Benedictines, and, when Julian fell seriously ill at age thirty, there is some indication that she was living in the convent, although not a cloistered one. A priest was present when she fell ill, and her mother was called to her bedside. Julian's illness seemingly was the catalyst that precipitated her move toward the solitary life of a hermit, for during her illness, she received sixteen revelations that she knew to be from God. She called these revelations, or visions, *showings*.

Julian later wrote in her book about many key concepts learned from her mystical experiences. In a medieval world that was enmeshed with images of judgment and damnation and of a God who was vengeful and exacting, Julian taught of a God who is merciful, slow to anger, and lavish in his love for all creation. In a time when humanity was divided into classes, Julian taught that all creation is one. When Christians viewed the Trinity in sharply defined, solely masculine images, Julian envisioned feminine images of God, such as those feminine images found in the Hebrew Scriptures: If God is Father, then so, too, is God "mother"; if God is Father, Son, and Holy Spirit, then so, too,

might God be creator, lover, and friend. And perhaps of most significance to Julian, of all her visions, was the certainty that God was telling her that "all shall be well." At a time when the world was mired in war, poverty, and plagues, God's assurance that all would be well gave her great comfort and peace, even as it may do the same for us.

As has been mentioned, Christianity in the twelfth century through the fourteenth century saw a Church that was suffering through tumultuous times, even to the point of being divided within itself. During this same time, however, women of great personal power and dignity rose to proclaim a prophetic message of unity, harmony, and respect for all of God's creation. It is not difficult to draw parallels between the world of the medieval mystics and our modern world. Nor is it hard to understand how the mystics' messages of ecological harmony, feminine inclusiveness, and cosmic unity resonate with contemporary theology. The mystics certainly have given to the Church and to the world a wonderful gift that is only recently being rediscovered.

Some Thoughts for Your Reflection

1. Do you see any parallels between the Middle Ages and our world today? If so, what are the similarities? How are the times dissimilar?

2. Saint Hildegard was not afraid to confront those who abused the power of their authority at the expense of the powerless. This advocacy for justice and mercy has always been one of the hallmarks of true religion. Who do you think needs an advocate today? In what ways is the Church addressing the needs of those who are disenfran chised? In what way(s) can you, as an individual, serve as an advocate to those who are in need?

3. Before his death, Joseph Cardinal Bernardin, seeing growing divisions within the Church, started a project titled *Catholic Common Ground*. The purpose of the *Catholic Common Ground* initiative, as envisioned by Cardinal Bernardin, was to find a place of compromise between areas of potential division within the Church. Mutual respect, active listening, and an appreciation of all that is held in common, as Christians, were key to Bernardin's project. Do you see yourself as a peacemaker? Are there areas within your life or your relationships with others that are in need of healing and peace? What can you do to find "common ground"?

4. Common to the experience of the mystics was the desire for solitude, whether through actually withdrawing from the world as Julian of Norwich did or by finding interior solitude through times of prayer and meditation as Saint Catherine of Siena experienced. How or where do you find your places and times of solitude? Do you find it difficult to create "sacred space" within your life? If the idea of creating a sacred space for prayer and meditation appeals to you, make such a place. If you are not able to create an actual physical place, can you create a space for moments of solitude in your life (perhaps when you are walking, driving to work, waiting in line, gardening, and so on).
5. Saint Hildegard of Bingen often referred to her visions as "being in the presence of the Living Light." Light a candle. As you watch the flickering flame, allow yourself to meditate upon this verse from Scripture that refers to Jesus: "As long as I am in the world, I am the light of the world" (John 9:5). Let the verse speak to your spirit. Allow yourself time to be in the presence of the Light.
6. The women that have been featured in this chapter all shared a wonderful ability to see the world from their own unique perspectives. In other words, they were women of vision, women who were true to their own experience and conscience even when others sought to dissuade them. To help you see things in a new way and from a unique perspective, try this exercise: Gather some art supplies; you may choose something as simple as a pencil and a piece of paper, a box of crayons, or a set of oil paints. Now look at any object around you, such as a lamp, a vase of flowers, a figurine, even a chair. Draw the object. Once you have finished, draw the object as if it were upside down, without actually moving it. Now try drawing the object, either upside down or right-side up, blindfolded or with your non-dominant hand.

Chapter Six

Life on a Pedestal

Madonna and Child

An Expanding Mariology

". . . Mother most chaste . . . Mother undefiled . . . Virgin most venerable . . . Virgin most powerful . . . Spiritual vessel . . . Mystical rose . . . Tower of ivory . . . House of Gold . . . Ark of the covenant . . . Gate of heaven . . ."

Excerpts from the Litany of the Blessed Virgin Mary

By the end of the Middle Ages—as reflected in the above litany that dates from the sixteenth century—devotion to Mary had developed into a complex system of belief that, quite literally, placed her on a theological pedestal. This Mariology included aspects of authentic prayer, pilgrimage, and apparitions and miracles associated with Mary, along with some rather unbelievable miracle stories.

Once there was a Flemish monk who was painting a picture of heaven and hell on the portals of his abbey. He was engaged in portraying the Devil as hideously as possible when his satanic majesty, appearing in person, begged the monk to paint him as a young and handsome man. The monk refused and the angry Devil pulled away the scaffold on which the artist was working. But, as the monk fell, a statue of the Virgin, in a niche below the portal, stretched out her arms and held him in safety until help arrived.

Marjorie Rowling, *Everyday Life in Medieval Times* (New York: Dorset Press, 1987).

Being held in the safety of the Virgin Mary's arms or protected under the mantle of her cloak were common and powerful

Coronation of the Virgin

images in medieval times, both in art and in the minds of the faithful. As previously noted, life was often hard, even brutal, filled with hardships of every kind, especially for those who were poor. Aside from the teachings of the German mystics and a few other notable exceptions, the theology of the Middle Ages saw God as harsh, punitive, and unapproachable and believed humanity was sinful and fallen. In contrast, the Virgin Mary represented mercy and compassion and was seen as infinitely approachable. The words of the following two prayers—composed in medieval times but still well known today—are excellent examples of Marian devotion and imagery from the Middle Ages. The *Memorare* (Latin for "remember") was composed in the fifteenth century. The second prayer, Hail, Holy Queen, dates from the eleventh century.

The Memorare

Remember, most gracious Virgin Mary, that never was it known that anyone who fled to your protection, implored your help, or sought your intercession was left unaided. Inspired by this confidence, I fly to you, O Virgin of virgins, my Mother. To you I come; before you I stand, sinful and sorrowful. O Mother of the Word Incarnate, despise not my petitions, but in your mercy, hear and answer me. Amen.

Hail, Holy Queen

Hail, holy Queen, Mother of mercy;
hail, our life, our sweetness, and our hope!
To you we cry, the children of Eve,
[Earlier wording: . . . poor banished children of Eve]
to you we send up our sighs,
mourning and weeping in this land of exile.
[Earlier wording: . . . in this valley of tears]
Turn, then, most gracious advocate,
your eyes of mercy toward us;
lead us home at last
[Earlier wording: . . . and after this our exile]
and show us the blessed fruit of your womb, Jesus.
O clement, O loving, O sweet Virgin Mary.
Amen.

As these two prayers and the miracle story that preceded them indicate, devotion to Mary was intense and personal during this time in history. The Virgin Mother was shrouded in mystery and majesty, even as she was felt to be intimately close and connected to the people. Of course, these concepts of Mary did not develop in a vacuum, but rather over centuries of the Church's examination and reflection on Mary's place in the history of salvation. In many respects, the biblical, historical Mary became lost in the developing theology that surrounded her. Mary of Nazareth, mother of Jesus, became Mary, Ever-Virgin; Mary, the New Eve; Mary, the Mediatrix (Mediator).

Layer upon theological layer, a Mariology was constructed that resonated with people's experience of Mary and what they needed Mary to be for them. By the end of the Middle Ages, this theological and social construction had become especially apparent. Mary had not only been placed on a theological pedestal, but on a pedestal that was so high that it was virtually unattainable for any human to reach. The manner in which this came to be and the impact of such devotion on the life of the people is an intriguing story. It is a story with many interesting twists and turns, as well as a story that continues to impact Catholic theology today.

As was noted in chapter 2, actual historical data regarding Mary is minimal. What we know of her, we know from Scripture. Unfortunately, after the ascension of Jesus, when Mary is mentioned as being in the upper room with the disciples (Acts 1:14), she is never mentioned again. Of course many stories and legends about her circulated through the early faith communities. The majority of these stories would have been known to the Gospel writers; however, only a few of them were recorded. And when the official canon of the Bible was agreed on, none of these scarce written accounts were added and none

are known with any degree of certainty to be factual. There is, however, a known historical record that does give us information about the development of Mariology. Part of this record pre-dates Christianity and, for clarity's sake, needs to be mentioned.

Sometimes devotion to Mary has been seen as nothing more than a substitution of the Virgin Mary for the goddess worship that was so prevalent in antiquity. While there does seem to be some connection, it is erroneous and an over-simplification to say that devotion to Mary merely replaced non-Christian goddess worship. Of course, goddess worship did exist in the non-Christian world, and it was a powerful and pervasive part of religious practice. Naturally the Christian community was well aware of this and used this knowledge to its advantage as the Church spread into the non-Christian world.

When faced with a non-Christian population that suddenly became Christian through mass Baptisms, the Church christianized many of the people's non-Christian feast days and celebrations. Rather than insisting that the newly converted give up celebrations that had always been an important part of their lives, the Church helped the new Christians change the focus of the celebration. It is not difficult, however, to see how this type of assimilation was confusing to some of the new Christian converts. Maurice Hamington notes this occurrence:

> *Goddess assimilation was actually encouraged by the Church because it was an excellent marketing strategy to [non-Christian] populations. In exchange for tolerating widespread devotion to Mary, the Church received a greater following. The history of goddess worship made Mary's assumption of various goddess legends anything but a simple transition. . . . Mary replaced [non-Christian] goddesses, but she never gained their status.*
>
> Maurice Hamington, *Hail Mary? The Struggle for Ultimate Womanhood in Catholicism* (New York: Routledge, 1995).

The Conception

In the catacombs in Rome, there is a fresco of the Virgin Mary holding the infant Jesus; the fresco dates from the middle of the second century. Also found in the catacombs were medals and coins with Mary's name inscribed on them and with petitions asking for her prayers. This type of archeological evidence certainly lends authority to those who would argue that Mary's place in Christian devotion was established early in Christianity and was much more than a substitution for goddess worship. Seemingly, Mary was seen—already in the early faith communities—in an intercessory manner. Her intercession was also generally sought under a title that represented some portion of her total being, such as Virgin or Mother, and it was almost always linked inseparably with the sacrifice of her Son.

By the end of the second century, such Christian writers as Tertullian, Justin, and Irenaeus were presenting Mary as a new Eve. They saw Mary as restoring, through her virtue and purity, what they felt Eve had lost through her disobedience and sin. This connection developed extensively over time and has had immense influence on Christian theology. (It is a connection that will be looked at in more detail later in this chapter.) By the fifth century, Marian piety was firmly entrenched in the religious experience of the Church. Monastic asceticism contributed to the rise in devotion to Mary, but so, too, did some official Church declarations.

When the Council of Ephesus in 431 endowed Mary with the title of *Theotokos*, or "Bearer of God," devotion to her increased dramatically. The council's true intent, however, was to clarify the Church's teaching regarding the divinity of Jesus. In other words, since Jesus was truly divine, even as he was truly human, then Mary, as the mother of Jesus, could logically be called the *Bearer of God*. Of course the council was dealing in theological concepts, while the common, ordinary Catholic understood the official declaration in devotional terms.

Twenty years later, the Council of Chalcedon further reaffirmed the dual natures of Jesus as they declared Mary to be *Aeiparthenos*, or "Ever-Virgin." Her perpetual virginity would, quite understandably, reinforce the divinity of Jesus because of the extraordinary events associated with his conception and birth. It was only two hundred years later at the Fourth Lateran Council that this teaching of Mary's perpetual virginity was elevated to the level of dogma.

As previously noted, Mary was always seen as an intercessor with God. As the mother of Jesus, she provided a maternal, counter-balance to a God who was increasingly seen as angry and distant. By the eighth century, Mary was even being thought of as a *co-redemptoris*, someone who, through her obedience, had brought God into the world and who, therefore, shared in the redemption of humanity. Like the linkage of Mary to Eve, the concept of Mary as co-redeemer (which has never been declared an official teaching of the Church) will be clarified further later in this chapter.

With this intense interest and study of Mariology developing at both doctrinal and devotional levels, it is not difficult to see how Europe, by the end of the fourteenth century, was literally adorned with churches and cathedrals dedicated to Mary.

> *Between 1170 and 1270 in France alone, over 100 churches and 80 cathedrals were dedicated to Mary. . . . In the first part of the twelfth century, a collection of apocryphal stories titled The Miracles of the Virgin appeared. . . . Devotion to Mary grew as miracle stories, previously the exclusive purview of the relics of saints, now became associated with Mary.*
>
> Hamington.

Marian Relics and Icons

In medieval miracle stories, statues and paintings, in accordance with iconodule belief, are constantly coming to life. . . . in a very popular tale, a woman begs the Virgin to spare her dying child, and to make sure seizes the Christ child from her arms as a hostage and only returns him to his mother on the recovery of her own child. . . .

The dynamic holiness of icons and relics did not just stir the soul to the contemplation of higher things, they also physically communicated the properties of their subject or owner. Images were alive, and so they could breathe life into the dying. Mary's peculiar qualities of bodily and spiritual integrity made her the supreme medium of healing and rendering whole again, and her shrines have always been thronged, since early Christian times, when, according to a tenth-century legend, the Empress Zoe had been cured by touching the [waistband of Mary] preserved in the Chalkoprateia church. . . .

Throughout the twelfth century, the flow of Marian relics increased prodigiously, and clergymen all over western Christendom discovered sacred and hitherto unknown remains of the Virgin in their sacristy treasuries. . . .

By the high middle ages, no scruple about the Virgin's assumed body impeded the discovery and veneration of physical relics. Whereas the Byzantines had concentrated on clothes the Virgin wore, western Christians revered her hair, her milk, and even her nail parings, which were kept in a red satin purse at Poitou.

Our Lady's hair was preserved at St. John Lateran and S. Maria sopra Minerva as well as in lesser churches throughout Rome; there was some in Venice, Bologna, Padua, Oviedo, Bruges, Assisi, St. Omer, Mâcon, in the Sainte Chapelle in Paris, at Montserrat, and at St. Denis, in shades of gold to red to blonde to black and in quantities that would have made a grizzly bear look hirsute. Her wardrobe took on fabulous dimensions, and fragments of her clothing or richly embroidered medieval dresses that had belonged to her hung in shrines in Rome, San Salvador, Marseilles, Toulon, Assisi, Arles, Novgorod, the Escorial palace, Limbourg, and Brussels. Soissons kept her slipper, which worked many miracles. The wedding ring she had worn as Joseph's wife was kept at Tuscany. And it was not the only one in Europe.

Marina Warner, *Alone of All Her Sex: The Myth and the Cult of the Virgin Mary* (New York: Vintage Books, 1983), 293–294.

Marina Warner's "tongue-in-cheek" commentary on the number and type of Marian relics and miracle stories that proliferated through the Middle Ages is a wonderful example of two very distinct elements at work within medieval times regarding matters of a spiritual nature. The first concerns the simple, even naïve, piety of the ordinary Christian of this time. This naivete contributed to a zealous type of religious fervor—the kind that would make even the aged and the infirm feel that they could make a pilgrimage to the Holy Land, for example, or that they could join in a crusade to free Jerusalem from the "infidels." It was exactly this type of fervor that fed the miraculous stories regarding the Blessed Virgin and that helped create a lucrative market for anything and everything that was passed off as a relic of Mary or of another saint. The people were hungry for belief in the closeness and the beauty of the spiritual realm. Their world was bleak, and the idea that a believer could be so close to Jesus, to the Virgin Mary, or to a saint (just through contact with a sacred relic or icon) gave many of the faithful a great deal of hope.

This leads to the second element of medieval piety, which was the general and pervasive feeling that humanity was wretched and deserving of God's wrath—an anger that could continue even for an eternity. Receiving sacramental forgiveness, doing penance, having a sincere sorrow for one's sins, atonement—none of it was sufficient to lessen the wrath of God in the mind of the medieval Christian. There was hope, however, in the indulgences that could be received by merely being in the presence of what was believed to be a holy relic.

> *The mere sight of the Vernicle [the cloth that tradition says was used by Saint Veronica to wipe the face of Jesus as he struggled toward Calvary] would earn for the pilgrim a 12,000-years' indulgence. To mount the 29 steps leading to the chapel where St. Peter sang his first Mass would remove 7,000 years from purgatory. By singing a Mass in the chapel where the bones of 10,000 martyrs were lying was believed to gain release from hell for a friend. A visit to the pillar on which Christ was bound, the sight of St, Thomas' cloak, or a glimpse of a piece of the True Cross, all of these actions had indulgences attached to them that were believed to erase thousands and thousands of years from [the medieval concept of] purgatory.*
>
> Rowling.

It is no small wonder that the making of relics became quite a profitable industry by those who had no compunction against fleecing the naïve and largely uneducated faithful. For this reason, paintings and icons became relics when they were credited as having been painted by the very hand of

Saint Luke, for example, or having been touched by Mary or another saint.

But because unscrupulous individuals gouged vulnerable medieval Christians, making money off their sincere but simple faith, does this mean that true Marian relics never existed? Were they merely physical manifestations of a deep need that was felt by Christians of the Middle Ages (even as it is seemingly felt by many today)? The answer to this is most definitely no, although the questions certainly require some clarification, both from a psychological level as well as from a theological perspective.

First of all, we know that relics (which in Latin simply means "remains") obviously were left on this earth by Jesus, by Mary, and by the saints, as they have been left by every living being or thing. These relics might include actual physical, bodily remains, such as those discovered by archaeologists. Also considered relics are those items that have had close physical contact with a saint or other holy person, such as articles of clothing or objects used by the person. Even objects that have merely been laid against a holy relic, such as a cloth, picture, or statue, become relics, although of a lesser degree.

In the case of Jesus (the ascension) and Mary (the assumption), the Church teaches that there are no bodily remains. With no body to venerate, those with a devotion to Mary sought whatever they could find that would bring them some closeness to the Blessed Virgin. During the Middle Ages, this lack of bodily remains led to relics being "found" that consisted not only of Mary's clothing, hair, and nail clippings, but also her teeth, breast milk, and tears. It was certainly a case of supply meeting demand. Sadly though, this type of superstitious, yet understandable,

collection and veneration of Marian relics ultimately did more harm than good, especially by the sixteenth century, which ushered in the Reformation movement.

Before we judge the Christians of medieval times too harshly, however, it may be helpful to draw a modern parallel regarding the veneration of relics and icons. First of all, it is only a natural and very human instinct to try to stay close to the memory of our deceased loved ones. Visiting and decorating gravesites and keeping mementos (things that belonged to, were used by, or that were cherished by our loved ones) is certainly natural to us. Not only does it help us feel close to the deceased person, it also helps keep our memories of them alive. It is a modern version of the practice in early Christianity of taking along a bone from a dead loved one's body if the deceased's family had to move, for example. It sounds macabre to our modern senses, but in that time and place, it made sense. We should be careful not to judge by contemporary standards practices such practices of ancestor veneration.

Today, popular culture also gives an example of this human need to feel close to those who have died, to honor their memory, and, perhaps, to feel an emotional (or spiritual) connection. This was evident as the entire world grieved openly when Princess Diana died in August 1997. Pictures and paintings of Diana, books and songs written about her, clothing that was once been worn by her, items she once used—all had immense value to those who wanted them. This was the way many people who loved Diana immensely chose to remember her. Of course, there were also those who capitalized on the grief of the people or on their naivete. So, too, did this occur in the Middle Ages regarding relics when people understood so very little compared to modern standards.

Madonna and Child Icons

But if relics of Mary, for example, are merely mementos of a beloved person—or in the worst-case scenario, outright forgeries—then how can it be that there are so many recordings of physical healings and miraculous events associated with these relics? Through the centuries, contact with relics has been associated with countless cures of human afflictions. In addition, intense spiritual conversions or reawakenings to faith have occurred.

Almost all of these miraculous events were meticulously examined by Church authorities and by experts in other fields. Some claimed miracles were dismissed as nothing more than a wishful projection by emotionally unstable or perhaps

misguided individuals. Some were attributed to a natural occurrence. (An example of this type of natural occurrence is the physical healing of a cancer victim through remission of his or her disease. While the remission may be miraculous, it is also possible that it could be the result of medical treatments that the person received prior to contact with a relic.) Some miracles have needed more study and investigation before a finding could be determined, while others gained (after intense study) an official declaration that the cure, event, or happening was truly miraculous. The Church is extremely careful in declaring some events to be miracles, and the process preceding a declaration is often lengthy and exhaustive.

The *Catechism of the Catholic Church* addresses the veneration of icons, and what it says can in turn be applied to relics.

> *Basing itself on the mystery of the incarnate Word, the seventh ecumenical council at Nicaea (787) justified against the iconoclasts [those who would destroy sacred images] the veneration of icons—of Christ, but also of the Mother of God, the angels, and all the saints. By becoming incarnate, the Son of God introduced a new "economy" of images.*
>
> *The Christian veneration of images is not contrary to the first commandment which proscribes idols. Indeed, "the honor rendered to an image passes to its prototype," and "whoever venerates an image venerates the person portrayed in it" [St. Basil,* De Spiritu Sancto *18, 45: PG 32, 149C; Council of Nicaea II: DS 601; cf. Council of Trent: DS 1821–1825; Vatican Council II:* SC *126;* LG *67]. The honor paid to sacred images is a "respectful veneration" not the adoration due to God alone.*

Religious worship is not directed to images in themselves, considered as mere things, but under their distinctive aspect as images leading us on to God incarnate. The movement toward the image does not terminate in it as image, but tends toward that whose image it is [St. Thomas Aquinas, S Th *II–II, 81, 3* ad *3].*

Catechism #s 2131–2132.

In the section on sacramentals, the Catechism makes the point that modes of popular piety, such as the veneration of relics, ought not to be ends in themselves. Rather, properly used, they should help the faithful participate more attentively in the liturgical dimension of the Church community.

The religious sense of the Christian people has always found expression in various forms of piety surrounding the Church's sacramental life, such as the veneration of relics, visits to sanctuaries, pilgrimages, processions. . . .

*These expressions of piety extend the liturgical life of the Church, but do not replace it . . . ". . . the liturgy by its very nature is far superior to any of them" [*SC *13§3].*

Catechism #s 1675–1676.

Marian Apparitions

The intercession of Mary throughout history has not been limited to relics but has also included apparitions, or appearances, of Mary.

> *From the Middle Ages on, as devotion to the Blessed Virgin became an ever more integral part of Catholic devotional life, word of apparitions has spread and given the Church hierarchy new challenges regarding the discernment of spirits. In modern times, each claim is checked by the local bishop, who may also appoint a commission to study the situation. While some apparitions have been recognized by the Church as authentic, such recognition does not mean that belief in the appearance of the Blessed Virgin Mary at a particular place and time is binding on all Catholics. It means only that the Church does not regard belief in the apparition to be misguided or harmful to the faithful.*
>
> Richard P. McBrien, gen. ed., *Encyclopedia of Catholicism* (New York: HarperCollins Publishers, 1995), 79.

> *From the Church's point of view, the most important aspect of a vision was not the private ecstasy, but the public message of divine approval that the descent of Christ or the Virgin on earth communicated to all the faithful. Through the experience of an individual mystic a whole locality, where the vision had taken place, was thereby blessed. Just as touching a relic, contemplating an icon painted by St. Luke, or treading the Via Dolorosa in Jerusalem could make the pilgrim feel in touch with the divine, so visiting places hallowed by the recent presence of*

the Virgin strengthens faith in the religion's continuity and endurance and efficiency.

Warner, 302.

Over the centuries, there have been many times when the Virgin Mary has seemingly appeared to people. Many of these appearances, such as the ones at La Salette and Lourdes, both in France, and at Fátima, Portugal, have received official Church recognition. The apparition of Our Lady of Guadalupe deserves special mention because of the significance it has had on the development of Christianity in the Americas.

The first apparition occurred on December 9, 1531, just slightly ten years after the conquest of Mexico. A young Aztec Indian, Juan Diego, whose native name was Singing Eagle was on his way to the nearby Catholic church just north of Mexico City. Juan had to pass by a hill consecrated to the mother goddess of the Aztecs; there he heard what he later described as a chorus of beautiful birds.

Then there was silence, and Juan saw a beautiful lady who seemed to radiate a luminous light; everything around her reflected rainbow-like colors. She spoke to Juan in his native dialect, asking him to come close. When he did, the woman told Juan that she was the "ever virgin, Mary, Mother of the true God who gives life and maintains it in existence" (McBrien, 79). Mary asked Juan to go to the local bishop and request that in her honor a small church be built at that place.

It is not difficult to understand the trepidation that this simple man must have felt as he approached the bishop's residence. One can also imagine the obstacles he encountered from those who worked for the bishop. Nonetheless, Juan persisted and eventually gained an audience with the bishop, who requested that he be given some proof of the truth of the vision. When Juan relayed this to Mary, she promised that on the next morning she would give him the proof he needed.

During the night, however, Juan's beloved uncle became ill—so ill that Juan feared that he might die. Juan decided it was more important to find a priest to bring his uncle the last rites than to meet the lady. To that end, Juan tried to circumvent the mountain by a different path, but the lady was there. She told Juan not to fear, that his uncle was at that very moment recovering from his sickness. Juan felt infused with a warm, comforting feeling, and he knew that the lady spoke the truth.

The lady instructed Juan to go to the top of the hill and pick the roses he found growing there. Juan was to put as many as he could carry in his *tilma* (a simple, coarsely woven cloak the native people wore). Of course, Juan must have doubted that he could gather any flowers, let alone delicate roses, in the dead of winter. Still, he trusted the lady, and, on reaching the top of the hill, he found beautiful roses growing on the frosty ground. Juan stuffed his *tilma* full and then hurried down the side of the mountain. In Juan's own words, when he brought the roses down to Mary, "she gathered them into her immaculate hands and then put them again into my mantle" (Warner, 303).

Once he gained entrance to the bishop's residence for a second time, Juan stumbled slightly, and the roses went tumbling out of his *tilma*. Embarrassed that he had been so clumsy, Juan looked to the bishop, only to find that the bishop and all the other persons gathered had dropped to their knees. It was then that Juan looked down at the front of his *tilma* and saw an image of the lady Juan had met on the hillside. Her complexion was dark, like that of the natives, and she wore a pink robe with

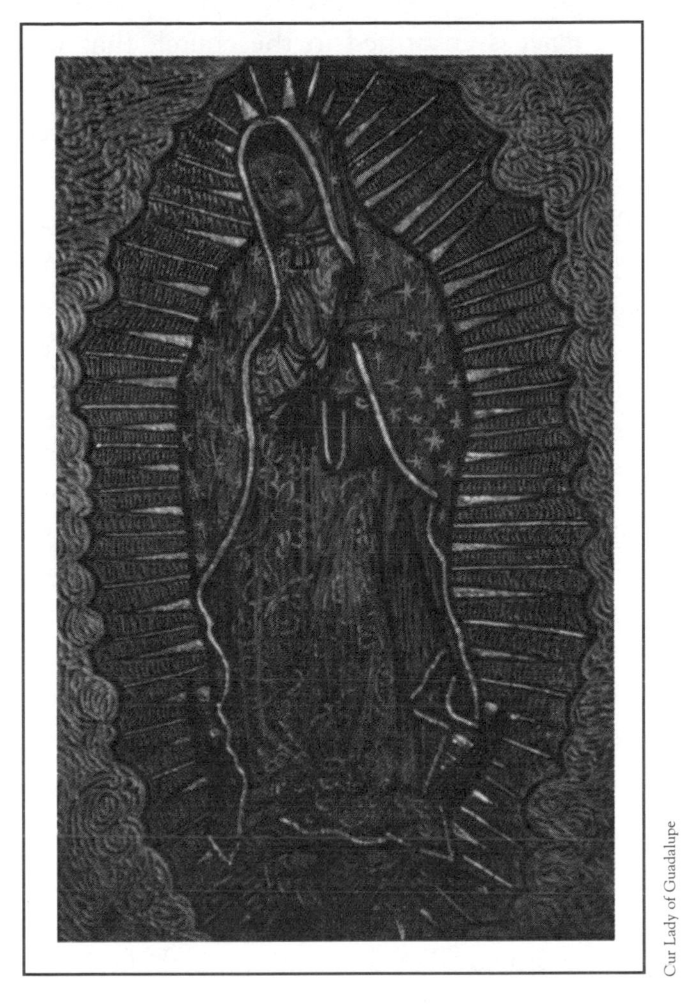

Cur Lady of Guadalupe

a turquoise mantle covered in stars and outlined in gold. Around her waist she wore a black cincture, and her feet rested upon a crescent moon that was being held up by the figure of a man.

To the indigenous Aztec peoples, the symbolism portrayed on the *tilma* had immense significance. The colors, body posture, cycle of the moon, black cincture that the lady wore—all conveyed, in its own symbolic language, that this lady was greater than the Aztec mother-goddess the people worshiped. So powerful was this image that, within a few years after her appearance to Juan Diego, more than nine million natives were baptized.

Today, the *tilma* is enshrined in the church that was built in Mary's honor and is surrounded by paintings and pictures that represent the countless cures believed to have occurred through the intercession of the Mary. Millions of people have journeyed to the church, where it is a tradition to enter on one's knees, if possible, as a sign of a person's deep respect for what God has accomplished through Mary. So many people have done so that a groove has been worn in the stone tiles on the floor of the church. Under the title "Our Lady of Guadalupe," Mary was proclaimed patron saint of all the Americas; her feast day is celebrated on December 12. Just as her appearance in the sixteenth century was cause for millions of conversions, the power of this apparition is still incredibly significant today, especially for the native peoples of the Americas.

More than any other event, the apparition of Mary to Juan Diego was a catalyst of conversion and a source of ethnic pride that helped Christianize Latin America. In Europe, the visions of mystics, the veneration of relics, and the apparitions of Mary were also extremely significant to the development of a Catholic faith that was richly imbued with Marian devotion. However, in Europe, all of these things, including the development of a secular code of chivalry, helped place Mary high upon a theological pedestal—a pedestal that the experience of Juan Diego contradicted. "Mary on a pedestal" had an impact on medieval society in Europe that was tremendous, especially because the pedestal that held Mary was not big enough to accommodate other women. If the entire Church had taken to heart the image of Mary portrayed in Our Lady of Guadalupe, much of the negative fallout might have been avoided.

The Effect of Mariology on Medieval Women

It took centuries for the European view of women to develop, influenced to a great degree by the Church. But the Church, of course, was also influenced by society. Hand-in-hand, the two arrived, by the Middle Ages, at an attitude toward women that was practically psychotic in its polarity. On the one hand, women were seen as the cause of the fall of humanity (Eve), the source of all evil, and even, as taught by Aristotle, as misformed males. The writings of many male theologians reflect this type of misogyny, including those of Tertullian in the third century, Augustine in the fifth century, and Aquinas in his early writings in the thirteenth century, to name a few. Of course, these theologians were writing from within their own historical and social perspective, which would have significantly shaped their attitudes toward women. Knowing this does nothing to validate the misogynistic attitude that permeated some of their writings, but it might help in our understanding of how viewpoints such as theirs were formed. The following words of Tertullian are an example of such a viewpoint.

> *And do you not know that you are each an Eve? The sentence of God on this sex of yours lives in this age: the guilt of necessity must live too. You are the devil's gateway; you are the unsealer of that forbidden tree; you are the first deserter of the divine law; you are she who persuaded him whom the devil was not valiant enough to attack. You destroyed so easily God's image, man. On account of your desert—that is, death—even the Son of God had to die.*
>
> J.A. Phillips, *Eve: The History of an Idea* (San Francisco: HarperSanFrancisco, 1985).

Fortunately, Tertullian's harsh and scathing words regarding women eventually lost ground to a different view. It was the growth in devotion to Mary that helped raise women from being seen as the epitome of depravity to the height of superiority. Listen to the adoration that is found in this writing from an anonymous medieval author.

> *Woman is to be preferred to man, to wit: in material, because Adam was made from clay, and Eve from Adam's side; in place, because Adam was made outside Paradise and Eve within; in conception because a woman conceived God, which man could not do; in apparition, because Christ appeared to a woman after the resurrection; in exaltation, because a woman is exalted above the choirs of angels, to wit, the Blessed Mary.*
>
> Rowling.

The evolution or progression of women from degradation to elevation is directly connected to the Virgin Mary. She was the New Eve, the Second Eve, the woman who through her obedience reprieved all womankind. The resulting sense of superiority of women was greatly enhanced by the knightly code of chivalry that developed in the twelfth century. This code virtually superimposed upon ladies of the upper class the virtues and qualities that men found so readily apparent in the Virgin Mary. Ordinary women (members of the merchant class and wives of serfs), however, were not honored in the code. Attributing the qualities of Our Lady (Mary) to women who were not considered ladies, merely women, was too much of a leap for the code of chivalry. Somewhere in between, dangling between heaven and hell, between the pit and the pedestal, is where the majority of medieval women resided.

The Effect of Mariology on Modern Women

When we remember all that we know about Jesus' love, compassion, and respect for women, it is difficult to understand how the Church arrived at a theology that saw woman as the cause of all evil in the world. Nonetheless, this is exactly what happened.

European social, political, and legal systems were also generally prejudiced against women in almost every respect. Together, Church and society arrived at a concept that linked womanhood to the base, the defiled, the imperfect, and the unredeemed. Woman somehow over the centuries became "lesser than," and because she was seen in this manner, all types of injustice and abuse were justified against her. From a theological perspective, this link was found in Eve.

As Mariology expanded, it was probably inevitable that Mary became linked with Eve, in the sense that Mary was seen as the New Eve. Where Eve was seen as self-seeking, Mary was all-giving; where Eve was seen as sinful, Mary was holy; where Eve was seen as openly sexual, Mary was pure and unsexual. This linkage of Mary to Eve was so firmly established by the fifth century that Mary was seen as the woman of the Apocalypse in chapter 12 of the Book of Revelation.

> *A great portent appeared in heaven: a woman clothed with the sun, with the moon under her feet, and on her head a crown of twelve stars. She was pregnant and was crying out in birth pangs, in the agony of giving birth. Then another portent appeared in heaven: a great red dragon, with seven heads and ten horns, and seven diadems on his heads. His tail swept down a third of the stars of heaven and threw them to the earth. Then the dragon stood before the woman who was about to bear a child, so that he might devour her child as soon as it was born. And she gave birth to a son, a male child, who is to rule all the nations with a rod of iron. But her child was snatched away and taken to God and to his throne . . . (verses 1–5).*

Today, Catholic theologians tend to see the woman of Revelation as more representative of the Church than of Mary. It is not difficult, however, to see how a connection to Mary was made, especially during the Middle Ages. Even today, this connection is still strong, as Mary is often referred to as "a woman clothed with the sun" or artistically represented wearing a crown of twelve stars. This type of representation of Mary is as powerful an image today as it was in medieval days. And it is this type of imaging of Mary that helped propel her onto her theological "pedestal."

For many Catholics today, Mary is still viewed on that pedestal. If that means that she is honored, respected, and loved as the mother of Jesus, who can argue with such devotion? But if being on a pedestal places Mary beyond her own humanity or raises her to a level of emulation that is literally impossible for women to achieve, then that presents a very serious dilemma.

Imagine for a moment . . . if Mary is on a pedestal because of her virginity, then what does that say to women today about their own sexuality? Does it convey a message that women are to be defined by their sexuality or that they are not to seed a healthy and holistic self-image that integrates their sexuality into their entire being? Does it imply that virgins are pure, while women who have chosen marriage and motherhood are not? But then, what of Mary's motherhood? Certainly her virginity is not more important than her maternity! The message that comes across to Catholic women is that Mary is honored for both her virginity and her maternity—for being a Virgin-Mother, an absolutely unattainable state of being for any other woman.

If Mary is on a pedestal primarily due to a particular role or title of honor, for example, as Virgin, as Mother, as Woman Clothed with the Sun, as Queen, and so on, then what about her humanity? Can she not also be honored as a young woman of faith who said yes to what she felt God was asking of her? Can she not be honored as a woman who probably struggled at times to deal with a pregnancy that she did not understand, who endured poverty, and who, for a time in her life, may have been a political refugee? Can she not be honored, as well, as a woman who aged and who no doubt endured all the physical changes that a woman's body goes through during the aging process? Can we honor Mary as a woman who most likely suffered the loss of her husband and who stood by her son, even when he was executed as a criminal of the state? Can we honor Mary in her aloneness and in her grief as a woman who lost, to death, the persons in her life whom she most loved?

Recall from the beginning of this chapter the excerpts from the Litany of Mary that honor her by some of her many titles. Mary has long been honored in Catholic tradition in this way, and there is nothing inappropriate in doing so. But perhaps we truly honor Mary best when we move beyond the titles to see her in the fullness of her humanity. In doing so, we might see a person to whom both women and men can relate because her experience of humanity resonates with ours.

It was to this very human Mary that God reached out. In other words, her humanness did nothing to estrange her from God, for she was made in God's image. She was, like all of God's creation, made from Goodness and for goodness. Imaging Mary in this way rather than as a New Eve might help end the estrangement of humanity from God. Imaging Mary in this way may also remind us that it is always God who takes the initiative, who always first invites. This is as true for Christians today as it was for Mary then.

Mary was also a person not only of faith, but of faithfulness. In her humanity, she probably struggled with all the unknowns that were part of her life. She said yes to God, but in doing so, her world was literally thrown into turmoil. She was an unwed mother-to-be in a culture that could have punished her with death by stoning. Imagine how she agonized over how to explain to her fiancé Joseph and to her family what even she did not fully understand. Scripture gives us only one brief glimpse into Mary's response to the knowledge that she was chosen to become the mother of the Savior. Her awe was expressed during her visit to her cousin, Elizabeth.

Praying Madonna

"My soul magnifies the Lord,
and my spirit rejoices in God my Savior,
for he has looked with favor on the lowliness of his servant.
Surely, from now on all generations will call me blessed;
for the Mighty One has done great things for me,
and holy is his name."

Luke 1:46–49

What we do not know about are the long and arduous months when, with all of her fears and her second thoughts, as well as her physical symptoms, Mary remained faithful to the vision.

Mary was also faithful to her relationships. While we honor individualism to the extreme, Mary was truly relational. In agreeing to be the mother of Jesus, Mary was agreeing to more than the nine months of pregnancy. She was agreeing to be there for the "long haul." She was committed not only to her child, but also to the heartbreaking choices her child would make. Her ability to stand with Jesus, even to the bitter end, was probably a tremendous comfort to him and a great source of strength. Mary, by her free choice to respond to God and then to live out that response in the best way that she knew how, is truly a model of faithfulness that everyone might emulate.

And finally, more than any other person who has ever lived, Mary entered completely into the Paschal mystery—that is, the life, death, and resurrection of Jesus. Within her body she literally sheltered the Son of God, so that, in his humanity, the first sound he heard was the beating of his mother's heart. Her body nourished his, feeding him so that he could ultimately be food for the world. She rejoiced with him, she wept for his pain, and she celebrated his resurrection. Mary was, by far, the first and greatest disciple, and her full and total experience of discipleship calls us to be true disciples. For these reasons and more, Mary ought not to be placed on a pedestal, but should be carried in our hearts.

Some Thoughts for Your Reflection

1. This chapter is titled "Life on a Pedestal." To give you an actual experience of what this might be like, if you are physically able to do so, try standing on a chair. (If you are not physically able to do this, then close your eyes and try to imagine standing on a chair.) Does your vantage point change? Do things look a little different from your pedestal? Allow some time to go by. How comfortable is it on a pedestal? Does your pedestal allow you much freedom of movement? Are you able to feel natural while you are on your pedestal? Do you worry about falling off? You may want to journal about what life on a pedestal might really be like or discuss with a friend some of your thoughts about this experience.

2. Is there anyone in your life that you have placed on a pedestal? If you have (keeping the previous experience in mind), would you say that it was a good thing? Is that person still on a pedestal, or has he or she "fallen" off? Were you a child when you placed someone on a pedestal? Do all children tend to do this? As a society, whom do we collectively place on pedestals? Would you like to be on one? What would be the negatives to being on a pedestal? What would be the positives?

3. Through the centuries, there have been many apparitions of Mary, some of which were officially recognized by the Church, such as the appearance of Mary to Juan Diego. Check out a book or a video about one or more of the apparitions that were mentioned in this chapter or research another one that captures your interest.

4. Tertullian certainly had some very harsh opinions regarding women. His opinions were, in fact, hateful as well as harmful. Nonetheless, he may have felt justified in his attitude because many people of his time shared a similar view. Is there any element within our society today that tends to hold such a hateful attitude against anyone else? Can you identify any specific groups? In your opinion, what can be done to change these attitudes?

5. As we have seen, Mary was commonly referred to in terms of roles or titles. In the next week, watch television with a critical eye toward the roles of women television portrays. You might find it helpful to keep a notebook handy to record your findings under titles: mother, virgin, wife, seductress, and so forth. You might be surprised by the number of times certain roles appear. Do you think that this type of stereotyping is basically harmless or harmful?

6. Take two big sheets of paper. Draw all of the roles your mother assumed in her life. Draw all of the roles your father assumed. Whose page is fullest? Whose page looks like it is the most fun?

7. Draw a cartoon with the theme of stereotyping, role-reversal, or being on a pedestal.

8. In your own words, and in your own way, compose a contemporary poem or prayer to Mary.

Chapter Seven

Reformation Theology and the Church's Response

Saint Teresa of Ávila

The Pendulum Shifts

Did you ever make a hanging mobile? Do you remember how even the slightest touch would cause a reaction that spread through the entire mobile? So delicately intertwined was each piece that, try as one might, it was virtually impossible to affect one part of the system without affecting it all. In many respects, the Reformation that divided the Christian Church into the Catholic Church and the Protestant Church was like that hanging mobile. It was not one person or one event that caused the ultimate division of the Church. But rather it was a series of interconnected events and a number of forceful and dynamic personalities that contributed to the chain reaction that eventually led to the division of Christianity.

The schism that split the Church was actually a long time in the making. In 1517, Martin Luther, in an act of conscience, nailed his Ninety-five Theses against the practice of indulgences on the church door at Wittenberg, Germany. Luther had reason to be critical of the Church hierarchy, which had been in trouble for a long, long time. The reasons for the Church's problems were complex, often political, generally self-serving, and ultimately (for the sake of Church unity) incredibly tragic. Like a pendulum that had swung too far in one direction, the Church had to swing back, seeking its balance. Sadly, that balance was not attained before the fabric of Christianity in the West was torn apart—a consequence that Martin Luther neither intended nor desired.

As the Middle Ages came to an end, Europe once again sunk into the darkness that characterized so much of its history. The relatively brief encounter that Europeans had with Greek knowledge during the twelfth century—knowledge that had come through contact with the Arabic world during the Crusades—was seemingly long forgotten. Europe of the fifteenth and sixteenth centuries was once again a dark and fearful place, where the portrayal of an angry God reigned supreme. In many people's minds, a God who was seen as so cold and inscrutable, so detached, as to have consigned his own Son to a torturous death was a God who was to be feared and placated. As hundreds of thousands of people died in wave after wave of plagues—the cause of which the people had no way of knowing—this negative image of God was reinforced.

Even the people's geographic concept of their world existed on the very edge of calamity. While there was a growing sense among some of the better-educated and well-traveled individuals that perhaps there was "more out there" than had yet been charted, maps of the vast unknown areas of the world carried a simple warning: "Here be dragons." This seemed totally feasible to the majority of the uneducated populace, for their world was already filled with the real demons and dragons of poverty, disease, and early death. Fear abounded, and the world was perceived as a place of trial and tribulation. People believed that they had so alienated themselves from God that the only way to reach heaven was to experience the hell they knew as earth.

Ascetics and, in addition, those monastics who saw the world as evil also viewed the body as evil. Fasting and flogging themselves toward heaven, they believed severe, self-inflicted bodily

punishments were the only way to sanctity. The majority of people, however, had little need for such severe penance, for their entire lives were being lived under the penitential sentence of poverty, brutality, and hardship. Holding fast to religious beliefs that were often· superstitious, the people sought to placate a wrathful God through other means. Many developed a very skewed understanding of religion and religious practice. For example, a pilgrimage to a holy site, such as Jerusalem, became not a means to deepen one's faith, but rather a way to gain release from the tremendous debt that was thought to be owed for past sins. Relics of the saints, whether authentic or not, became objects to ward off evil. Even prayer took on a magical significance in the sense that people felt God's mercy could be manipulated by saying a certain number of prayers in a certain manner.

Many Christians felt so far removed from God that even Mass and the reception of Communion was seen as beyond their sinful grasp. Instead, many devout Christians sought simply to get a glimpse of the Eucharist at the moment of consecration and were satisfied that this was all the closer they dared to approach the Lord. To accomplish this, the truly devout journeyed from church to church so as to be present at the moment when the consecration of the bread and wine occurred. (Not seeing themselves as worthy to receive Communion, these Christians believed that at least Christ, under the sign of the sacred elements, could be adored from afar.) To make the practice of witnessing the sacred moment of consecration more possible, bells were rung before and during the consecration. The fact that the Mass was in Latin, unknown to most, gave even greater importance to this moment. Thus, for some, the Mass was reduced to a "magical moment," with its true significance lost in the hurried shuffle of pilgrims who only saw themselves as penitential onlookers. Many Christians felt so unworthy and spiritually separated from the Divine that the Church mandated that the faithful receive Holy Communion at least one time during the course of a year.

The violence that was endemic to the Middle Ages also, quite understandably, affected everyone who lived during this time. While some ascetics and many of the vowed religious used self-flagellation as a penance and a means to get closer to God, it was not unusual for the common people to physically punish their children. This was justified as a way to "beat out the devil" that might be seeking to insinuate itself inside the body and soul of the children. For the same reason, those who held a slightly higher position within society and had authority over servants or apprentices frequently had them whipped, either privately or publicly. People who were believed to be heretics or witches were burned at the stake if they would not recant their evil ways. Criminals, even those whose crimes were as simple as an inability to pay a debt, were subjected to torture and imprisonment. All of this, of course, was done for the good of the person's soul, in the hope that, through punishment and chastisement, those who had fallen off the narrow path to heaven would be saved from an eternity in hell.

Europe, by the end of the Middle Ages, had endured hundreds of years of violence, so it is not too surprising that violence played a strong role in the fabric of society. The early invasions by the Germanic peoples; the wandering bands of thieves and murderers who preyed on unfortunate travelers; the princes who rose to power and then waged war on each other, on their subjects, and even on emperors and popes—all contributed to an escalating cycle of violence.

The Church was also at battle. Political turmoil had embroiled the Church for generations, as political authorities sought to control the Church and make it a puppet of the emerging nation-states. Also, Christian ethics and canon law (the law of the Church) were often in direct opposition to secular law. The greatest battle that the Church faced, however, was an internal one, and this battle had to be waged on several fronts.

One recurring concern of the Church was that of heretical teachings. The Fourth Lateran Council in 1215 requested that secular authorities assist in the elimination of heresy. Pope Gregory IX took this further when he established specific procedures for use when identifying heresies and heretics in Europe. Tribunals traveled into Germany, France, and Italy in search of those suspected of heresy. If found guilty, heretics were punished with public penances or imprisonment or, for those who stood firm in their beliefs, even death. By 1252, Pope Innocent IV went so far as to approve torture, if necessary, in the Church's quest to eradicate heresy. The use of torture and severe punishment was condoned if done "for the greater good," which the Church believed was the defense of the faith and the salvation of the heretic's soul. Often it was Christian visionaries—mystics—who came under the closest scrutiny and were branded as heretics.

The waves of inquisitions that swept through the Church increased and decreased according to whatever at the time was viewed as contrary to the faith. Two sad examples of the Church's response to heresy are the Spanish and Roman Inquisitions. The Spanish Inquisition sought to disclose and punish those Christians who had converted from Judaism or Islam but who were suspected of still practicing rituals of their previous religions. Quite likely a majority of the new converts did choose to maintain some aspects of their former religion because they had converted under economic and social pressures, rather than through a true sense of conversion.

The Roman Inquisition, established by Pope Paul III in 1542, was part of the Church's response to the Protestant Reformation. Not only were many lives torn apart and lost due to over-zealous inquisitors, but the Roman Inquisition also was responsible for the formation of the Index of Forbidden Books. Catholics were banned from reading books that were placed on the Index without first obtaining special permission from their local bishop.

Today, with the hindsight of historical perspective, the Inquisition is seen for what it was—an incredibly tragic period in the history of the Church. It was a time when the Church—with its back against the wall—thought the only way to keep the faith safe against what it viewed as false teachings was through severe and aggressive measures. In a world that was exceedingly harsh and violent, the Church reflected the times. Sadly, the Inquisition institutionalized fanaticism and torture against people who dared to think or act in a way that did not conform to the prevailing theological standard. Few would disagree that the era of the Inquisition, to this day, is a terrible commentary on a Church that claimed to follow Jesus.

But the battle against heresies was not the only war waging within the Church during this time. Humanism, celebrating humanity's accomplishments, developed in the sixteenth-century. Humanists bridled against the medieval Church's heavy, authoritative hand and taught that humanity was in control of its own destiny rather than merely a manifestation of God's divine will. In other words, the accomplishments of humanity stood as accomplishments in their own right, not because God deemed them into existence. To the Church, this appeared to be a direct threat, a philosophy that discounted both God and the Church.

The development of the printing press and a rising middle-class that was becoming more literate and informed helped set the stage for a cataclysmic confrontation with the Church. Rather than a few hand-copied manuscripts in the possession of scholars, monastics, and bishops, books now became available to the common, middle-class citizen. Inside these books was a wealth of information that expanded people's minds and stirred a new appreciation for independent thought. As people became more informed and knowledgeable, their criticism and dissatisfaction with society grew. The Church, long intertwined with governments, was not immune to this criticism and was, in fact, quite frequently its greatest target.

One of the greatest criticisms of the Church was the status of the clergy, many of whom were uneducated and seemingly without authentic vocations to the priesthood. After the plagues the Church in Europe faced a serious shortage of priests at an opportune moment for many men to increase their status in society. Some very-unqualified men joined the priesthood, while others were appointed by secular rulers to positions of authority within the Church. Understandably, the results were often catastrophic. To further fuel the fire of dissatisfaction, many of the hierarchy of the Church were living lives of opulent luxury, similar to royalty. This, quite naturally, was offensive and scandalous, especially to those who were poor, people who could not help but contrast their meager existence with the splendor of the hierarchy.

Yet, even while the hierarchy of the Church became increasingly entrenched in power, politics, and outright corruption, the heart and the soul of the Church remained—those persons who heard the voice of Jesus calling to them and did their best to follow. Such persons kept the true essence of Christianity alive in one of the darkest times in the history of the Church.

Mystics of this time, such as Saints Teresa of Ávila, Elizabeth of Portugal, and Bridget of Sweden, experienced visions that lifted them above the low level at which much of the Church seemed to be mired. Repeatedly, however, the hard, male hand that held the reins of ecclesiastical and secular power did its best to restrain such women. Often women were easily dismissed by labeling them as theological threats to the Church (as many of the mystics of this time were) or calling them mentally unstable (as in the case of Saint Rose of Lima, Peru). But their voices could not be silenced and their presence could not be ignored.

Saint Catherine of Genoa

Saint Catherine of Genoa's given name was Caterinetta Fieschi. A introverted and solitary woman, Caterinetta desired to live a religious and spiritual life. Already at the age of thirteen, she tried to join a convent near her home, but she was rejected, due to her young age. At the age of sixteen, she was forced into an arranged marriage that served as a merging of two prominent Genoese families who had been politically estranged—her family and that of her husband-to-be, Giuliano. Giuliano seemingly did not want the marriage either, for he spent the first eleven years of matrimony indulging his own desires; he was frequently away from his wife and often unfaithful to her.

At the age of twenty-seven, Caterinetta had a vision of Christ (the first of many such visions) that lifted her out of the misery of her marriage. Overwhelmed by a knowledge of the vast goodness and love of God, she gave away most of her possessions, made a complete confession of her sins, and began attending daily Mass to receive the Eucharist. (Remember that frequent reception of the Eucharist by the laity was practically unheard of during this time.) Caterinetta also began visiting a nearby hospital to care for those who were sick, often taking on the hardest and least wanted jobs herself.

Perhaps the beauty of Caterinetta's soul and her compassionate care for those who were less fortunate finally caught the attention of her husband. Guiliano underwent a complete conversion and,

by 1475, joined his wife in her ministry. Two years later, however, Guiliano died after confessing to Caterinetta what she already knew—that he had been unfaithful to her and, in his unfaithfulness, had fathered a daughter, Thobia. Seeing past her husband's unfaithfulness, Caterinetta, through her generous spirit, helped provide and care for Guiliano's child as well as for the child's mother.

The woman who came to be known as Catherine of Genoa died in 1510, just seven years before Martin Luther triggered the Reformation of the Church by posting his Ninety-five Theses. In a time when many in the Church hierarchy were alienating the people, Catherine showed the Church what faithfulness was all about.

> *Though her family tree included two popes (Innocent VI and Hadrian V) and one of her cousins was a prominent cardinal, she never showed a hint of interest in ecclesiastical affairs. Contrast the works of Genoa and the works of Rome: While Catherine was nursing plague victims and cleaning house for the sick poor of her city, popes of that era concentrated on the business of the Italian Renaissance, promoting the splendors of art and architecture. This occupied their energies to the extent that the murmurings of discontent across Christendom were either ignored or dismissed as being of no consequence.*
>
> *In the quest for beauty one pope's papal crown cost two million francs. Another, Alexander VI (one of the notorious Borgias), added not only to the glory of Rome but to the bank accounts of his children and grandchildren as he distributed Church wealth among them. To pay for all the luxuries, indulgences as well as ecclesiastical offices were sold, and the murmurings grew to rumblings.*

Still, the papacy neglected the conditions—indeed, aggravated them—which would lead to the Protestant Revolt soon after Catherine's death.

Joanne Turpin, *Women in Church History: Twenty Stories for Twenty Centuries* (Cincinnati, OH: Saint Anthony Messenger Press and Franciscan Communications, 1990), 126.

As someone who truly modeled the Christian ideals of loving and compassionate presence, Catherine ought to be better known, for her story is one of witness to the Christian message at a time when much of the official Church had forgotten it. Her life is an example of the heights that the human spirit can achieve, even while living a simple and obscure life. She gave to the Church a special gift that can still be appreciated today. That gift is a reminder that the Church (and every member of the Church) is called to holiness. The Church celebrates the feast day of Saint Catherine of Genoa on September 15.

Martin Luther

The catalyst that sparked the Reformation that changed the Church forever was Martin Luther. He was born into a world of political power struggles and Church corruption, heresies and inquisitions on the feast of Saint Martin's Eve, November 11, 1483. Martin initially studied law, as his parents hoped he would become a lawyer, but he left his studies to become a monk after a near-death experience.

> *Martin Luther was a complicated man. On the one hand he was lively, cheerful, fond of song and companionship, and on the other hand, stubborn, brooding, fearful of the wrath of God, given to tormenting introspection and self-inflicted punishments, all in pursuit of spiritual grace. If the social flux determined his place in the world, the medieval ethos of the God of wrathful judgment had a hold on his character. Entering a religious order must have seemed to him the obvious way to acquire the peace of mind he so desperately sought.*
>
> Edith Simon, "The Reformation," *Great Ages of Man* (Alexandria, VA: Time-Life, Incorporated, 1966).

Martin Luther received his doctorate in theology in 1512 from the University of Wittenberg, Germany, and was offered a professorship there. A person of true integrity, he was deeply disturbed by the corruption he saw within the Church. Of particular concern, Martin felt, was the sale of indulgences. An indulgence is the remission of temporal punishment for sin that remained

after a sin had been forgiven by God. People believed they could receive the benefit of an indulgence through saying certain prayers, doing good deeds, visiting religious shrines, and so on.

The problem for Luther was associated with the commonly held belief that indulgences could be purchased. It was believed that one could receive an indulgence by giving alms to the Church. Under Pope Urban II, Christians who unable to participate in the Crusades could receive an indulgence for giving money toward the cause. Or a busy merchant who paid for another person to journey to a holy site on behalf of the merchant would receive the indulgence for the visit to the site. By the time of Luther, a complicated tariff system of indulgences was formulated. In this system, a specific dollar amount in value and in payment was attributed to specific good deeds. The good act was not actually executed by anyone but rather paid for by the penitent.

When Luther formulated his Ninety-five Theses, he hoped that the ensuing academic debate would help clarify the Church's teaching regarding indulgences, as well as help eliminate the scandalous practices associated with them. Never could he have imagined what was to come, for he did not desire a break within the Church that he loved. In Luther's own words:

> *Had I known when I began to write, what I am now aware of, namely that people proved hostile to the Word of God and opposed it, I assuredly would have remained silent, for I never would have been so bold as to attack the Pope and all people.*

Geoffrey Barraclough, gen. ed., *The Christian World: A Social and Cultural History* (New York: Harry N. Abrams Incorporated, 1981).

In January of 1521, four years and three months after posting his Theses, Martin Luther was excommunicated from the Church. For a time he was considered a criminal of the state but eventually was able to resume his career as a teacher. After publicly renouncing his former beliefs regarding monasticism and priestly celibacy, Luther, in 1525, married a former nun named Katherine von Bora. Unfortunately, the process that led to Luther's eventual excommunication had as much to do with miscommunication and politics as it did with theological concerns. In the end, Luther's desire to reform the Church had begun the process that led to its division in the West.

During the next two decades, Luther continued to teach, preach, and translate Scripture into the vernacular (which, thanks to the printing press, finally allowed the Bible to be available to the general populace). Over time Luther grew increasingly bitter toward the Church that, he felt, never officially addressed his efforts at reform. As the leader of the Reformation, Luther's ideas and beliefs quickly spread throughout Europe, gaining many followers.

Church Response to Luther

The Catholic Church countered Luther's criticisms and his written treatises as well as the movements of other reform theologians, such as Ulrich Zwingli and John Calvin, with several internal reforms. This attempt by the Church to contain the damage done to it by the Reformation is known as the Counter Reformation or the Catholic Reformation. Probably most evident event in this reform is the Council of Trent, which met in three different sessions between 1545 and 1563. Luther, however, died in 1546, just one year after the convening of the general council he had so desperately wanted to resolve issues almost thirty years before.

Martin Luther's goal was to reform, not split, the Church in the West. Many of the reforms he sought were addressed when the Council of Trent convened. However, the Reformation continued to split Christianity into many factions, a problem that was also discussed during the Council of Trent. The reasons for the splits were many and varied. The concepts of the Reformation were embraced or altered according to the unique differences in European culture and experience. Quite often, the emergence of nationalism played a significant role in how Reformation theology was interpreted. While the Council of Trent went a long way toward eliminating abuses within the Church, it was not able to deal adequately with the split from the Church. The Council reaffirmed Catholic orthodoxy, especially the doctrinal issues that were disputed during the Reformation, including belief in the Real Presence of Christ (transubstantiation) and the issue of justification with God.

Although there was great variance among the reformers regarding the Church's belief that Jesus is truly present in the Eucharist, Reformation theologians generally saw the Eucharist as more symbolic than substantive. To counter this, the Catholic Church adapted practices that stressed the Real Presence of Christ, such as kneeling before the Eucharist and not allowing anyone's hands but those of the priest to touch the sacred bread and wine.

Regarding the issue of justification, the Catholic Church clarified its teaching that humanity, only through the sacrifice and merit of Christ, is freely offered the gift of faith. Whereas Reformation theologians tended to see humanity as sin-filled and fallen, made only "acceptable" in God's sight, the Catholic Church proclaimed humanity to be redeemed, holy, and grace-filled through the gift of faith. In addition, the Church saw this gift as one that, by its very nature, invited a response. That response, according to Catholic theology, would be a life of faith that is accompanied by good works and actions. Unfortunately, in common understanding, Protestants favored faith and Catholics favored good works, and neither allowed room for the inclusion of the other in their interpretation of justification.

On the positive side, the Council of Trent reaffirmed belief in the seven sacraments of the Church; the reformers generally accepted only two—Baptism and Eucharist—because the origins of these two sacraments are very clearly found in Scripture. In addition, the council reaffirmed priestly celibacy and the practice of indulgences, although it condemned the abuses that had become endemic to both. Papal authority was also bolstered, and Church organization improved. By clarifying the doctrines and dogmatic beliefs of the Church, as well as practical expressions of belief that were rooted in tradition, the Council of Trent provided a clear and concise theology that the Church could fall back on and defend in the coming centuries.

Women Defenders of the Faith

Teresa de Cepeda y Ahumada was one defender of the faith, although she could have easily been a victim of the Spanish Inquisition. We know this woman today as Saint Teresa of Ávila, one of the Church's most beloved and intriguing saints. Born into a wealthy family, Teresa nonetheless desired to join a convent. The problem was that she desired to become a nun for all the wrong reasons. Teresa believed that the convent was a place where she could do penance for what she felt were her overwhelming sins, thus assuring for herself a place in heaven. She also saw the convent as a place where she could flee to avoid marriage. Teresa's father was vehemently opposed to her becoming a nun; nonetheless, she joined the Carmelite Convent of the Incarnation in 1535 at the age of twenty-one.

Eventually Teresa's father had a change of heart, and his financial support allowed Teresa to live a very comfortable life within the confines of the convent. During this time it was often the practice that those women whose families could provide for them were able to live in comfort and relative ease. For example, women with family financial support had their own private rooms and favorite foods, as well as beautiful clothing and jewelry to wear. This initially suited Teresa quite well, although her idea of vowed religious life would indeed change.

Although she led a deep, prayerful life, Teresa struggled with her vocation for almost two decades, feeling as if she had not surrendered herself completely to God. At the age of forty, she experienced a life-altering spiritual conversion when she saw an image of the wounded Christ as she prayed. Filled with intense sorrow for what she perceived as her lack of love for God, Teresa prayed for the grace to follow the Lord more faithfully.

Teresa spent the remainder of her life forming seventeen reformed convents and fourteen priories. These religious communities followed the early Rule of the Carmelite Order, which was very austere in nature. This reform, however, did not come easily, for at first there was great suspicion regarding Teresa's motives. Many of the sisters in Teresa's convent felt as if she was trying to put herself above them, contrasting their comfortable lifestyle against the simplicity of her own. (Teresa personally adhered to such a harsh and penitential lifestyle that she used a stone for her pillow and slept without covers on her bed.) She did not, however, ask such severe penance of the sisters who followed her into the reformed Carmelite Order. They were required to adhere to rigorous fasting, intense prayer, and simple clothing, which would have included the absence of shoes had it not been for Teresa's intercession. (She insisted that her nuns wear a simple sandal. Nevertheless, today Teresa's reformed Carmelite Order is known as the *Discalced* Carmelites, which means "barefooted.")

As a mystic who experienced visions of Christ's presence, Teresa was also a suspected heretic, according to the Spanish Inquisition. Fortunately, no serious investigation ever materialized, and Teresa was able to live a relatively long and deeply spiritual life that helped spark the Catholic Reformation in Spain, countering the Protestant theology that was spreading so rapidly throughout the rest of Europe. Teresa wrote extensively about her experience of a mystical union with God. One of her books, *The Interior Castle*, is a treasury of insight into the journey of mystical life.

Saint Teresa of Ávila died in 1582, was canonized in 1622, and declared the first female Doctor of the Church in 1970.

Teresa of Ávila inspired a renewed Catholic piety that helped counter the growing divisions within Christianity. In 1540, the Church also benefited from the formation of a new religious order for men, called the Society of Jesus. Although the Jesuits, as they are commonly known, were not formed specifically to defend the Catholic Church against Reformation theology, that quickly became one of their main objectives. By the time their founder, Ignatius of Loyola, died in 1556, the Society numbered one thousand members. Within fifty years, that number swelled to almost sixteen thousand.

The Jesuits infused within Catholicism a spark of enthusiasm that had—with a few notable exceptions, such as Teresa of Ávila—been absent from the Church for too long. The Society focused on education, and the combination of their loyalty to the pope and Church teachings and their fervor helped reclaim many areas of Europe that had become Protestant. The order's missionary nature also helped move the Church into new and uncharted areas, such as India and Central and South America, where the Church was able to reach people who had never heard the gospel of Christ proclaimed. The first Jesuits arrived in South America in 1549. No doubt a young girl named Isabel de Santa María de Flores y del Oliva (known today as Saint Rose of Lima) was a direct beneficiary of the Jesuits' missionary zeal.

Rose was born in 1586 in Lima, Peru, to an impoverished family. Of Incan and Spanish ancestry, she was a beautiful woman, but it was a beauty that Rose found deeply disturbing. This probably was so because she knew that her beauty would lead her into a marriage that she did not desire. Rose was so desperate to avoid

Saint Rose of Lima

marriage so that she could follow a religious vocation that she scoured her face with hot peppers, causing her skin to blister and appear blotchy. She also hardened and dried her lips and the skin of her hands by applying lime to them.

Feeling a spiritual connection to Saint Catherine of Siena, Rose became a Third Order Dominican and chose to follow Catherine's example by living in relative isolation at her parents' home. At the age of twenty, Rose took a vow of virginity and moved into a small building in her parents' garden, which had

supplied the flowers that, as a child, she sold to help support her family. She spent her days in prayer and penance and experienced mystical visions. When she did venture from her home, she often wore a crown of thorns and dragged a heavy cross as an act of public penance.

Naturally, Rose's severe penances and her mystical experiences concerned Church officials. It was not long before she found herself the subject of ecclesiastical inquiry. Not surprisingly, even her closest friends found her choices in life hard to accept; many shunned and ridiculed her. Through it all, Rose remained true to the life to which she felt called. In addition to her solitary prayer life, she also cared for those who were poor and ill—especially those who were slaves.

What caused the death of young Rose in 1617 at the age of thirty-one is unknown. History tells us, however, that Rose suffered for many years from some type of painful illness. She was the first canonized saint of the Americas, canonized in 1671.

Today, we might label Rose a masochist for the hard life of penance she inflicted upon herself, or we might assume that she suffered from a severe psychological or affective disorder. But at the time she lived, it was believed that the burden of the pain the body experienced relieved some of the painful burden the soul carried. Penitents believed they were relieving themselves from the crushing burden of sin they carried. Often men penitents of this time who reached the level of sainthood were considered exceptionally pious and holy because of the acts of self-mortification they chose. Women penitents, on the other hand, were often labeled hysterical, or in the case of Rose, insane and unstable, for practicing similar penances.

The Results of the Counter Reformation

Today Catholic Christians in many parts of the world are able to trace their religious roots directly to the missionary activities of Jesuits, Franciscans, Dominicans, and others, as the Church sought to recover from the divisions caused by the Protestant Reformation. Quite understandably, as many areas of Europe were initially "lost" to the Catholic Church, it sought new worlds to convert. But the Church did not let go easily of its hold within Europe either. Just as Reformation theology, by virtue of its newness, brought an excitement to the religious experience, so, too, did the Catholic Church as it emerged from the Reformation.

The Council of Trent provided a clearly defined theology that made the teachings of the Church more easily understood, even by those who were not well educated. From this better understanding of Church teaching came a renewed piety and vigor as well as an appreciation and embracing of orthodoxy. The Jesuits helped through their enthusiastic teaching of the faith as they established new schools. Even the art and architecture that emerged from the rubble of the medieval Church rose to a height that inspired the soul. Known as *baroque*, this artistic style is generally recognized as a part of the Counter Reformation. The baroque style overwhelmed, even as it inspired. It was designed to impress Christians with its display of riches and power and to convince the faithful that the Church stood as the one and only true Church, linked inseparably to God.

> *All the means of salvation had to be represented dramatically: the Madonna, the saints and revered relics, the Mass and the host. Baroque churches displayed many images. Some showed Christ the Redeemer. His suffering on the cross was often linked with the host on the altar. Other images stressed the Trinity. But above all, the images exalted the Virgin, as the Madonna, as Queen of heaven, as the Immaculate Conception, assumed into heaven. Other images portrayed the mystic fervor of the saints, whose piety and asceticism provided examples for the faithful. . . . Baroque art built on the style of the Renaissance, but added the effects of light and darkness. It can be called a "naturalism of the supernatural." It stressed that we live in an open world, where communication is possible between earth and heaven, with the Virgin and saints interceding.*
>
> Tim Dowley, *Eerdmans' Handbook to the History of Christianity* (Grand Rapids, MI: William B. Eerdmans Publishing Company, 1977).

There is an old saying that "too much of a good thing is no longer good," and this certainly was true of the baroque artistic style of the Counter Reformation. Although it inspired the spirit, it also tended to lose the focus of Christ, the center of the Church. Instead, the focus or message of the baroque style was often scattered everywhere, with saints glorified and the power and richness of the Church showcased. Within a few generations, the Church and the world entered the period of Enlightenment, which focused on human reason and philosophy rather than on religion. The emerging threat to the Church was the growth of Humanism, which celebrated the intellect over the spirit and challenged belief in a God whose existence could not be proved through science or reason.

Some Thoughts for Your Reflection

1. Violence characterized much of the Middle Ages, and the effects of this violence permeated every aspect of people's lives. Do you believe that we are living in a violent world? If so, what effect does violence (or the response to violence) have on our society? What effect does it have in your life on a personal level?

2. Jesus said, "Blessed are the peacemakers, for they will be called children of God" (Matthew 5:9). Do you ever see yourself in the role of a peacemaker? If so, how are you a maker of peace? In what ways would you like to be a peacemaker? Can you identify someone whom you characterize as a peacemaker? Do you feel that the role of peacemaker carries any special responsibilities or burdens?

3. Although Martin Luther never imagined the consequences of posting his Ninety-five Theses on the Church door at Wittenberg, it, nonetheless, must have taken great courage for him to do that. What do you think Christianity would be like today if Martin Luther had never taken this step?

4. Catherine of Genoa was also a reformer of Christianity, but in a different way. Her lifestyle reflected the holiness and goodness of spirit that should be evident in all people of faith. When people look at you, how is your faith reflected in your actions and in the life choices that you make?

5. Close you eyes and think about yesterday. Allow the events of the day to unfold in your mind. Now open your eyes and make a list of every action you did (no matter how small) that was a reflection of your Christian faith.

6. If you are in a group setting, you may want to try the following activity. (You will need a sandal for this exercise and a person who will act as leader.) Form a circle. Dim the lights, if possible, and have soothing, prayerful music playing in the background. Pass the sandal around the circle from person to person, never skipping anyone and always handing, never tossing, the sandal. Do this reverently, for the sandal represents the sandal that Jesus once wore. As this is being done, the leader should read the Beatitudes from the fifth chapter of Matthew, verses 3–11. As the leader finishes the Scripture reading, the person who is holding the sandal at that moment is the person who, that week, will be "walking in the footsteps of Jesus" by trying to live out the Beatitudes in his or her life. Have that person report to the group at the next meeting on what the week was like for him or her.

Chapter Eight

Women and the Teachings of the Magisterium

A Definition of Terms

The word *magisterium* comes from the Latin word *magis* and means "to master." In current usage, the word *magisterium* is commonly associated with the hierarchy of the Catholic Church, who are entrusted with teaching and authority. This hierarchy includes the pope, individual Catholic bishops who are responsible for the Christian doctrine that is taught within their particular diocese, and the college of bishops when they act in solidarity and in communion with the bishop of Rome (the pope) through an episcopal conference or a synod or a council.

Through these means, specific issues are often addressed—by the pope in encyclicals and the bishops in pastoral letters to Catholics. These documents are meant to teach and instruct the faithful and help form the collective conscience of the Church. Catholics have a responsibility to listen to what the pope and bishops address in a particular document, to do their best to understand what is being taught, and to give assent to the teaching. The role of conscience, however, plays an extremely important part in this process of assent, since, ultimately, each individual must stand before God, responsible for the choices he or she made in life. Since the pope and bishops usually teach in a non-definitive way (not declaring a dogma of faith), an individual who has been thus informed but who cannot, in good faith, accept a particular teaching, is bound to follow his or her informed conscience.

The teaching office of the Church resides with the pope as head of the college of bishops and with the bishops in union with the pope and especially in an ecumenical council. When the pope as head of the bishops speaks *ex cathedra* (which in Latin means "from the chair"; figuratively speaking, the chair of the first pope, Saint Peter, from which episcopal authority, through Christ, originates), and when the bishops speak in council or otherwise as a group in union with the pope, proclaim by a definitive act a doctrine, or teaching, on faith or morals, that teaching is infallible. Through apostolic succession and with the special assistance of the Holy Spirit (which the Church believes will not allow the faithful to be led into error through false teaching), dogmas of faith are considered to be without error, or in other words, infallible. The bishops gathered at the Second Vatican Council explained the extent of infallibility in this way:

> *Although the bishops, taken individually, do not enjoy the privilege of infallibility, they do, however, proclaim infallibly the doctrine of Christ on the following conditions: namely, when, even though dispersed throughout the world but preserving for all that amongst themselves and with Peter's successor the bond of communion, in their authoritative teaching concerning matters of faith and morals, they are in agreement that a particular teaching is to be held definitively and absolutely [Cf. Vatican Council I, Const. Dogm.* Dei Filius, *3: Denz 1712 (3011) . . .]. This is still more clearly the case when, assembled in an ecumenical council, they are, for the universal Church, teachers of and judges in matters of faith and morals, whose decisions must be adhered to with the loyal and obedient assent of faith [Code of Canon Law, c. 1322–1323].*

> *This infallibility, however, with which the divine redeemer wished to endow his Church in defining doctrine pertaining to faith and morals, is co-extensive with the deposit of revelation, which must be religiously guarded and loyally and courageously expounded. The Roman Pontiff, head of the college of bishops, enjoys this infallibility in virtue of his office, when, as supreme pastor and teacher of all the faithful—who confirms his brethren in the faith (cf. Lk.22:32)—he proclaims in an absolute decision a doctrine pertaining to faith or morals [Cf. Vatican Council I, Const. Dogm.* Pastor aeternus: Denz *1839 (3074)].*
>
> "Dogmatic Constitution on the Church," *Vatican Council II: The Conciliar and Post Conciliar Documents*, Austin Flannery, Gen. Ed. (Collegeville, MN: The Liturgical Press, 1975), #25.

Note that infallibility does not apply to every statement or teaching of every pope or council throughout the history of Christianity. Nor does it imply that a pope or council is impeccable (without sinfulness). And it does not mean that the pope or bishops are infallible, but rather that, through the desire of God, the pope and the bishops in union with him have been granted the gift of infallibility for the good of the Church, when he or they specifically define a dogma and proclaim it to be infallible. As mentioned in chapter 2, in the history of Christianity, infallible declarations have been infrequent.

Today, as can be expected in a Church with hundreds of millions of people, there is much controversy over some Church teachings. There is also confusion in the minds of many about what criteria must be present for a teaching to be considered infallible, with many people incorrectly assuming that all Church teachings are infallible. This becomes an especially sensitive topic in regard to moral teachings and issues that are of special concern to many women in the Church. There are some in the Church who argue against the belief that the pope or bishops can ever teach with infallibility. As a result of the confusion, the primacy of the role of conscience and the individual's right to dissent from non-infallible Church teaching is not well understood. Not surprisingly, confusion among the people, often primed by errors in the reports of the secular media, puts theologians, with their prophetic role in ecclesial life, under some scrutiny by the magisterium. Naturally, this is a cause of concern for many in the Church, especially those whose lives are directly associated with Catholic colleges and universities, including those who write or teach theology.

In this chapter, these issues and others, especially teachings of the ordinary magisterium that directly impact women's involvement in the Church will be examined in some detail. These are the teachings that were not pronounced in a definitive way (infallibly), but which, according to the Catechism, call for religious assent, though not the assent of faith (#892). First, however, it would be helpful to see how the current hierarchical structure of the Church came into existence, for it actually evolved over time as the Church came to a greater understanding of itself and of its mission in the world. It was also further developed and refined as the Church responded to theological, social, and political concerns that, throughout history, were often a threat to the Church's very existence.

The Development of the Hierarchy

The Church, as it is experienced today, is in many respects organized very differently from the community of believers who long ago personally knew, loved, and shared in the ministry of Jesus. That community initially saw itself as deeply rooted in Judaism, for that was the religion of Jesus, as it was the religion of the first disciples of Christ. The followers of "The Way" believed that all who followed Jesus were gifted with the Spirit; social and cultural constraints, such as gender and ethnicity, were not issues of divisiveness among them. This soon changed, however, and disputes arose between Gentile and Jewish followers over Jewish dietary regulations and whether or not non-Jewish male converts needed to be circumcised according to Jewish Law. Cultural considerations and restraints eventually also became an issue as some sought to limit the role of women within the communities of believers.

The conflicts regarding dietary regulations and male circumcision were brought for resolution to the apostles at the Council of Jerusalem. At this gathering, Peter recalled the vision he had been granted earlier that convinced him that Gentiles should be accepted into the community. Then James, who headed the community in Jerusalem, made the judgment to allow Gentiles to be admitted without the requirements of Judaism. As we shall see, the second dispute regarding full and equal gender partnership in the Church, according to many, has still not been adequately resolved.

There was recognition among the apostles that Peter's vision communicated the will of God to them. Over time, Peter, whom Jesus had chosen, was held in special honor. *Apostolic succession* refers to the continuation of Jesus' mission through those who were chosen by the apostles and commissioned by them with the laying on of hands. They in turn commissioned others, and so on, down through the centuries. Today the bishops, with the pope, the successor of Peter, as their head, are the successors of the apostles.

By the latter half of the second century, bishops were already taking responsibility for and governing specific geographic areas. In addition, Church synods and councils were called to help clarify Church doctrine and respond to heresies that arose frequently. These gatherings, modeled on the first Council of Jerusalem, recognized that true unity existed only when there was unity among the bishops and that the ultimate authority of the Church was seated with the pope in Rome. (After the fall of Jerusalem, the center of the Church shifted to Rome, and both Peter and Paul preached and died there.) Because the Church was significantly influenced by the Roman family structure, in which the exercise of authority and leadership was the sole prerogative of the father, the structure of the Church developed in a similar way. A strong, centralized system of authority was also a necessity because, for much of its early history, the Church was "under siege."

The threats to the Church were both internal and external and included, over the centuries, heresies such as Gnosticism, Arianism, and Jansenism; hostile invasions of Christian territories; the decimation that resulted after the bubonic plague; and political alliances and infighting. The fact that the Church was able to survive at all is testimony to the Spirit and the unity the Spirit brings. The hierarchical structure of the Church has often been likened to that of a human skeleton

which provides the underlying support for the rest of the body. And it is a good analogy, in the sense that one can easily see how necessary a skeletal structure is for the existence of any living organism. But if such an analogy is used to describe a part of the Church, then it must be taken to its logical conclusion, for a body is comprised of more than bone. Using this comparison, the Church also consists of muscle and sinew and blood and skin. It moves and breathes and is constantly in a process of self-renewal. Only when the body loses the ability to regenerate itself does it die. Throughout the history of the Church, there has always been a tension and the need for balance between the rigidity of the hierarchical "skeleton" and the fluidity of the rest of the body that, in its totality, we call the Body of Christ—the Church.

This was especially apparent from the Middle Ages well into the twentieth century. The Church during this period had to react to many threats, some of which were mentioned in the previous chapter. This led to a reactionary stance that can be likened to a Church with its guard up and its back against the wall. This stance resulted in an exaggerated concept of papal authority which filtered down and settled into a clericalism that tended to see things only in black and white and bordered on absolutism. Prior to the Second Vatican Council (1962–1965), this was the experience of the "modern" Church. Hundreds of years of Church members being passive recipients led further to an understanding of Church primarily in terms of those who were ordained leading those who were not ordained. Power, holiness, and a call to ministry were believed to reside in the realm of those who were ordained. For the rest of the Church, "paying and praying" became the understood role of the laity, and, as a result, the Church was in danger of forgetting that it was the People of God, the Body of Christ.

The Second Vatican Council did its best to call the Church back to a sense of the true mission with which it had been entrusted by Christ—to proclaim and to be a sign of the kingdom of God. The Church is to be a servant Church, a compassionate community of the faithful who embrace those in need; it is to be collegial in nature, comprised of people who see themselves as equal in dignity and grace and who then act as such. It is to be so imbued with the presence of God that Christ will be reflected in the loving actions of its members. The words of one of the premiere documents of the Second Vatican Council express this sentiment well.

> *The Church, "like a stranger in a foreign land, presses forward amid the persecutions of the world and the consolations of God" [St. Augustine.* Civ. Dei, *XVIII, 51, 2:* PL *41, 614], announcing the cross and death of the Lord until he comes (cf.* 1 Cor. *11:26). But by the power of the risen Lord she is given strength to overcome, in patience and in love, her sorrows and her difficulties, both those that are from within and those that are from without, so that she may reveal in the world, faithfully, however darkly, the mystery of her Lord until, in the consummation, it shall be manifested in full light.*
>
> "Dogmatic Constitution on the Church," *Vatican Council II: The Conciliar and Post Conciliar Documents*, #8.

This reference, like most official writings of the Church, projects the ideal. These writings proclaim the goal toward which all Christians should strive or the fullness of a teaching that the faithful should accept—even as they acknowledge how limited humanity often is in responding fully and completely, by the very nature of our humanness. We are not perfect, nor do we love perfectly or understand completely. Nonetheless, the magisterium of the Church, its bishops in unity with the pope, has a responsibility to instruct Christians in matters of faith and morals. This magisterial responsibility, especially as it resides in the papacy, has always been present but was defined and ratified during the First Vatican Council (1869–1870). The document *Pastor Aeternus* underscored the papacy's juridical primacy as well as the infallibility of the teaching office of the pope. The Documents of the Second Vatican Council made clear the role of the college of bishops and ecumenical councils, as well as the pope, in the infallibility issue (cited earlier).

There is some irony in the fact that so often in Church documents (such as the one just cited) as well as in common usage, the Church is referenced in the feminine. Ironic because at times these very documents, as they pertain to women, have limited or diminished the Church's understanding of the dignity of women. This was especially true of many early, non-biblical Church writings, which, of course, should be seen in a proper historical context, but which, nonetheless, were often misogynistic to the extreme. Most operated from the premise that women were created by God as "lesser men," as inferior to males both physically and intellectually. Often the entire female gender was condemned as spiritually bankrupt due to "the sin of Eve." It was from this mindset that the following writings originated.

> *It is not permitted for a woman to speak in the church (1 Cor 14:34–35), but neither is it permitted her . . . to offer, nor to claim to herself a lot in any manly function, not to say sacerdotal office.*
>
> Tertullian, *The veiling of virgins* 9, A.D. 206.

> *[W]hen one is required to preside over the Church and to be entrusted with the care of so many souls, the whole female sex must retire before the magnitude of the task . . . .*
>
> *The Priesthood* 2:2, A.D. 387.

"The man is the head of the woman" (1 Cor. 9:3), and he is originally ordained for the priesthood; it is not just to abrogate the order of the creation and leave the first to come to the last part of the body. For the woman is the body of the man, taken from his side and subject to him, from whom she was separated for the procreation of children. For he says, "He shall rule over you" (Gen. 3:16). For the first part of the woman is the man, as being her head. But if in the foregoing constitutions we have not permitted them to teach, how will any one allow them, contrary to nature, to perform the office of the priest?

The Apostolic Constitutions, A.D. 400.

Many of the early writings of theologians and councils, such as the ones just cited, may have been so opposed to the idea of women serving in a priestly function because they were condemning what was already localized or perhaps even common practice. In other words, why would there have been such a need to instruct against something that was not occurring? This seems to be the case, as Tertullian called women "heretics" if they exhibited any of the gifts of the Holy Spirit.

It is of no concern how diverse be [the heretics'] views, so long as they conspire to erase the one truth. They are puffed up; all offer knowledge. Before they have finished as catechumens, how thoroughly learned they are! And the heretical women themselves, how shameless are they! They make bold to teach, to debate, to work exorcisms, to undertake cures.

Demurrer Against the Heretics 41:4–5, A.D. 200.

Of course, some are quick to point out that these ancient writings originated in a different time and culture. And, although they helped shape the mindset of the Church for generations, nonetheless, writings such as these should be viewed within their proper historical context. The point is well taken, as Christian Scripture, with the example of Jesus, has always viewed women as equal to men simply by virtue of the fact that both women and men are made in God's image. Through the Sacrament of Baptism, all are equal in dignity before God. The magisterium today views many of the contentious issues, such as the ordination of women, as unrelated to equality. As we shall see through a brief look at some historical and recent Church documents and teachings, the issue of women in the Church is complex in nature, vast in scope, and truly begging for resolution.

Occasionally, there are moments within a person's lifetime in which there is an instantaneous recognition that what is happening (or about to happen) will be life changing, monumental in scope, or even earth shattering. Pope John XXIII had such an insight when he convened the Second Vatican Council in 1962. In fact, the pope was so convinced that the Holy Spirit was urging the Church toward this moment in time that he called the council a "new Pentecost." Sadly, though, Pope John XXIII died after only one session of the council, but his vision of what the council was meant to accomplish was mirrored in all of its documents, particularly the final one. Issued in December 1965, the preface of "The Pastoral Constitution of the Church in the Modern World" (*Gaudium et Spes*) begs that the Church be seen in a new way, so that "it might be fashioned anew according to God's design and brought to its fulfillment" (#2). In chapter 2 of the document, the council recognized that, in order for the Church truly to change and be fashioned anew, it was imperative that the social order also change.

> *The social order and its development must constantly yield to the good of the person, since the order of things must be subordinate to the order of persons and not the other way around, as the Lord suggested when he said that the Sabbath was made for man and not man for the Sabbath (Mark 2:27). The social order requires constant improvement: it must be founded in truth, built on justice, and enlivened by love: it should grow in freedom towards a more humane equilibrium [Cf. John XXIII, Litt. Encycl.* Pacem in Terris: *AAS 55 (1963), p. 266]. If these objectives are to be attained there will first have to be a renewal of attitudes and far-reaching social changes. The Spirit of God, who, with wondrous providence, directs the course of time and renews the face of the earth, assists at this development (#26).*

The document also speaks to the essential equality of all persons.

> *. . . forms of social or cultural discrimination in basic personal rights on the grounds of sex, race, color, social conditions, language or religion, must be curbed and eradicated as incompatible with God's design. It is regrettable that these basic personal rights are not yet being respected everywhere, as is the case with women who are denied the chance freely to choose a husband, or a state of life, or to have access to the same educational and cultural benefits as are available to men.*
>
> "The Church in the Modern World," *Vatican Council II: The Conciliar and Post Conciliar Documents, #29.*

These three excerpts from "The Pastoral Constitution of the Church in the Modern World" give the core essence of this prophetic document's call for equality of all persons. It also, however, is an excellent example of how the Church, even as it tries

to move humanity toward new ways of thinking and of relating, is still a part of the very fabric of society that it seeks to change. The above reference to a woman's right to freely choose a husband is an excellent example of this fact. It may seem constraining and sexist to the extreme to western ears, but it must be remembered that the council addressed the universal Church and that, in many parts of the world, such a freedom was denied to women.

The Church is not separate and apart from the world. Even as it influences society and culture, it is itself being influenced. The importance of this fact cannot be underestimated and begs to be acknowledged, for it is a crucial point, especially as it pertains to the issue of women in the Church. Keep these three excerpts in mind as we consider the tensions that are present in the Church today, as the Church seeks to respond to the issue of the changing roles of women, both in society and in the Church.

Of Spirit, Giftedness, and Service

Imagine, if you can, what the hope of "a new Pentecost" of Second Vatican Council was like. In describing Pentecost, the event that is noted as the beginning of the Church, the author of the Acts of the Apostles says that the Spirit of God descended upon the group of believers with such power and might that those who witnessed the Spirit-filled disciples marveled at the change and wondered if it were the result of excessive drinking (Acts 2:1–13). No doubt that was the only logical conclusion the onlookers could make, for the world had never seen anything like it before. Imagine the excitement and the pure joy of the believers who witnessed firsthand the power of the Lord! This experience was so overwhelming that Scripture tells us thousands of people believed and were baptized that very day.

Now try to intuit what Pope John XXIII meant when he said that Vatican II was a "new Pentecost" for the Church. If he truly felt led by the Spirit in calling the council, we need to allow the power of his words to be heard anew. His words can today enflame our hearts and the heart of the Church. But if a "new Pentecost" is to sweep through the Church, shaping it anew, then the logical question is, what shape will this renewed Church take? Perhaps the answer lies in the hope that the Church, guided by the Holy Spirit, is being called into new ways of being. If this is so, then the Church's ultimate response to the role of women in the Church will be a response that is

true to the best of its Tradition. It will be a response that is made with integrity and justice and is based on the praxis of Jesus. This may ultimately mean that, as the Church struggles to interpret anew the intent of the Lord, it will need to let go of those things that hinder the movement of God's Spirit. How this will be accomplished and how Tradition, practice, and mission will be interpreted are the cause of many tensions in the Church today.

Of course, the image of Church hierarchy that has been presented in this chapter thus far is not the only model of Church. There are many, but there is one model that pre-dates all others. The model that Jesus gave us is a model of his actual physical presence to his followers, which later shaped the early Christian community gathered in his name. It is the experience of the earliest faith community, who were graced with the spirit of his presence and comforted, formed, and led by their memories of Jesus.

How easy it is, centuries later, to forget that the earliest "Church" was a community of people who knew Jesus personally! The members of that faith community knew what Jesus' voice sounded like; they knew what made him laugh, as well as what upset him. They knew his favorite stories and the foods he liked. They saw Jesus, the Son of God, work miracles when he cared for the multitudes who flocked to him, and they saw him struggle with his own human limitations of fatigue and physical weakness. They no doubt felt his anguish and his joy. Then, as a growing awareness of Jesus' mission to the world unfolded before their eyes, his friends and supporters grieved and despaired over his impending death. Imagine the immense joy when they realized that Jesus conquered death—that he truly was the Messiah for whom they had waited.

Because this early faith community knew Jesus, they were able to create, with the grace of the Spirit, a community that was true to his ideals and to his actions. For believers today, that long-ago community may present our most authentic manifestation of what Jesus meant for his Church to be. It is a model based on the very Spirit of God; it is "Church" at its best. This is the Church experienced in the first and second generations after Christ's life, death, and resurrection.

Effused with the Holy Spirit, this community was aware of its giftedness and its call to acts of service in Christ's name. The early Church defined these three hallmarks of the community (the *kononia*) as *pneuma*, *charisma*, and *diakonia* (all Greek terms). We call these hallmarks *spirit*, *gift*, and *service*, and like the early faith communities, we acknowledge that all these blessings are to be used for the sake of the kingdom. As the Church today struggles with potentially divisive issues, it's beneficial to revisit this premiere model of community. The issue that seems to be most in need of resolution is whether or not women should be ordained to the priesthood.

The Elephant in the Living Room— a.k.a. the Issue of Women's Ordination

Few would argue that gender equality in the Church is solely limited to or defined by whether or not Catholic women should be ordained. Equality of discipleship goes far beyond even this crucial issue. Nonetheless, the ordination of women is at the center of a growing controversy that holds the potential to become increasingly divisive if it is not adequately addressed. In May 1994, somewhat ironically on the Solemnity of Pentecost, Pope John Paul II issued the apostolic letter *Ordinatio Sacerdotalis*, "On Reserving Priestly Ordination to Men Alone." It appears that the pope's intent was to make a definitive statement that would end all further debate and all theological discourse on the subject. But rather than quelling the mounting theological storm, the letter and a follow-up clarification by the Vatican office of the Congregation for the Doctrine of the Faith created even more controversy. As we shall see, these documents broadened the dialogue on the issue of ordination to include that of papal authority and infallibility as well as the authority of the magisterium in general.

The English translation of *Ordinatio Sacerdotalis*, taken from the Latin, is only eleven paragraphs in length and, for the most part, is a reaffirmation of previous Church teaching on the subjects of ordination, the priesthood, vocation, and Tradition. In addition, the last two paragraphs are of special significance

because they move the Church into uncharted theological waters regarding infallibility, the role of conscience, and papal authority.

> *Although the teaching that priestly ordination is to be reserved to men alone has been preserved by the constant and universal Tradition of the Church and firmly taught by the Magisterium in its more recent documents, at the present time in some places it is nonetheless considered still open to debate, or the Church's judgment that women are not to be admitted to ordination is considered to have a merely disciplinary force.*
>
> *Wherefore, in order that all doubt may be removed regarding a matter of great importance, a matter which pertains to the Church's divine constitution itself, in virtue of my ministry of confirming the brethren (cf. Luke 22:32), I declare that the Church has no authority whatsoever to confer priestly ordination on women and that this judgment is to be definitively held by all the Church's faithful.*

The release of this apostolic letter caused a swift and clamorous response in many theological circles. Some hailed the instruction as long-awaited and much-needed, while others greeted the pope's statement with great dismay. Almost all, however, were asking a collective question: What exactly did the pope mean when he stated that "this judgement is to be definitively held by all the Church's faithful"?

The confusion and clamor of different voices demanding clarification or, quite often, providing their own clarification through individual interpretation of the document, swirled through Catholic colleges, universities, and seminaries. Nor was the Catholic laity, in general, oblivious or untouched by the theological debates sparked by the pope's apostolic letter, thanks in a large part to the secular press, which provided its own interpretation of things. It came as no great surprise, therefore, when the Congregation for the Doctrine of the Faith issued a follow-up statement. What was surprising, even shocking to many, however, was what the Congregation said.

Released on October 28, 1995, the congregation's document was a response to a *dubium*, an official question that the congregation received requesting clarification on exactly how the pope's reference to "definitively held" was to be understood. Regarding the teaching in *Ordinatio Sacerdotalis* that the Church had no authority to ordain women and therefore never could, the congregation declared the teaching to belong to the "deposit of faith." (The reference to the deposit of faith simply means that the magisterium—in this case, the pope—contends that its decision is based on the teaching of Jesus as found in Scripture and as experienced in the apostolic Tradition.) For this reason, the Congregation for the Doctrine of the Faith contends that the order of a male-only priesthood is to be considered as infallibly taught.

The response to the *dubium*, which intended to put an end to future discussion on the topic of women's ordination, has only fueled the fires and expanded the debate. Writing in the December 9, 1995, issue of the periodical *America*, Ladislas Orsy SJ responded with the following:

> *In the ordinary dialectics of the life of the church, the reception of the document should follow, not in the sense of legal ratification, but in the sense of intelligent absorption. In this process, the "universal body of the faithful who have received the anointing of the holy one [and] cannot be mistaken in belief . . . from the bishops to the last of the faithful of the laity" [see the Second Vatican Council's "Dogmatic Constitution on the Church,"*

#12] must assess the authority of this document (otherwise they cannot properly obey it) and must understand the message (otherwise they cannot correctly respond to it).

Infallibility cannot be delegated. It is a charism granted to the pope . . . no other office or body in the church can possess it. The assistance of the Holy Spirit cannot be transferred. . . . A non-infallible organ of the Holy See, on its own authority, does not have the power to modify in any way the doctrinal weight of a papal pronouncement. It has, however, the right to publish its own view, which must be received with the respect that is due to that office. . . . The Code of Canon Law, too, has a cautionary rule for these matters: "No doctrine is understood to be infallibly defined unless it is clearly established as such" [Canon 749].

Ladislas Orsy, "The Congregation's 'Response': Its Authority and Meaning," *America* (9 December 1995): 4.

Pope John Paul II, seemingly, had no intention of making a dogmatic pronouncement over the issue of women's ordination, as he was not speaking *ex cathedra*. Furthermore, the bishops of the Catholic Church had not been able to give a unanimous assent in their teaching that the exclusion of women from the priesthood is a divinely revealed truth that is contained in the deposit of faith. Such a criteria, as well as consultation with the magisterium and with theologians, would generally have been part of the necessary process before the promulgation of a dogma. This is so because such a dogmatic statement would have demanded that Catholics accept the pope's instruction as being without error. If that were the case, then the faithful would have been obliged to give a definitive assent of faith to the teaching. Perhaps the pope recognized that even long-standing tradition does not necessarily equate infallibility. Many would argue that this is especially true regarding the tradition of the Church that has banned women from ordination.

The Place of Tradition in Church Teaching

As relational beings, something inside us longs for tradition and ritual. Time-honored traditions make us feel good, such as going to Grandma's house for Christmas or gathering for the yearly Fourth of July family reunion. Appealing to tradition can also make a powerful argument, as anyone knows who has ever tried to implement a new way of doing things, only to be met with the plaintive cry, "But we've never done it that way before!" It seems that as lovers of tradition, we are also inherently suspicious of change. This is true in our own experience, as it is true for the Church.

All religions, like families, observe traditions, such as fall festivals and regular gatherings for worship. No matter how familiar, well attended, or comfortable these events may be, they are all observances that are subject to change. The type of tradition that will be our focus, however, is generally designated by a capital "T." This Tradition concerns the transmission of beliefs and rituals that define who we are as a community of believers. In this sense, Tradition conveys God's revelation through the experience of the Church's entire witness, worship, and life.

An example of this Tradition is the belief that Scripture is the divinely inspired word of God. The Church has always held this to be true, even when biblical scholarship and exegesis allowed for a greater role for historical and cultural factors in

the shaping of the Bible. By its very nature, Tradition conveys revelation and demands continuity with the past, but it also allows for new ways of knowing and experiencing that revelation. This is so because Tradition is not carved in stone, no matter how static and unchanging it may at first appear to be. In other words, the Tradition of the Church changes (without compromising Truth) because the Tradition of the Church is alive.

In the first sentence of *Ordinatio Sacerdotalis*, Pope John Paul II makes a powerful appeal to the Tradition of the Church in the framing of his argument against female ordination: "Priestly ordination, which hands on the office entrusted by Christ to his Apostles of teaching, sanctifying and governing the faithful, has in the Catholic Church from the beginning always been reserved to men alone." For many, the pope's document could have ended there. Not only had a strong appeal to Tradition been made, but also an appeal to divine authority. In other words, things are the way they are because God wants them to be this way.

The pope is correct in making such a claim, for Jesus did not entrust any sacramental or authoritative office to women. He never ordained any women as priests. (Jesus did choose and send out his apostles to continue his mission. The presumption of the Catholic Church is that he, in that sense, ordained them, but the priesthood as we know it developed over time.) It was in the second century when an order of bishops to succeed the apostles developed, and it was probably not until the third century that the order of priests to assist the bishops became well established.

An argument could be made regarding the use of the term *apostle*, for an apostle is one whose primary function is to give witness to the resurrection. The fact that none of the Twelve were present at the empty tomb and that Jesus chose to appear first to the women would technically make them apostles. But this type of theological semantics does not really do justice to the subject at hand, because, while accurate, there is seemingly a greater truth. That truth is that Jesus did not choose any women to be among the Twelve, and because he did not, the Church feels justified in following his example.

Of course, as we have learned, the fluidity of the first generations of Christians seemed to allow for the ministry of women. For example, as Christians gathered together in the early "house churches," women presided just as men did, depending on whose home it was. And not only does Scripture give hints of a time when women were active in appointed, ecclesial ministry, but there is documentation to prove such a claim.

> *Already at the beginning of the third century, women had been recognized as deaconesses in the church. Origen explained the text in Romans concerning Phoebe by saying, "This text teaches with the authority of the apostles that even women are instituted deacons in the church. . . ." Hands were imposed on them as for other clerics, as the bishop prayed: O Eternal God, Father of our Lord Jesus Christ, Creator of man and of woman, who replenished Miriam with the Spirit, and Deborah, Anna and Huldah; who did not disdain that thy only-begotten Son should be born of a woman; who also in the tabernacle of the testimony and in the Temple did ordain women to be keepers of the holy gates, do Thou now look down upon thy servant who is to be ordained to the office of deaconess, and grant her the Holy Spirit, that she may worthily discharge the work that is committed to her to thy glory and the praise of thy Christ.*
>
> Paul Bernier, *Ministry in the Church: A Historical and Pastoral Approach* (Mystic, CT: Twenty-Third Publications, 1992).

Seemingly in disregard to the historical evidence of women serving in a clerical role at one time in the history of the Church, the pope restates in *Ordinatio Sacerdotalis* many of the apologetics that were used eighteen years earlier in a declaration by the Congregation for the Doctrine of the Faith called *Inter Insigniores*. In that document Mary, the mother of Jesus, is held up as further proof of Jesus' intent that the eventual development of the priesthood was to be restricted to males only.

> *Yet, we must acknowledge that in the matter under discussion there is a whole set of facts which point in one direction and make it all the more surprising that Jesus did not in fact entrust the apostolic office to women. His own mother was intimately associated with the mystery of her Son and her important role is brought out in the Gospels of Luke and John, yet she was not called to the apostolic ministry. This fact led the Fathers to propose Mary as an example demonstrating Christ's will in this matter. Pope Innocent had stated the same teaching at the beginning of the 13th century when he wrote: "Even though the Most Blessed Virgin Mary surpassed all the apostles in worth and perfection, yet the Lord gave the keys of the kingdom to them and not to her."*
>
> Sacred Congregation for the Doctrine of the Faith, *Inter Insigniores: Declaration on the Question of Admission of Women to the Ministerial Priesthood* (Washington DC, 1976), #2.

Pope John Paul II refers to the same logic as found in *Inter Insigniores*, but he stresses that the fact that Jesus would not confer ministerial priesthood on his Blessed Mother must not be used as an argument against the equality and the dignity of women. This is not surprising when one considers that Pope John Paul II, in 1988, promulgated *Mulieris Dignitatem*, an often-beautiful apostolic letter on the dignity and vocation of women. Those who criticize the document generally do so on the grounds that the pope seems to see women's role in society and in the Church as primarily experienced through motherhood (or through consecrated virginity). Motherhood, according to the pope, finds its culmination in the very motherhood of Mary. Furthermore, the pope makes reference to the powerful effect that women can have on society through the proper education of their children.

In *Ordinatio Sacerdotalis*, the mother, virgin, and martyr roles the pope sees as belonging to women and that do not allow for the possibility of ordination are ". . . to be seen as the faithful observance of a plan to be ascribed to the wisdom of the Lord of the Universe" (#3). It is certainly difficult to counter an argument that is claimed to have validity because it comes directly from God. Nonetheless, those who do question the argument have often cited cultural considerations as the reason that Jesus did not choose any women to be among his apostles. This certainly may have been a factor—maybe even the true reason for his decision—but we have no way of knowing this with any certainty. And the question would then have to be asked, "Why would Jesus bow to the prevailing culture in this matter when, in every other way, he did not mind going against the prevailing culture?"

With special regard to his mother Mary, some point to the fact that perhaps Mary did not have a vocation to the type of ecclesial ministry that would come to be called the priesthood. Her vocation was of an entirely different sort. Perhaps she was not called to consecrate the Body and Blood of Christ on an altar because, in a very deeply profound way, her body once was the altar from which the world received the Body of Christ.

But the same logic that applies to vocation would then naturally follow in regard to Jesus' choice of apostles. The argument could be made that while Jesus chose only men, this was no more significant than the fact that he selected those who were called to this ministry—those for whom it was a vocation. After all, at that time, he did not have a large pool of people who were close to him from whom he might choose. Critics of the "Christ-chose-only-men model" are also quick to point out that he chose only Jewish men as apostles. Then, using this type of logic, would it not follow that only Jewish men are called to the priesthood, because that was the example of Jesus?

Not found in *Ordinatio Sacerdotalis*, but of profound importance to the theology that contributed to it, is the argument that women cannot be ordained because they cannot represent Christ's maleness to the Church.

> *Christian priesthood is thus sacramental in nature. The priest is a sign, the supernatural efficacy of which derives from ordination. The meaning of the sign must be perceived and the faithful should be able to grasp it readily. The whole sacramental system is based on natural signs whose power to signify is intimately connected with the psychology of man. As St. Thomas puts it, "sacramental signs signify by reason of a natural likeness." This criterion of likeness must be applied, moreover, to persons no less than to things. Since, then, Christ's role must be sacramentally represented in the Eucharist, the "natural likeness" required between Christ and his minister would be lacking if Christ were not represented by a male. Otherwise it would be difficult to perceive the image of Christ in the minister, since Christ was and remains a male.*
>
> *Inter Insigniores* (1976), #5.

This reasoning is seldom used today, as the Church finds it difficult to defend. It is Christ's humanity that is represented at the altar, not his maleness—just as a priest's color of skin and eyes, his height, or a personal disability should not detract from the association the faithful would make: "And the Word became flesh and lived among us" (John 1:14). But as we know, the introduction of something or someone new, no matter how welcome the change might be for some people, is never easy.

This has frequently been the experience of Protestant denominations whose leadership voted to admit women to the clergy. It is not uncommon in such denominations to see women clergy struggling with such issues as being continually channeled into parishes that find it difficult to retain a resident pastor or being assigned to a large parish as an associate pastor but not as pastor. Often when the male pastor relocates, the female pastor is passed over for consideration as pastor. Many women ministers also complain of sexism that is occasionally displayed by members of a congregation. Some have even endured verbal and emotional abuse that led to their ultimate decision to relocate to a different parish, hoping that things will be better in a new situation.

As Protestant congregations find that women ministers are not only competent and equal to the task, but often bring a perspective to their ministry that is unique and refreshing, the situation tends to improve. From the Catholic perspective, change is not easy, especially when it involves a matter as serious as changing tradition. However, Rose Hoover gives some insights into what happens when a tradition becomes a negative.

In the call to holiness, that is, the call to represent Christ in the world, the Church has not traditionally held women to a lower standard than men—on the contrary. Nevertheless, whether or not the intention is there, the all-male priesthood and the arguments proposed in its favor do suggest that women are a lesser image of Christ than men. . . . Does it matter whether or not women were at the Last Supper, or whether their role in early Christianity included priesthood? The questions are important, but for the discussion of ordination in today's Church they cannot be decisive. For the restriction of the priesthood to men is primarily a negative tradition, based on an omission, not on Jesus' unambiguous instruction. It is also a subsidiary tradition, not at the heart of the gospel mystery. Finally, considering what we know today about human beings and about the gospel, it is a tradition that has become a stumbling block . . . a scandal to the world, and a detriment to the handing on of the Church's constant Tradition.

Rose Hoover, "Consider Tradition: A Case for Ordaining Women," *Commonweal* (29 January 1999): 17.

In 1994, the National Conference of Catholic Bishops approved a pastoral reflection on women that was several years in the making. Called *Strengthening the Bonds of Peace*, its purpose was to bring not only clarity to the issue of what role women play within the Church but also to stress the importance of women's participation. In a sense, the pastoral reflection was presented as a means to open and continue the dialogue on this issue. Quite understandably, the bishops' intent was to present that dialogue as framed within the context of current Church teaching by the magisterium. The bishops also promised to continue their reflection, study, and dialogue regarding the issue of the role of women within the Church.

From that commitment came, in 1998, the statement of the NCCB Committee on Women in Society and in the Church called *From Words to Deeds: Continuing Reflections on the Role of Women in the Church*. This statement presents three goals that are considered essential to the promotion of an increased awareness, not only of the dignity and equality of women, but also of their importance to the continuing life and mission of the Church. Those three goals are to appreciate and incorporate the gifts of women in the Church, to appoint women to Church leadership positions, and to promote collaboration between women and men in the Church. Perhaps of most significance to the complex, diverse, and potentially divisive issue of women's ordination is the statement on the following page.

> *Finally, we must nurture the spiritual foundation on which collaboration rests. This means individual and group prayer, time for reflection and faith sharing, and attentive listening to the Spirit in our midst. Prayer, the sacraments, charity, and service are, in an extended sense, collaboration with God and with those whom we serve. Collaboration is much more than just a way to accomplish certain tasks. Since God calls each of us to holiness, and since we become holy in and through our relationships, collaboration is a means for becoming who God wants us to be.*
>
> Committee on Women in Society and in the Church, National Conference of Catholic Bishops, United States Catholic Conference, *From Words to Deeds: Continuing Reflections on the Role of Women in the Church*, (Washington, DC, 1998).

Ultimately, "who God wants us to be" is the question that the Church needs to ask itself. Are we tied to a tradition that originated out of misogyny, fear, and sexual constraints, which were part of a long-ago societal structure that is confining the direction the Spirit would have the Church take now? Is the Church's limitation on the faith response that women may make not only a sin against women—the sin of sexism—but also a sin against God's Spirit? Is it truly right that there are seven sacraments within the Catholic Church but that women are allowed to receive only six of them? Or is the Church correct in its interpretation of the will of God in this matter of crucial importance? Have we, as Church, come to such a sense of clericalism that we have linked ministry primarily to ordination? Perhaps it is time for the Church, both individually and collectively, to make a long-overdue examination of conscience on this matter. Only through prayer, dialogue with each other, theological reflection, and genuine collaboration will this happen.

Some Thoughts for Your Reflection

1. As a child, were you ever told that you could not do something because of your gender? Have you ever felt personally excluded from a group or organization because you were female or because you were male? How did this make you feel? Have you ever practiced techniques of exclusion regarding other persons? If so, how do you think your actions made the other person(s) feel?

2. How do you personally feel about the issue of women's ordination to the Catholic priesthood? To help you clarify your thoughts, you may want to divide a large piece of paper into three columns. In column 1 write your feelings on this issue; in column 2 actual reasons why women should not be priests (be specific); in column 3 reasons why women should be allowed to join the priesthood. Now look over your list. How many items in columns 2 and 3 have more to do with feelings than actual reasons? If you are in a group setting, try to debate the issue.

3. The Church teaches that the issue of women's ordination is not about equality. Can you think of some professions that once were limited to men? Why do you think they changed, and has this change been beneficial?

4. The Catholic Church is much bigger than just the United States experience. How do you think Catholics in other parts of the world would receive women priests?

5. Do you think it would help our relations with Protestant Churches if the Catholic Church ordained women? What would happen to our relations with Orthodox Churches who do not allow women priests?

Chapter Nine

The Feminine Experience of Church

Sister Thea Bowman

Tessie's Story

Her name was Sister Theresa, but just about everyone called her Tess or even Tessie. She liked the name *Tessie* better, and the informality of it seemed to suit her. Everyone in the parish said that she was "wonderfully down to earth," while the clerics that came and went tended to describe her as "a wonderful example of a post-Vatican II woman religious." Tessie keyed in on the "wonderful" part and tried not to think too much about what the other stuff might mean. She sometimes had a sinking feeling that what the priests really meant was that she was a nun who no longer dressed like one (even though she still often wore the shoes) and who really did not know her place.

Well, maybe that was the problem after all, because Tessie was no longer sure of her place. For thirty-seven years she had been a member of her religious order, and she hoped to be able to see thirty-seven more (although she was the first to admit that this was entirely in the hands of God). Still, Tessie could honestly say that even through the turmoil of the sixties and seventies, when she saw so many of her friends and associates leave her order and other orders as well, she never had those doubts about her chosen life. And she was glad, too, because she remembered how heart-wrenching it was, going through it as a friend. She could not imagine surviving such a crisis if she was going through it herself. No, what bothered Tessie, and bothered her to the very depths of her soul, was wondering what direction her ministry was to take now—now, after she

was dismissed by the pastor and parish council of the church where she ministered as pastoral associate for the past six years.

Everyone was nice about it. In fact, they went out of their way to praise Sister Theresa for her years of dedicated service to the people of Holy Trinity Parish. It was just that now there was a priest available who could serve as associate pastor. "You understand," they told her, "don't you?" And the truly ironic part was that she did, even though the abruptness of their announcement and decision came as a shock to her. She understood how the parish would have trouble meeting two associates' salaries. And she understood why, in spite of all that she did at Holy Trinity, a priest's presence would be preferable, as he could administer the sacraments. But what she did not understand was why no one at the parish council meeting—even Father Michael—seemed to recognize the sacramental nature of what she had been doing all along.

As Tessie left the council meeting, on her walk home, she allowed her thoughts to drift to some of the people who had graced her life in the past few years. (She always thought of it in such a way, too, even though she knew that people generally saw it as her gracing their lives.) Quite often they seemed to feel especially grateful to her, even expressing a sense of indebtedness. But Tessie would have none of that; no, it was she who was indebted to the people of Holy Trinity. They had opened their hearts and homes to her—even their very souls. She felt so privileged to have had the opportunity to know them.

As her spirits drooped and her ears still rung with the sound of her abrupt dismissal, a part of her wondered if her presence would really be missed at all. Almost as soon as that thought

entered her mind, she pushed it aside as coming from a false sense of pride. What she had done, she had done through the grace of God and in God's name, and she was glad! It really was not at all an issue of whether or not the parishioners recognized this fact, although she truly thought that many of them did. She would miss them, for in the presence of their need, she had been standing on holy ground.

Before the night was over, in the relative comfort of her tiny apartment, Tessie relived much of the past six years. She searched for God's presence in it all, looking for some pattern, some way to discern where it all might be leading. She had always thought that she knew, but tonight she was no longer quite so sure. In the darkness of the living room, with only the moonlight filtering in through the lace curtain at the window, she sat in silence and remembered. And she cried to think that what she had done could be so easily dismissed. (There was that pride again. Even in her pain, she smiled to think that she would really have to work on that. But not tonight, Lord; please not tonight.)

As she rocked in her squeaky old hickory rocker, she could not stop the tears that came from the depth of her soul. Just for tonight, she allowed herself the very understandable emotion of grief. And she cried to feel that what she had done for so many years must be thought of as "lesser than" when compared to the sacramental ministry of a priest. She dared to whisper the words aloud into the quiet darkness of the room that she, too, had presided at countless sacraments, though not in any way that the Church officially recognized. But Tessie knew in her heart that, through her ministry, she had helped bring Christ's healing presence to many people. How many times, over the years, had she baptized with her tears of joy or compassion? How many times had she healed with the warm touch of her hands, forgiven by the softness of her words, or anointed by the love that flowed forth from her heart? She loved these people and would always feel blessed that they had loved her in return. It was enough. It would suffice. Enough of feeling sorry for herself.

Tessie knew that the pastor and the parish council expected her to go back to the motherhouse. It only made sense, as she did not really have too many options available to her. After all, if she was not working at the parish, where else could she work in this relatively small Midwestern town? Returning to the motherhouse for a while was probably a good idea. She could recoup there, regain her balance, and have some time for reflection. Yes, the motherhouse was probably a very good idea—only by 4 A.M., Sister Theresa knew that she had absolutely no intention of going there. Not if she could receive permission from her religious order to stay.

The idea had come to her like a gentle surety that overcame her and quieted her troubled heart. Tessie attributed the rightness of this feeling to coming from God. She was absolutely sure of this part of her plan, for this feeling was familiar to her, and never had this type of rightness of feeling led her astray. This was right. This was the desire of God. As dawn came, Tessie fell asleep, confident that everything was in God's hands. All she had to do was work out the details (and she was good at that).

As it turned out, Sister Theresa was right in her conviction that God was leading her into a new ministry—and where God led her specifically was to North Franklin Avenue. It was there that the children lived (if you could call it living). Such a low

profile did the children have that it had been only two years ago that Tessie had even learned of their existence. They were mostly teenage girls, but sometimes boys as well, who roamed the streets at night in groups of two or three. The north end of Franklin was closest to the nearby army base, the pawn shops, the liquor stores, and more than a few rundown hotels. It just wasn't a place where anyone would want to visit, let alone live. And for the most part, people pretended not to see what was going on there, if they noticed the situation at all.

It took five months before the home that Tessie fashioned for the children was ready. It would have taken much longer if it had not been for the great charity and care of the people of the community, and most especially the people of Holy Trinity parish. Once word got out (which took about two minutes) that Sister's contract was not going to be renewed, the parishioners literally overwhelmed her with care and with their contributions of money, time, and talent. Even the house for the children, which Tessie later named Saint Anne's, was given to the cause. Long, long ago, it had been an elegant home, but at the time it was donated, it was close to being condemned. Nonetheless, with all of the help she received, the house was a godsend.

Of course it was not in Tessie's nature to sit back and wait for anything to happen. While the house was being renovated, she and several mothers and grandmothers from Holy Trinity and two of the Protestant churches in town began an outreach to the children. It wasn't easy. Some of the teens were suspicious that anyone would want to help them without wanting something back; others refused to admit that they needed any help at all. But for those children who could trust enough to take a risk, safe places were found; medical care and counseling was provided, which eventually led to the formation of a community-based mission clinic; educational and technical training was provided; and, whenever possible, family ties were reestablished and strengthened.

Sister Tessie never lived to see the full culmination of what she had set in motion. Tragically, she was killed in a car accident two years after Saint Anne's opened its doors. But her legacy of loving intervention on behalf of the forgotten and victimized children lives on in countless ways. Most especially, her legacy lives on in the lives of the children she helped. If you were to visit the house today, you would see one of her favorite pictures hanging in the entrance foyer. It is a picture-portrait of Sister Tessie surrounded by some of the first children of Saint Anne's. Her smiling visage serves as a reminder to everyone of what faith and compassion can do—maybe especially when it comes in the guise of a wonderfully down-to-earth woman who didn't know her place and who liked to wear nun's shoes.

A Litany of Saints

Dorothy Day

The earthiness of Sister Theresa's approach to the sharp change in direction imposed on her ministry would have appealed greatly to another saintly woman of the twentieth century—Dorothy Day. In her spiritual autobiography *The Long Loneliness*, Dorothy admits that she "had been around."

Born in Brooklyn Heights, New York, in 1897, Dorothy Day was a woman ahead of her time or, perhaps more appropriately, a woman who rose to greatness in her own time. There are many facts about Dorothy Day that are of incredible interest, but facts alone never capture the essence of anyone, especially someone of such personal power and spiritual grace. It is important to note some fundamental facts about her life, however, not only because they can provide courage to those who struggle with their own personal demons, but because her life is certainly outside of the course that most persons would consider a path to holiness. Perhaps Dorothy Day's way was the prophet's path, often misunderstood, frequently criticized, but so desperately needed as a witness to the world.

As a journalist living in Greenwich Village in the 1920s and 1930s, Dorothy associated with people who shared her radical social views. However, after the birth of her daughter Tamara, she underwent a powerful spiritual conversion. In 1927, Dorothy converted to Catholicism and was baptized. Five years later, she met the French peasant-philosopher Peter Maurin, whose life had a profound effect upon hers. He was able not only to help Dorothy understand, on a deeply personal level, the religion she had embraced but also understand her unique place within the Church and society.

It was with Maurin that Dorothy Day co-founded the Catholic Worker Movement. The objective of the movement was solidarity with those who were poor and oppressed—the people society often overlooked or did not see at all. Although the original concept of the Catholic Worker Movement was Maurin's, it was Dorothy Day's enthusiasm, practicality, and perseverance that not only embodied the ideals they shared but also allowed the movement to flourish. For example, as a means of earning money to support the movement, Dorothy started publishing a newspaper titled the *Catholic Worker*, which sold for one penny per copy. She opened what she called a "house of hospitality" for those who needed place to sleep and food to eat. It was also in her original hospitality house that intellectuals, including many of her fellow workers, gathered to discuss politics, philosophy, religion, and so forth. Always a motivating factor in such discussions was how these systems and beliefs impacted those who were already disenfranchised within society.

Dorothy Day and the Catholic Worker movement's followers viewed themselves as the leaven that could change the social order. Dorothy believed deeply, as did Maurin, in Christian personalism, a philosophical view that stressed the dignity of each and every person. She identified so deeply with those who were poor that she embraced a lifestyle of voluntary poverty. The gospel ideal of justice was a great motivator in Dorothy Day's life, for she believed that no one would be won over to Christianity until Christians began to live what they professed.

Dorothy Day

For Day, to live poorly meant to share the life of the poor: "Let us love to live with the poor because they are especially loved by Christ." Each person who represents himself or herself to us—rich, middle class, or poor—must be given love, "not because it might be Christ . . . but because they are *Christ."*

Day's staunch views on pacifism drew a deep line between the Church's just-war teaching and gospel nonviolence. She shared with Saint James the view that the roots of violence are fear, lack of forgiveness, and greed. Fear leads us to strike out at enemies; it may even help to create them. Day believed the Catholic Worker must be a school of non-violence. The young volunteers who came in search of their vocation, she wrote, "learn not only to love with compassion, but to overcome fear, that dangerous emotion that precipitates violence." They may go on feeling fear, but they know the "spiritual weapons," as she called them, of self-discipline, willingness to take up the cross, forgiving "seventy times seven," and readiness to lay down one's life for one's fellows to overcome it. Here, prayer and daily Mass were the best offense. From her own testimony of sitting through nights of threatened violence in the racially divided South in the 1960s, it is prayer that "gives courage."

Patrick Jordan, "An Appetite for God: Dorothy Day at 100," *Commonweal* (24 October 1997): 12.

Dorothy Day's views of justice, peace, and nonviolence often brought her into direct conflict with those in authority. This was true regarding her relationship to the Catholic magisterium at the last session of the Second Vatican Council in 1965. As the bishops debated the Church's teaching on modern warfare, Day gathered with a small group of women to fast, on water only, for ten days.

*Dorothy did not like to fast (she said her besetting sins were gluttony and sloth), and made sure she had filled her senses by going to the opera (*Cavalleria Rusticana*) before the fast. Her report in the November 1965* Catholic Worker *included the daily schedule of the group and concluded as follows: As for me, I did not suffer at all from the hunger or headache or nausea which usually accompany the first few days of a fast, but I had offered my fast in part for the victims of famine all over the world, and it seemed to me that I had very special pains. They were certainly of the kind I had never had before, and they seemed to pierce the very marrow of my bones . . . and I couldn't feel that I had been given some little intimation of the hunger of the world. God help us, living as we do, in the richest country in the world, and so far from approaching the voluntary poverty we esteem and reach toward . . . may we try to do more in the future.*

Jordan, 12.

Jean Vanier, founder of L'Arche (a community for mentally challenged young adults) and an author and advocate for the oppressed within society, once described a meeting that he had with Day.

I was in New York and I felt ill at ease. I needed to find places and people with the Holy Spirit living in their hearts. . . . Later, I met Dorothy Day. She is not very young any more, but she remains a symbol of the kind of person who, practically without means, struggles for justice and truth and does not let herself be crushed by the gigantic mountain of tyranny, despair, and luxury. She lives in an area where there had been several murders recently. Her house is always open to the out-of-work, to beggars, to the poor of all kinds. We had a cup of tea in the main room, surrounded by some of these poor people. Dorothy is dressed very poorly, and her face is lined with years of struggle. But her eyes are illuminated by the living love which dwells in her.

Jean Vanier, *Be Not Afraid* (Mahwah, NJ: Paulist Press, 1975).

Day's pacifist views were at the heart of the American Catholic peace movement as the Vietnam War raged through the '60s. She was a supporter of an individual's right not to be forced by one's government into committing acts of violence to which a person was opposed. Her witness to peaceful protest through the withholding of a portion of one's income that would be used by the government to support war was also prophetic and put her under great scrutiny and criticism.

Nonetheless, Dorothy Day persevered until she died in 1980 at the age of eighty-three. Because of her, the Catholic Worker movement influenced the formation of such social justice organizations such as Pax Christi USA, the Catholic Peace Fellowship, and the American Pax Association. Today the Catholic Worker movement in the United States, begun in 1933, is stronger than ever and is expanding into several other countries. "As Dorothy prayed in Rome: 'Give us, O Lord, peace, and joy, so that we in turn may give them to others'" (Jordan).

Elizabeth Ann Seton

If Dorothy Day was a model of perseverance (even though she felt that she lacked the quality of perseverance), she looked to saintly women who had gone before her and were models of courage and holiness. We are encouraged to do the same. Naturally, there are many women from whom we might choose (including grandmothers, mothers, and favorite aunts). But in addition to your personal women of faith, there are those who have been recognized, in a special way, by the Church. Some of them have even been given the official status of "saint," such as Elizabeth Ann (Bayley) Seton and Maria Francesca Cabrini, whom we know as Mother Frances Cabrini. These women played significant roles in laying the foundation for the United States Catholic Church.

Elizabeth Bayley became a Catholic at a time and place when such a choice was rare, unless for the sake of marriage. Born into a financially secure family in New York City in 1774, she nonetheless knew tragedy early, for her beloved mother Catherine died when Elizabeth was three. Tragedy seemed to follow Elizabeth, but it was interspersed with times of great personal growth and achievement. This pattern continued for the rest of her life, so much so that, in her later years, Elizabeth once said, "Tribulation is my element."

When she was nineteen, Elizabeth married William Seton, and their lives were fast-paced, yet blessed, for the next ten years. Elizabeth and her husband, both members of the Episcopalian Church, had five children and a successful business. Elizabeth was also very active in social work, and in 1797, she founded the Society for the Relief of Poor Widows with Children. Life was very pleasant for the Seton family until William contracted

tuberculosis. As a result of his ailing health, his business began to fail. The family physician suggested an overseas voyage as a possible cure for his illness, but sadly, Elizabeth's husband died while they were in Italy.

Elizabeth was twenty-nine years old when her husband died, and she was left with five children to support. Although she felt alone, Elizabeth was uplifted and inspired by the deep Catholic faith of an Italian family who befriended her during this difficult time. When she returned to the United States, Elizabeth, against the staunch opposition of her family and friends, became a Catholic in 1805. She now felt a calling to become a nun but thought that her need to raise her children would prohibit such a thing from happening. Four years after she became a Catholic, however, the rector of Saint Mary's Seminary in Baltimore invited her to open a school for girls. Seeing no reason why motherhood should preclude Elizabeth from pursuing her dream of becoming a vowed religious, the rector urged her to establish a new religious order. On June 2, 1809, Elizabeth Ann Seton donned the habit of the newly established order of the Sisters of Saint Joseph.

Elizabeth was named mother superior of the order, and the following year, with four companions, she opened the first parochial school in the United States in Emmitsburg, Maryland. Tragedy struck again, however, when Elizabeth's daughter, Anna Maria, died of tuberculosis that same year. Elizabeth's grief was overwhelming, only to deepen further when her youngest daughter contracted the same dreaded illness and died in 1816. Soon after this, Elizabeth became aware that, she, too, was sick. In spite of her grief over the loss of her daughters and her own failing health, she managed to care for her other children and see to the needs of her religious order.

Sister Elizabeth Ann Seton

Despite Elizabeth's personal tragedy, the Sisters of Charity of Saint Joseph, as the order was now called, continued to grow in numbers. When there were eighteen members, Mother Seton was able to send some of the sisters to Philadelphia to establish an orphanage, the very first of its kind in the country. Soon she opened and staffed another Catholic orphanage in New York City. The new order spread so rapidly through the United States that by the time of Mother Seton's death in 1821, there were already twenty communities in existence. (Not all of them were in the United States, however, as the order had spread to South America and Italy as well.) The work of Elizabeth's Sisters of Charity included tending to the wounded on the battlefields of the Civil War. In her memory and for love of God, the order also went on to found hospitals, homes for the elderly, orphanages, and schools for the deaf.

Pope John XXIII beatified Mother Seton, and Pope Paul VI canonized her in 1975, making her the first U.S.-born, canonized saint. In her relatively short life (she died at the age of forty-six), Elizabeth clung to her belief that God's will directed the events in her life; this belief helped her through so many tragedies, which in turn gave her the ability to see and attend to the suffering of others.

> *Saint Elizabeth Seton once said, "We must be so careful to meet our grace. If mine depended on going to a place to which I had the most dreadful aversion, in that place there is a store of grace waiting for me—what a comfort. We must be so careful to meet our grace." Her fervent lifelong prayer truly was "Thy will be done," and she proved her faith through nearly every action of her life. While she experienced great suffering, she never grew bitter because she came to see that without suffering we cannot understand love. . . . Through her suffering she learned about love, and through her love she served God with all the faith and love she had. What more could we possibly ask of a saint?*
>
> Anne Gordon, *A Book of Saints: True Stories of How They Touch Our Lives* (New York: Bantam Books, 1994).

Frances Cabrini

Maria Frances Cabrini was born in Italy in 1850, the youngest of thirteen children. As a little girl, she dreamed of going to China to become a missionary when she grew up, but her frail health precluded that. Frances had always been a petite child (her small size hiding a strong will and a fiercely independent spirit), but when in adolescence she contracted smallpox, her health became even more tenuous. No religious order wanted to take her in, feeling that she was not physically strong enough to endure the harsh lifestyle of a vowed religious. It took quite a while, but Maria Frances eventually became a nun.

Frances Cabrini

The bishop of Lombardy, Domenico Galmini, needed someone to take over a small orphanage for girls in the town of Codogno, for word had come to him that conditions were not good at the orphanage. He thought of Maria Frances, who was thirty years old and a teacher. The bishop's concerns about the orphanage were well founded. When Maria Frances accepted the bishop's invitation and went to the orphanage, she discovered that the children were living in squalor and that the nun who was in charge was mentally disabled. Within a short time, she also discovered that the headmistress of the orphanage was misappropriating funds, which explained why the children were living in such dreadful conditions. From the moment she entered the door of the orphanage, Frances took charge with love and a determined effort to change things for the better. This included not only seeing to the children's physical and emotional welfare but also to their education and spiritual care.

Her "delicate health" not withstanding, Frances did such a wonderful job at the orphanage that the bishop became convinced that she might be physically strong enough to become a nun after all. In fact, he was so impressed that permission was granted for Frances Cabrini to start a new religious order called the Institute of the Missionary Sisters of the Sacred Heart. Several of the girls from the orphanage joined Frances and made religious vows in 1880. By 1887, due to the overwhelming popularity of her order, Mother Cabrini established six additional convents in Italy.

Having proven herself and her ability to the bishop and to the pope, Frances hoped that her life-long dream of becoming a missionary to China would be granted. This was not to be, however, for the pope asked Mother Cabrini to travel, not to the Far East, but rather to the West to the United States. Her mission was to help the flood of Italian immigrants who were trying to assimilate to a new culture, a new language, and a new way of life that was not their own. Mother Cabrini accepted her new mission, and in 1889, she and several of her sisters set sail for New York.

When the sisters arrived in New York, no one met them at the docks, as they had been told to expect, and hence, they were on their own to find affordable accommodations. They found such a place, but unfortunately, it was little more than a vermin-infested tenement. The conditions were so bad that the sisters had to take turns staying awake through the night to be sure that rats would not crawl across them as they slept. It did not take Mother Cabrini long, in the following days, to find the residence of the archbishop. Soon she and her sisters were at his doorstep. The archbishop was emphatic that the sisters would have to return immediately to Italy. Mother Cabrini was just as emphatic that they stay.

Things were quite difficult in this new environment for Mother Cabrini and her sisters. For starters, it was their understanding that they were to staff an orphanage that was established to care for children of Italian immigrants. Actually, to their dismay, the sisters discovered that no such orphanage existed. (Apparently there was an argument between the archbishop of New York and Countess Cesnola, who was a great benefactress of the Church, and she withdrew her financial support of the proposed orphanage.) Unwittingly, her decision put the sisters in a tenuous position, for upon arriving in New York, they not only had no place to stay but also no means of employment. They found themselves little better off than the immigrants whom they had come to help. Perhaps, however, that was the secret of their success.

Many Catholic immigrants traveled to the United States during this time looking for opportunity and wealth. But, too often, upon arriving, they were forced to settle into bleak and impoverished lives. Most spoke no English, had very little money, did not understand the culture, were often persecuted for their religion, and were frequently victimized by unscrupulous landlords and employers. They generally lived in buildings that were barely habitable and fell victim to the common illnesses of poverty, such as malnutrition, pneumonia, and influenza. Despair chipped away at whatever hopes they had that life in the United States would provide a new beginning; instead they often found a tragic ending.

Into this harsh environment came Mother Cabrini and her sisters. They, too, had practically nothing, except a deep faith that God would provide. Their faith was well founded, and it probably was a comforting example and reminder to the people of God's great love and compassion to those who suffer.

Being a practical woman, Mother Cabrini started making plans for the orphanage that they had been sent to staff and that was so desperately needed. After Francis learned the true reason the orphanage had never materialized, she immediately went to see the countess. Mother Cabrini's determination and unwavering faith in her mission won the countess over, and soon the orphanage was established. Of course, this was only a beginning for Mother Cabrini, as she saw so much that needed to be accomplished to ease the plight of immigrants. Speaking very little English herself, she nonetheless became well known and deeply respected by many of the people of New York City for her untiring efforts on behalf of the city's poor people. Newspapers helped increase public awareness of Mother Cabrini's unceasing efforts and made her a figure of public stature (in spite of her diminutive size).

Mother Cabrini's business sense was so astute that she saw her missionary efforts in America expand over the next twenty-eight years in numerous orphanages, hospitals, schools, and convents. By the time of Mother Cabrini's death in 1917, the order that she had founded had begun to work in eight other countries. This was quite a legacy of love to be left to the world from a woman who had been so easily dismissed many years before as someone who was not fit for the religious life.

Kateri Tekakwitha

We have no way of knowing, but in all likelihood, Mother Cabrini probably never heard of Kateri Tekakwitha, who lived in North America in the seventeenth century. Kateri's unique story illustrates how powerful the call to serve the Lord can be and the great sacrifice it can sometimes cost. This is especially true when a person's call to follow Christ leads them on the mystic's path, as was the case for Kateri. Further complicating matters for her was the clash of cultures and ethnicity as transplanted European culture came face to face with the indigenous culture of the Mohawk people.

In her book, *Kateri Tekakwitha: Mystic of the Wilderness*, Margaret Bunson explains that Kateri's world was framed within the context of a world that was far more ordered and structured than we might imagine today. The forest wilderness of the Iroquois (the larger clan of which Kateri's people, the Mohawks, belonged) was a world of beauty and abundance, but also a world of great potential peril. The "woodland warriors" of the group (usually men but also sometimes women of exceptional skill) took care of the hunting for the village and served as sentinels against any dangers that might threaten the community. The rest of the people cultivated the crops, gathered nuts, berries, honey, and tubers, or made repairs to the lodgings, cured deer hides, made clothing, and so on. Everyone had a unique place and purpose within Mohawk society, and everyone had a voice, because all members of the tribe contributed according to their ability.

By the time of Kateri's birth in 1656, the Iroquois population was about 25,000 people, with the nation divided into a confederation of five groups: the Mohawks (numbering approximately 5,000 members), the Oneidas, the Onondagas, the Cayugas, and the Senecas. Each village was overseen by a matriarch, and everyone in the village worked for the good of all and could count on the care and the support of an extended family. This system worked very well for the Mohawk people, and for the most part, the nation managed to live in relative peace and harmony with neighboring groups. However, as Europeans came into the Iroquois territory (French fur traders followed by Jesuit missionary priests and French soldiers), significant conflicts arose.

Blessed Kateri Tekakwitha

The most devastating, by far, was purely accidental. The Europeans introduced smallpox to the Iroquois, who had absolutely no resistance against the disease. Many of Kateri's nation were wiped out by the disease, including her parents, leaving Kateri orphaned at four years of age. She also contracted the illness. Although smallpox did not kill Kateri, her face was severely scarred, and she was partially blinded. Her father's brother took her in, as was the custom, and since Kateri's father had been chief, her uncle now assumed that role.

The first decision Kateri's uncle made was to leave their village site and relocate, as a community, to a different place, leaving behind any vestige of the illness and the despair that the people had known. As she grew older, Kateri had increased contact

with the Jesuits and was drawn further into a faith that her people did not understand and that, at times, seemed to directly oppose their beliefs. Kateri chose not to take a husband, a decision virtually unheard of in Mohawk society; for it seemed to counter the plan of the Great Spirit. To have the power within one's body to give birth and help the Mohawk people increase and prosper—and then to choose not to do so—was incomprehensible. But Kateri stood firm in her choice, despite often being ostracized and tormented by her people until they finally acquiesced to her wishes.

On Easter Sunday, 1676, at the age of twenty Kateri was baptized. She chose to live at the Mission of St. Francis Xavier near Montreal, Canada, where she taught children, cared for those who were ill and aged, and lived a life of increasing penance and prayer. As has been noted in the lives of other holy people, severe bodily mortification was common at this time. Kateri was such a person. As she felt drawn deeper and deeper into mystical union with God, she seemed to have less and less concern for anything other than the spiritual realm. When she was cautioned by her priest to ease her penances, which were taking a physical toll upon her body, she obeyed. In the end, Kateri's life was not long, perhaps shortened by her harsh penances, which included kneeling in the snow, walking barefoot in the dead of winter, and sleeping on thorns.

On March 25, 1679, Kateri made a vow of perpetual virginity and chastity. It was her desire to live out the remaining days of her life espoused to Christ, just as the nuns had chosen to do. The following year, Kateri died at the age of twenty-four. But prior to her death, her people, as well as the missionaries and other non-natives, had come to recognize within her a deep and abiding holiness.

Kateri was not aware of a major role in history of the Native Americans, although she had a predisposition to understanding that her life would not end in the grave; not in the usual sense of hoping for salvation, resurrection and life everlasting but in the manner of continuing as God's Servant in the world even when her life's breath had faded. She was like an eagle flying directly into the sun, being consumed, being blinded and still flying, soaring and making her way toward the Uncreated Light. . . . Such an individual confounds the world, especially if she is raised up by God in the wilderness, in an age that does not afford her or her people the sort of considerations that they are due. . . . She was prepared for her death, as she was prepared to work as God's servant beyond the grave.

Margaret R. Bunson, *Kateri Tekakwitha: Mystic of the Wilderness* (Huntington, IN: Our Sunday Visitor, 1996).

It appears that God did indeed choose Kateri Tekakwitha to help bring the gospel message to the Iroquois people, for almost immediately after her death, the first of many miracles occurred. Kateri, who was severely scarred in her early life from smallpox, was restored to great physical beauty upon her death. To the amazement of everyone, her scars vanished, the frail appearance of her body disappeared, and her skin glowed as if it was radiant. After her burial, those who were brought to her grave received physical healing. When an object she had used, such as her moccasin or blanket, was taken to those too sick to travel, they were cured. Novenas and other prayers were offered in her honor, and a common feeling arose among the people that they had been in the presence of a saint. Her native people called her the *Thaumaturge*, the "healer of the New World," and by common accord, she was venerated by the people. As the number of cures mounted, they were authenticated and recorded by Church authorities, who passed along the information to Rome. It was not until 1942, however, that she was officially recognized as venerable. A prayer for the canonization of Kateri Tekakwitha has been approved; it reads:

> *O God, who, among the many marvels of Your Grace in the New World did cause to blossom on the banks of the Mohawk and of the St. Lawrence, the pure and tender Lily, Kateri Tekakwitha, grant we beseech You, the favor we beg through her intercession; that this Young Lover of Jesus and of His Cross may soon be counted among her Saints by Holy Mother Church, and that our hearts may be enkindled with a stronger desire to imitate her innocence and faith. Through the same Christ our Lord. Amen.*
>
> Bunson.

The Jesuit priests and the sisters who ministered to the native peoples of North America felt called to a very special vocation that often opened them to criticism by European whites, based largely on cultural ignorance and racial prejudice. But they were even, at times, exposed to mortal danger at the hands of the people they sought to help. For example, within Kateri's lifetime, three Jesuit priests lost their lives at the hands of the Mohawk people. This occurred at a time of heightened tensions between the Europeans who were moving into Iroquois territory and the native people who already lived there. And, as has been noted, Kateri Tekakwitha also suffered abuse and torment because her people initially could not understand her choices in life. This is quite understandable, for as cultures and belief systems come into close contact with each other, they often clash—sometimes with tragic results. The life of a missionary is frequently dangerous, whether in another land or within the subcultures and ethnic groups of a person's own nation.

Rose Philippine Duchesne

Rose Philippine Duchesne was born in France in 1769. At the age of nineteen, she entered the Visitation order (a congregation of contemplative women, which was founded in France by Jane Frances de Chantal and Francis de Sales in 1610). Thirteen years later, however, in 1801, her desire to serve as a missionary led her to change affiliation, and she joined the Congregation of the Religious of the Sacred Heart (known today as the Society of the Sacred Heart). Her missionary spirit led her to the United States, where, in 1818, she established the first convent of her order in this new nation. She went on to found several other schools and orphanages and to minister to the Potawatomi nation at Sugar Creek, Kansas. The holiness that resonated throughout her life was so evident to everyone that the Potawatomi gave her a name that is translated as "The Woman Who Prays Always." Rose Duchesne died in 1852 and was canonized in 1988.

Katharine Drexel

Blessed Katharine Drexel felt called to the missionary life, too, even though she was born in 1858 into a life of wealth and social privilege. Katharine was drawn to a life of service to those who were poor and oppressed within the United States. Pope Leo XIII recognized her call to a vowed religious life and encouraged her to follow her vocation, giving her life in service and her inheritance for those in need. After joining the Sisters of Mercy, Katharine felt a call to a special ministry among the Black and Native Americans. In response, she asked for and was given permission to start a new religious order. Reflective of its time, the new order was called the Sisters of the Blessed Sacrament for Indians and Colored People. Upon its establishment in 1891, the order took on the mission of helping those in need in every way, especially through education that could potentially lift men and women out of poverty. Katharine Drexel founded many schools on Indian reservations and, in 1925, established the first U.S. Catholic university for African Americans, Xavier University, located in New Orleans, Louisiana.

Katharine Drexel

Thea Bowman

Thea Bowman was born in Yazoo City, Mississippi, in 1937, and was given the name of Bertha. She often referred to her family as an "ecumenical family." During the time she was growing up, racial division and oppression, especially in the South, was institutionalized. Schools were segregated, as were swimming pools, restaurants, public restrooms, and water fountains. Signs on many of these places designated them for "whites only" or for "coloreds only." It was a time when blacks literally had to "move to the back of the bus" in accord with the law. But in the Bowman household, all people were treated with equal respect and dignity, and those who would perpetrate violence through racism, religious prejudice, or any other method, were people for whom the family prayed.

Thea was a firsthand witness to the genuine love and compassion that her parents not only taught, but lived. Her family stories were rich in pride and heritage. Her grandfather, a freed slave, moved his family to Tennessee so that his children could receive an education. Relocation was necessary because in the state where they had been living, blacks could not attend school with whites, and, tragically, there was no school for blacks. Because Thea's grandfather held education in such high regard, her father was educated as a physician. He received his education and training in the North, where there were more opportunities for career advancement. But rather than stay in the North, Thea's father chose to return to the South, to Canton, Mississippi, where there was not a black doctor in the entire county. He chose to serve the people in Mississippi because blacks were often refused medical treatment by white doctors.

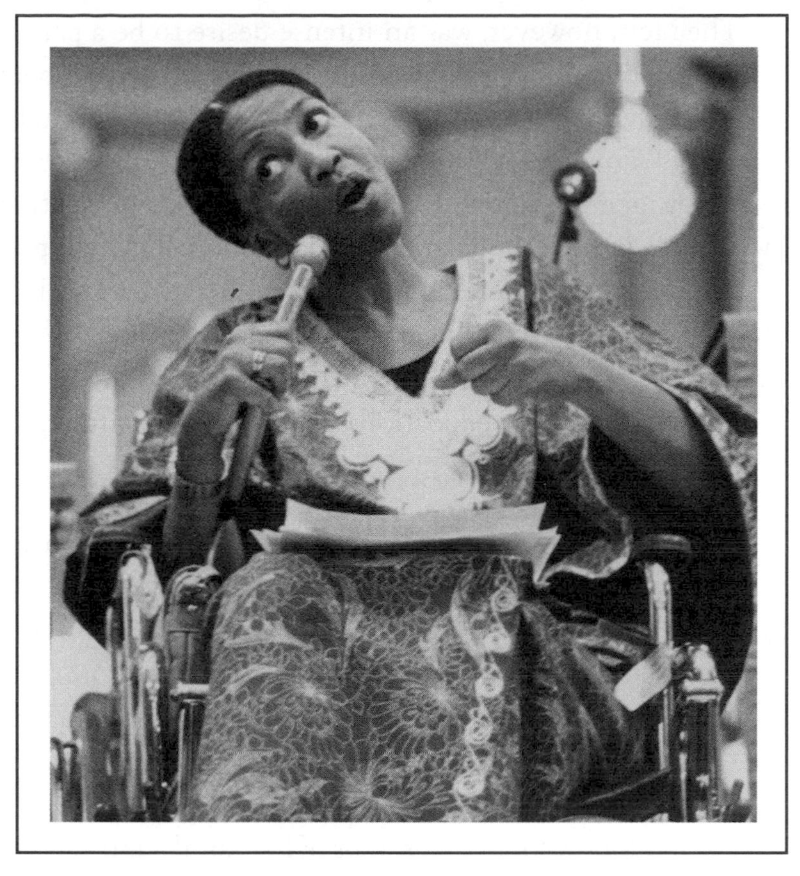

Sister Thea Bowman

Thea remembered well the day that "the Catholics came." The entire town was filled with all kinds of rumors about the real reason the Franciscan Sisters of Perpetual Adoration (and Northerners, at that) were moving to Canton. The actual reason was to staff a school there, but many people in Canton initially felt that the sisters had little or no business doing do. They were seen as "interlopers" and as people whose Catholic beliefs and practices were held in some suspicion. For example, the people of Canton heard that Catholics spoke in tongues (Latin Mass), and most of Canton's citizens initially wanted nothing to do with the sisters or the school, although they were generally too polite to make their feelings known.

What Thea felt, however, was an intense desire to be a part of such a faith community that would care so very much about those who suffered in body, mind, or spirit. And it did not take the town of Canton long to accept and welcome the sisters. It also did not take Thea long to know with total certainty that she wanted to be a Catholic and, one day, a nun. The first part of her unfolding vocation took place while she was still in elementary school, when she was received into the Catholic Church. Then, when she was fifteen, Thea left for La Crosse, Wisconsin, to finish her education and become an affiliate of the Franciscan Sisters there.

It was 1952, and at that time, Thea was the only African American woman in the entire religious order. She was also transplanted into a northern culture that was very alien to her experience and that was also primarily an Anglo culture. She missed the exuberance and the natural enthusiasm for life that was so readily apparent in the black, southern culture of her home. She missed the stories and the songs. She, no doubt, felt homesick and lonely for the closeness of her family and friends. Thea felt, however, that this was a small sacrifice to make. It was in La Crosse that Thea took her new name, leaving her given name of Bertha behind and choosing Thea in honor of her father, Theo. It was also in La Crosse that she received her undergraduate degree at Viterbo College, a college founded and run by the Franciscan Sisters. As difficult as it must have been for her at times, Thea found her experience in La Crosse to be a time of many blessings.

Thea went on to receive her master's degree and then her doctorate in English literature at the Catholic University of America in Washington, DC. It was there that she had her first experience of African American Catholicism, and her spirit soared with a new appreciation of black history and culture.

According to Thea, it was in Washington that she first learned to celebrate who she was as a black, American, Catholic woman and to feel a natural integration of all the different aspects of her person. It was also in Washington that she learned that she, who was a perpetual student, always wanting to learn, was also called to teach others. Thea did this not only by serving as a teacher but also by educating and uplifting others through her lectures, stories, and music. Her enthusiasm for her cultural heritage was the driving force behind the establishment of the Institute for Black Studies at Xavier University.

Two themes dominated in Thea's teaching and in her presentations. The first was that each person needs to know and appreciate who he or she is, for God created each one of us. Therefore, we are unique; we are special; we are loved; we are somebody. Second, all of us, unique and special, must unite our hearts as one—otherwise, we are not "Church" to anyone, but rather a sacrilege. Thea felt that each individual needs to assume personal responsibility to reach out to others and be "Church" to them. She presented a liberating message of empowerment—of what the Church could truly be—if only everyone would strive to do their best, if they would seek to befriend and love each other for the love of Jesus.

Sister Thea died in 1990 at the age of fifty-three. Six years before her death, she was diagnosed with cancer and given three months to three years to live. She was stunned by the news, naturally, but chose to face death as she faced life—with joy and with hope in her heart. Even in her illness, or perhaps especially through her illness, Thea witnessed to her tremendous faith by maintaining her lecture schedule—spreading the good news through her words and song and her message of hope that the world can be transformed through the

love of God, self, and others. She admitted that God's love and the love of the people whom she met sustained her and strengthened her to continue her ministry in spite of her illness. The people who knew her best said that it was as if Sister Thea could read a person's soul or see inside a person's heart. Obviously, what she saw in the people she met was good and holy, for that is exactly how gently she treated each person. She cherished them.

Mother Teresa of Calcutta

In India, where Mother Teresa lived for most of her life, the people revered her as a holy person. When she passed in a crowd, many people reached out to touch the hem of her sari, the edge of her sandal, or even the place where her footstep had fallen.

Mother Teresa earned such reverence and respect because of the tremendous respect and care that she showed, without exception, to the people of India. Without a doubt, she was one of the most beloved and inspiring examples of Christian ministry to those who were poor and oppressed, sick and dying, that the world has ever seen. She was loved and respected by Catholics and Protestants alike, by Hindus and Buddhists and Jainists, and by people with no religious affiliation at all. She was the recipient of countless awards, commendations, and other honors, including the Nobel Peace Prize, awarded in 1979. Upon her death in 1997, all the people of India grieved, as did the world.

Mother Teresa was born Agnes Gonxha Bojaxhiu in 1910, in Skopje, Yugoslavia. At the age of seventeen, she joined the Sisters of Loretto in Ireland and, soon after, was sent to Calcutta, India, to teach. In 1948, she left the Sisters of Loretto to establish, with papal approval, the Missionaries of

Mother Teresa

Charity, a community of sisters, brothers, and priests whose ministry it is to serve "the poorest of the poor." Today, the Missionaries of Charity can be found in many countries of the world, including the United States. Their ministry continues to expand, due in no small part to the example of their foundress, Mother Teresa.

In a video titled "Work of Love," Mother Teresa said that the work that she and her missionaries do is simply their love for Jesus put into action. When they see someone who is hungry, they recognize that this person is hungry for more than just food, but also for love. When they see someone who is naked, they recognize that he or she also needs to be clothed with human dignity and respect. When they see that people are homeless, they know that those persons are also carrying the burden of feeling rejected, unwanted, and unworthy.

For the Missionaries of Charity, an active yet contemplative order, the first lesson that Mother Teresa taught was that the missionaries were to learn to "pray the work." In order to do that, they first would need to learn to pray.

> *The beginning of prayer is silence, when God speaks to your empty heart and you listen. Then, from the fullness of your heart, you speak to God and God listens. Once that lesson is learned, then what is done is done with Jesus, it is done for Jesus, and it is done to Jesus. For every person that is met, it is Jesus who is in need.*
>
> *Mother Teresa of Calcutta: Work of Love*, ex. prod. Vernon Robertson, Catholic Communication Campaign, video.

In Mother Teresa, the world saw true discipleship, and the world took notice, not only by the accolades given to her (which she never sought), but also in the knowledge that such a depth of discipleship was actually possible. Perhaps after her love for God, her greatest love was her ministry to those who were destitute and dying. In them, she saw Christ. It was her greatest honor to be able to bring them into her mission and to nurse them back to health. If that was not to be, she saw to it that their final days or hours were not spent alone, not spent in despair, and not spent without the comfort of human touch. For those young mothers who felt burdened by the birth of another child, she begged them not to abandon their children or to abort them, but rather to "bring them to me, and I will be their mother." The stories of Mother Teresa's great love, wisdom, and compassion fill countless books. Many examples of what she believed and sought to teach others can be found in her own words:

> *I picked up one person—the first person—but if I wouldn't have, then maybe I wouldn't have picked up the other 42,000.*

. . . And once having picked someone up, we need to teach that person to walk—to give them a means to care for themselves and for their families so that they may know human dignity and worth. . . . The whole work, all that we do, is only one drop in the ocean, but if we do not put in that drop, the ocean would be one drop less. . . . How do you change the world? You begin by changing yourself—your outlook, how you touch and care for things, how you learn to first recognize God within yourself, so that you can then see God in others. . . . Just begin, just begin, just begin.

Mother Teresa of Calcutta: Work of Love.

Jean Donovan

For Jean Donovan, her vocation as a lay missionary led her to El Salvador in August of 1979.

Despite a worsening of violence, the general feeling among North Americans volunteering in El Salvador seems to be that they are relatively safe. The native clergy and native church-workers involved with the poor are objects of reprisal. . . .

Jean has come to this troubled land to join a mission team recruited from her diocese in Cleveland, Ohio. She leaves behind in the States her parents, her brother, close friends (including a special man in her life) and a career job with a prestigious accounting firm.

Both before and after she decides to join the mission team, Jean wonders why God has chosen her to make a commitment so far removed from anything she's ever known before. The only answer the 26-year-old woman gets is a deep down sense that she's made the right choice.

Joanne Turpin, *Women in Church History: Twenty Stories for Twenty Centuries* (Cincinnati, OH: Saint Anthony Messenger Press and Franciscan Communications, 1990), 166 and 167.

Jean Donovan

By December of 1980, Jean Donovan was dead. By the standards of the world, her choice in going to El Salvador to work for peace and to care for the country's political refugees was nothing less than tragic. And in the sense that a beautiful person's life was lost, with so many possibilities yet before her, it was incredibly tragic—especially for the people closest to her who, no doubt, grieve their loss every day. Her family and friends may have received some comfort, however, in knowing that Jean was doing what she wanted to do with her life and that she was at peace, confident that she was where she was meant to be, doing what God called her to do.

Jean Donovan and her three companions and coworkers—Ursaline sister Dorothy Kazel and Maryknoll sisters Ita Ford and Maura Clarke—are modern-day martyrs. They join the long list of martyrs, who throughout the history of Christianity, have given the ultimate sacrifice of their very lives as they went about doing the work of the Lord. "Blessed are the peacemakers . . ."

Some Thoughts for Your Reflection

1. Dorothy Day firmly believed that the roots of violence originated in fear, lack of forgiveness, and in greed. Can you apply her belief (theory) to any situation of violence or of potential violence that exists in our world today? Some areas of concern include racial intolerance, religious intolerance, gang involvement, warfare, and the growing disparity between the world's rich and the poor.

2. Elizabeth Ann Seton once said, "We must be so careful to meet our grace." What does this statement mean to you? Where will you find your grace? You may want to spend some time journaling about this.

3. Thea Bowman learned at an early age the stories of her family, and she recognized the events that literally changed the future for her family. What events have shaped your family? Your friends? Yourself? Do you know your family's story?

4. According to Mother Teresa, "the whole work, all that we do, is only one drop in the ocean, but if we do not put in that drop, the ocean would be one drop less." From this statement, write a poem or story or song, draw a picture, or choreograph a dance that reflects this truth in your life.

5. Many of the people featured in this chapter were missionaries. If a missionary were to come to your town, where would he or she be most needed? Have you ever considered that you could be such a missionary?

6. When Mother Teresa was asked, "How do you change the world?" she replied, "You first begin by changing yourself." What things in your life may be holding you back from changing the world? Make a list. Are you willing to let go of any of these things? What attitudes, behaviors, or actions do you have that are positive in nature and would be valuable assets in changing the world? Make a list. (You may find some of the same qualities on each list!)

Chapter Ten

Visions for the Future

"I Have Called You by Name; You Are Mine."

As we know, in Scripture the female disciples of Jesus were often given no name and no voice. If a woman was mentioned by name, it was often in reference to whatever connection she had to a man, such as being a wife or a daughter. Frequently, in the culture of the time, a woman had few rights and was often considered little more than property or a possession.

In many parts of the world today, women endure conditions that are not too different from those just mentioned. For the most part, these women live in developing countries, where they are nameless and faceless, for the rest of the world often takes little notice of them. But their struggles for equality in society and in the Church are of indescribable importance. Often Catholic American women are reminded that "the Church is bigger than just the United States." The fact that women in some other countries have not achieved the level of "equality" that Catholic women in the United States supposedly have is often used as an argument against seeking greater gender-equality within the Church at all. There is some truth in this argument, but generally, it is an old and worn-out "truth."

It cannot be denied that social, political, and legal conditions in many other countries of the world often debase women and keep them within societal structures that limit not only their basic human rights but also their God-given gifts to the world. But it must also be remembered that within the next couple of generations, the white, European Church and the Church of North America will gradually become less important than the

Church of the "third" world. Population shifts and demographics tell us as much. The Catholic Church is going to be younger and poorer, and it is going to be a Church that will need to recognize the names, the voices, and the faces of its women who comprise far more than half its membership. No matter where they live, no matter what their cultural experience or educational opportunity, the Spirit of God is moving among the women of the world, calling them to greater discipleship—calling them by name. It would do the Church well to listen.

Francis Bernard O'Connor CSC did a study (as part of the Kellogg Institute for International Studies at the University of Notre Dame) that included a statistical survey, a questionnaire, and interviews with women on four continents, from the countries of Uganda, Bangladesh, Brazil, and the United States. What she found was an awareness on the part of the women, not only of their own repression within their specific culture, but also of the repression that many of them feel within the Church. Each woman's issues, opinions, and feelings arose out of her own personal and unique experiences, and so they are her own, even though there are common threads of shared awareness that weave through the stories.

What the women in developing countries do tend to share is a desire for the Church to stand with women against that which oppresses them. When the Church, itself, is guilty of representing the cultural status quo, the women who were part of the study were not afraid to call the Church to accountability. There was a general awareness that, while Jesus had come to liberate those who were poor and to call both men and women into discipleship, too often the Church of these women was not even close to living up to that ideal. In each country, the women endured forms of oppression, marginalization, and diminishment. Understandably, these conditions existed in varying forms and in different degree, but they were present in all countries. Sister O'Connor's study found the following information.

The Women of Uganda

In Uganda, a woman is considered to be the property of her father until she becomes, through marriage, the property of her husband. Once married, it is her duty to produce children so that the family will have the necessary labor to work the fields and help maintain the clan. Since she is "property," the Ugandan woman is not free to make her own decisions, nor does she have a right to ownership of anything. For that reason, she can never own or inherit the very fields that she works to sustain her family. Since her husband is the only one who is allowed to sell what is produced, men control whatever money is made.

The average Ugandan woman's workday is between twelve and eighteen hours long. This usually includes a walk of up to five miles a day to gather the firewood and water that is necessary for the needs of her family on that day. She does this while caring for her children. An education is generally not available to women, nor is communication with the "outside" world, since in rural areas, the only means of communication is a radio, and most women have no access to one.

The men of Uganda are allowed to have more than one wife, and about half of them choose to do so. For the remaining half, a monogamous marriage does not necessarily translate into a faithful one, for male faithfulness is not highly prized in Uganda's male-dominated culture. The men who frequently leave their wives to go to the cities in search of work often are

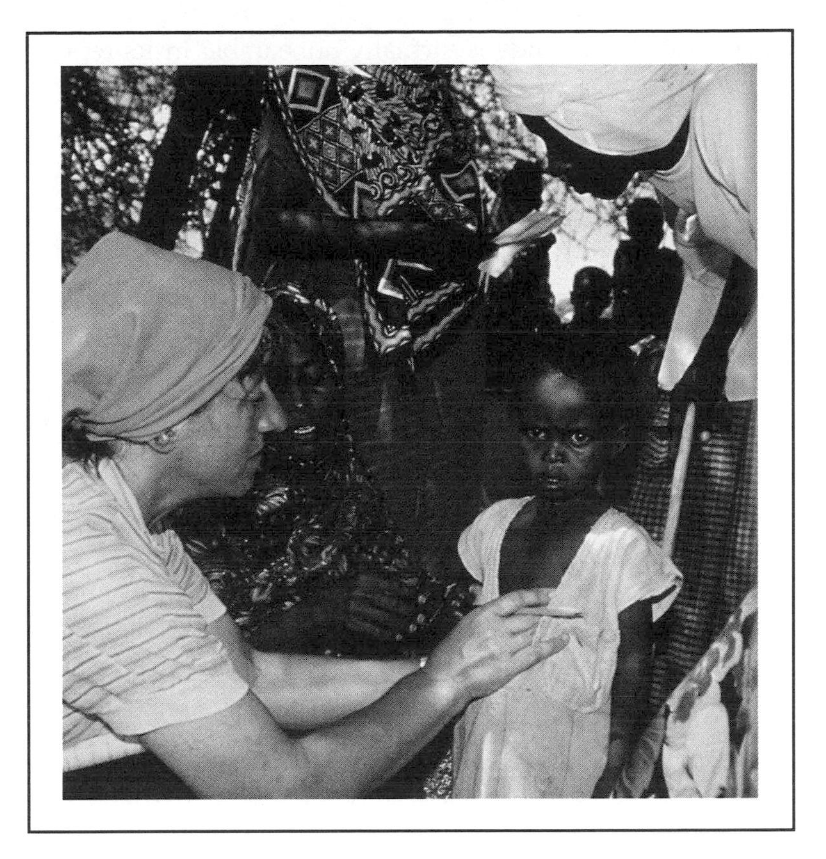

unfaithful. The number of AIDS cases is increasing in Uganda, and women are especially vulnerable to the disease. Because of this, many women are literally faced with a life-and-death dilemma.

> *Either they accept an unfaithful husband along with the possibility of contracting AIDS or reject him and face starvation for themselves and their children. The overall demographic impact of AIDS has not been sufficiently studied as yet. However, the increase in AIDS deaths of both women and men between the ages of twenty-five and forty may set the stage for a nation of orphans and elderly in the next generation.*
>
> Francis B. O'Connor, *Like Bread, Their Voices Rise! Global Women Challenge the Church* (Notre Dame, IN: Ave Maria Press, 1993), 41.

The situation in Uganda is virtually unbearable in its repression and victimization of women. Yet when women turn to the Church for guidance and assistance, they are often victimized again, in the sense that the Church in Uganda all too frequently reflects the attitudes of that society.

> *Ninety-six percent said that they believe Jesus wants his church to treat women and men as equals. Well over half of the women felt that the church is either not living the message of Jesus for women or there were times when it does not. . . . The church's lack of appreciation for women was evidenced when only thirty-nine percent said they feel their pastor and bishop want full participation of women.*
>
> *Not unlike the woman in the gospel who came out of the shadows to touch Jesus' garment and was cured of her blood disease, women of Africa are driven by a similar sense of hope. Ugandan women were born and many are still living in the shadows of history. . . . They are suffering from an incurable disease, that of being diminished, devalued and excluded by their male counterparts, both lay and cleric. In reaching out her hand, the gospel woman becomes the symbol of all the women who, conditioned and habituated to insignificance, still find in themselves a small flame of unexplainable hope that things may be different, and reach out towards what they recognize in some way as the fire that lighted the flame.*
>
> O'Connor, 51.

The Women of Bangladesh

There is an old saying in Bangladesh that goes like this: "Educating your daughter is like watering another man's field." Socially conditioned from infancy to believe that they are inferior to men, the women of Bangladesh struggle to step outside of such limiting and debasing barriers. It is not an easy task.

> *The fact that the total life situation of a woman in Bangladesh is highly dependent on her status within a family as daughter, wife, or mother cannot be overstated. A woman in Bangladesh society has no name or identity of her own. Before she is married, a woman is not called by her own name, but is known as "Peter's daughter." After marriage, she is designated as "Andrew's wife," and when she has born a son, she is known as "Joseph's mother." Out of respect a wife never speaks her husband's first name. She, however, is nameless and seems to have no identity in and of herself.*
>
> O'Connor, 56.

Bangladesh is an Islamic nation with a population of over 110 million. Of these 110 million people, 10 percent are Hindu, and less than .02 percent are Catholic. It must be noted that within Catholic families, women have a greater degree of freedom, although this is often relative. (A "greater degree of freedom" in a country that has very little freedom for women is still next to nothing.) It was during the war of independence in 1971, however, that Catholic women, by necessity, moved into positions and roles that had previously been closed to

them. With this movement from the home to the marketplace, so to speak, came a greater awareness of the status of women in both Bangladesh society, in the Church, and in the world.

Once having achieved some small measure of expanded roles and increased status within society, it was difficult to step back. For that reason, many Catholic girls now receive an education—not so much because a father feels that his daughter deserves an education, but because he realizes that an educated daughter can bring more money into the home, either through employment or by obtaining a favorable marriage.

Since Catholics in Bangladesh are such a minority, women frequently marry outside of their faith, often to Muslim men. In Bangladesh, a Muslim has the right to seclude a woman in his household through the imposition of *purdah* (veiling). This custom is much more than merely covering a woman's face; it can include restricting a woman's movements to the point that she is a virtual prisoner in her own home. Marriage to a Muslim man also means the renunciation of her Catholic faith, so this is a very serious issue for Bangladesh families. Many Catholic men in Bangladesh feel that the solution is for the law to give them more rights to impose increased limitations on the few freedoms Catholic women have.

> *In spite of their experiences, over 96 percent of the women indicated they believe Jesus Christ wants his church to treat women as equals with men. Eighty-five percent feel that they deserve to be treated as an equal by their priests. For women to feel they deserve equal treatment and to experience it are two different things. The highly educated women were significantly more aware of their unequal treatment. There is a correlation between the heightened level of awareness that results from*

education and the understanding of what it means to be treated as an equal in the church.

O'Connor, 63.

Paradoxically, the uneducated and primarily non-Catholic women of Bangladesh often seem to have arrived at some measure of peace within themselves regarding the way things are.

In her book Women, Tradition and Culture, *Malladi Subbamma, a prominent Indian woman journalist and writer . . . refers to their self-designation as* kue ka meyndak *(frogs in a well)—people with intellectual and physical horizons limited to the tiny patch of sky directly above their heads. How can any woman who is oblivious of the chains that bind her desire freedom?*

O'Connor, 57.

The Women of Brazil

Brazil is a country of over 155 million people, and it is comparable in size to the continental United States. Of the 155 million people, about 90 percent call themselves Catholic, and 75 percent of the population is urban. Many people in Brazil are of mixed race, with approximately 55 percent being primarily white, 38 percent brown, 6 percent black, and a tiny percentage of the population Asian.

The prevailing reality for women in Brazil is that, no matter how gifted, talented, educated, or beautiful a woman is, she is still oppressed at virtually every level of Brazilian society, whether in the home, the school, or the church.

> *Brazilian society is characterized by* machismo, *a Hispanic form of male dominance and aggressive behavior. Men are free, willful and powerful, while women are subject to limitations of all kinds, ranging from male control over their private lives to their restricted position in society. Women are invariably considered in relationship to the home. Even though they are present and fulfill important roles in the home and society, they are invisible because their presence does not count. Women are often seen as non-persons in society, oppressed by a father, then abused by a husband and finally deserted by a son. In reality they become daughters without fathers, wives without husbands and mothers without sons. Without a relationship to one of these male figures, they are "no one."*
>
> O'Connor, 70.

Brazil, like most Latin American countries and, in fact, most developing countries of the world, has serious economic problems. Because of the existing conditions, women have had to leave their homes to help support their families. This has broadened many women's horizons and opened their minds to new possibilities.

One of the new possibilities is serving as facilitators in *base de comunidades* (base communities or small faith communities). These small faith communities are so popular and leadership is so needed that nearly 80 percent of these communities are led by women. This is possible, however, because most men do not participate in these communities. Therefore, the women are "the church." The fact that the base communities exist at all is partially due to the severe priest shortage in Brazil. Visits by priests are few and far between, so the communities of faith fill some portion of this void.

> *Women theologians and Scripture scholars all over the world are pointing to the example of the way Jesus treated women in his day and are asking, "Why doesn't the church follow the example of Jesus?" In Luke 13:10–17, the story is told about Jesus curing the woman who had been bent over double for eighteen years. She immediately stood up straight and glorified God. And that, says Maria De Groot, can only happen after you are raised up. "You can participate in the community where only men have leadership and can speak, but you do it as someone who is bent over and distorted. Only if you are lifted up by the power of Jesus does your own song awaken."*
>
> O'Connor, 68.

A century ago, Elizabeth Cady Stanton, traveled the world searching for the source of women's subordination and

dependence on men. She felt that she had found it in the institution of religion, which so very often failed to live up to the very best of its own ideals.

> *What power is it that makes a Hindu woman burn herself on the funeral pyre of her husband? Her religion. What holds the Turkish woman in the harem? Her religion. By what power do [some] Mormons perpetuate their system of polygamy? By their religion. Man, of himself, could not do this; but when he declares, "thus says the Lord," of course he can do it. So long as ministers stand up and tell us that Christ is the head of the church, so is man the head of the woman, how are we to break the chains which have held women down through the ages?*
>
> O'Connor, 142.

The Women of the United States

Increasingly, many Catholic women in the United States who desire to be part of a Church that recognizes their gifts (and then who work toward that desire) are criticized for doing so. They often are given labels that have the word *feminist* attached, and the labels usually are not meant as compliments. Nonetheless, these women continue to call the Church to accountability for the teachings, traditions, and practices that they see as contrary to the gospel message of Jesus.

In the Vatican II documents, such as "The Church in the Modern World," Christian feminists, Christian womanists (or whatever title they may be given, if titles are necessary), find support for the cause of greater gender-equity within the Church.

> *At all times the Church carries the responsibility of reading the signs of the time and of interpreting them in the light of the Gospel, if it is to carry out its task. In language intelligible to every generation, she should be able to answer the ever recurring questions which men ask about the meaning of this present life and of the life to come, and how one is related to the other.*
>
> "Pastoral Constitution on the Church in the Modern World," *Vatican Council II: The Conciliar and Post Conciliar Documents*, Austin Flannery, gen. ed. (Collegeville, MN: The Liturgical Press, 1975), #4.

It takes a great deal of courage to challenge the Church that you love and want to serve. Yet today, more than ever, women in the United States and all over the world are doing exactly that—not because they want power, but because they want equality.

> *Feminist theology has unmasked the sexist structures of Church language, theology and social policies. It is fundamentally challenging the Church to recognize the distortion of the Christian message created by the Church's patriarchal socialization, and to reconstruct its social patterns, language and theology to affirm the full humanity of both women and men.*
>
> O'Connor, 144.

Women in the United States comprise 57 percent of the Church, and a much higher percentage of those who are actively involved. Fifty-seven percent translates to approximately 33 million Catholic women. Women are involved in the Church in a hundred different ways, and most agree that equality and true discipleship go hand in hand.

> *Women crying out for inclusion are offering the church the opportunity to become whole. For centuries the church has been and is walking on one leg, seeing with one eye, hearing with one ear, speaking from half a heart and functioning with half the intellectual resources available to it.*
>
> O'Connor, 29–30.

Women's inclusion would provide a wholeness that is not yet present and a healing that is so desperately needed. In many ways, the Church of today is at a crossroads. Whether it chooses to step back into time, trying to regain a sense of itself that never was complete, or whether it has the courage to press forward into a wholeness that has not yet been experienced by the Body of Christ, only time will tell.

Women throughout the centuries have had more than enough time to weep, to keep silence, to wait, to submit, and to sit in the pews. Today, thousands of women the world over feel that the time is over and now is the time for them to rejoice, to speak up, to act, to preach, to rise up and claim their rightful place in the church. The time is now. The women are rising and the Church will be blessed!

O'Connor, 163.

A Litany of Women for the Church

Dear God,
creator of women in your own image,
born of a woman in the midst of a world half women,
carried by women to mission fields around the globe,
made known by women to all the children of the earth,
give to the women of our time
the strength to persevere,
the courage to speak out,
the faith to believe in you beyond all systems and institutions
so that your face on earth may be seen in all its beauty,
so that men and women become whole,
so that the church may be converted to your will
in everything and in all ways.

We call on the holy women
who went before us,
channels of your Word
in testaments old and new,
to intercede for us
so that we might be given the grace
to become what they have been
for the honor and glory of God.

Saint Esther, who pleaded against power for the liberation of the people,
Saint Judith, who routed the plans of men and saved the community,
Saint Deborah, laywoman and judge, who led the people of God,
Saint Elizabeth of Judea, who recognized the value of another woman,

Saint Mary Magdalene, minister to Jesus, first evangelist of the Christ,

Saint Scholastica, who taught her brother Benedict to honor the spirit above the system,

Saint Hildegard, who suffered interdict for the doing of right,

Saint Joan of Arc, who put no law above the law of God,

Saint Clare of Assisi, who confronted the pope with the image of woman as equal,

Saint Julian of Norwich, who proclaimed for all of us the motherhood of God,

Saint Thérèse of Lisieux, who knew the call to priesthood in herself,

Saint Catherine of Siena, to whom the pope listened,

Saint Teresa of Ávila, who brought women's gifts to the reform of the church,

Saint Edith Stein, who brought fearlessness to faith,

Saint Elizabeth Seton, who broke down boundaries between lay women and religious by wedding motherhood and religious life,

Saint Dorothy Day, who led the church to a new sense of justice,

Mary, mother of Jesus, who heard the call of God and answered,

Mary, mother of Jesus, who drew strength from the woman Elizabeth,

Mary, mother of Jesus, who underwent hardship bearing Christ,

Mary, mother of Jesus, who ministered at Cana,

Mary, mother of Jesus, inspirited at Pentecost,

Mary, mother of Jesus, who turned the Spirit of God into the body and blood of Christ,

pray for us. Amen.

Bibliography

Barraclough, Geoffrey, gen. ed. *The Christian World: A Social and Cultural History*. New York: Harry N. Abrams Incorporated, 1981.

Bernier, Paul. *Ministry in the Church: A Historical and Pastoral Approach*. Mystic, CT: Twenty-Third Publications, 1992.

Bunson, Margaret R. *Kateri Tekakwitha: Mystic of the Wilderness*. Huntington, IN: Our Sunday Visitor, 1996.

Committee on Women in Society and in the Church, National Conference of Catholic Bishops, United States Catholic Conference. *From Words to Deeds: Continuing Reflections on the Role of Women in the Church*. Washington DC, 1998.

Day, Dorothy. *The Long Loneliness: An Autobiography*. San Francisco: HarperSanFrancisco, 1981.

Dowley, Tim. *Eerdmans' Handbook to the History of Christianity*. Grand Rapids, MI: William B. Eerdmans Publishing Company, 1977.

Durka, Gloria. *Praying with Hildegard of Bingen*. Winona, MN: Saint Mary's Press, 1991.

Flannery, Austin, gen. ed. *Vatican Council II: The Conciliar and Post Conciliar Documents*. Collegeville, MN: The Liturgical Press, 1975.

Gasnick, Roy M. *The Francis Book: A Celebration of the Universal Saint*. New York: Macmillan Publishing Company, Incorporated, 1980.

Gordon, Anne. *A Book of Saints: True Stories of How They Touch Our Lives*. New York: Bantam Books, 1994.

Hamington, Maurice. *Hail Mary? The Struggle for Ultimate Womanhood in Catholicism*. New York: Routledge, 1995.

Hoover, Rose. "Consider Tradition." *Commonweal* 126 (29 January 1999): 17.

Jordan, Patrick. "An Appetite for God." *Commonweal* 124 (24 October 1997): 12.

Kraemer, Ross S. *Her Share of the Blessings: Women's Religions among Pagans, Jews, and Christians in the Greco-Roman World*. New York: Oxford University Press, 1994.

Maloney, Robert P. "Models of Being Holy." *America* 176 (1997): 17.

McBride, Alfred A. *The Story of the Church: Peak Moments from Pentecost to the Year 2000*. Cincinnati: Saint Anthony Messenger Press & Franciscan Communications, 1996.

McBrien, Richard P. *Catholicism*. San Francisco: HarperSanFrancisco, 1994.

McBrien, Richard P. *The HarperCollins Encyclopedia of Catholicism*. New York: HarperCollins, 1995.

Mother Teresa of Calcutta: Work of Love. Vernon Robertson, ex. prod. Catholic Communication Campaign, video.

O'Connor, Francis B. *Like Bread, Their Voices Rise! Global Women Challenge the Church*. Notre Dame, IN: Ave Maria Press, 1993.

Ohanneson, Joan. *Woman: Survivor in the Church*. San Francisco: HarperSanFrancisco, 1983.

Orsy, Ladislas. "The Congregation's 'Response': Its Authority and Meaning." *America* 173 (9 December 1995): 4.

Perkins, Pheme. *Reading the New Testament: An Introduction*. Mahwah, NJ: Paulist Press, 1988.

Phillips, John A. *Eve: The History of an Idea*. San Francisco: HarperSanFrancisco, 1985.

Ricci, Carla. *Mary Magdalene and Many Others: Women Who Followed Jesus*. Minneapolis: Augsburg Fortress Publishers, 1994.

Rowling, Marjorie. *Everyday Life in Medieval Times*. New York: Dorset Press, 1987.

Senior, Donald, gen. ed. *The Catholic Study Bible: New American Bible*. New York: Oxford University Press, 1991.

Simon, Edith. "The Reformation," *Great Ages of Man*. Alexandria, VA: Time-Life, Incorporated, 1966.

Turpin, Joanne. *Women in Church History: Twenty Stories for Twenty Centuries*. Cincinnati: Saint Anthony Messenger Press & Franciscan Communications, 1990.

Uhlein, Gabriele. *Meditations with Hildegard of Bingen*. Santa Fe, NM: Bear & Company, 1983.

Vanier, Jean. *Be Not Afraid*. Mahwah, NJ: Paulist Press, 1975.

Wahlberg, Rachel C. *Jesus According to a Woman*. Mahwah, NJ: Paulist Press, 1975.

Warner, Marina. *Alone of All Her Sex: The Myth and the Cult of the Virgin Mary*. New York: Vintage Books, 1983.

Index

A

B

C

D

E

F

H

I

J

K

L

M

O

P

Q

R

S

T

V

W

Photo Index

Hildegard von Bingen. Credit: CNS, page 134.

Bridget of Sweden. Credit: Culver Pictures, page 143.

Saint Catherine of Siena by Carlo Dolci, Dulwich Picture Gallery, London. Credit: SuperStock, page 144.

Madonna and Child by Bellini, Brera Gallery, Milan. Credit: Culver Pictures, page 153.

Coronation of the Virgin by Enguerrand Quarton, Musee de L'Hospice de Villeneuve, Les Avignons. Credit: SuperStock, page 155.

The Conception by Giovanni Battista Tiepolo. Credit: SuperStock, page 159.

Madonna and Child, Icons. Credit: SuperStock, page 167.

THE CROSIERS/Gene Plaisted OSC, page 173.

Praying Madonna by Giovanni B.S. Sassoferrato, The Cummer Museum of Art and Gardens. Credit: SuperStock, page 181.

Saint Teresa of Ávila, colored lithograph. Credit: Corbis/Bettmann, page 185.

Saint Rose of Lima. Credit: Culver Pictures, page 205.

THE CROSIERS/Gene Plaisted OSC, page 211.

THE CROSIERS/Gene Plaisted OSC, page 227.

Sister Thea Bowman. Credit: CNS, page 243.

Dorothy Day. Credit: Archdiocese of Dubuque, page 252.

Saint Elizabeth Ann Seton by Joseph Dawley. Credit: Corbis/Bettmann-UPI, page 257.

Frances Xavier Cabrini. Credit: SuperStock. page 259.

Blessed Kateri Tekakwitha by Sister M. Fides Glass. Credit: Corbis/Bettmann-UPI, page 264.

Mother Katharine Drexel. Credit: CNS, page 269.

Sister Thea Bowman, photo taken by Denise Walker. Credit: CNS, page 271.

Mother Teresa of Calcutta. Credit: Corbis/Bettmann-UPI, page 275.

Jean Donovan. Credit: CNS, page 278.

Bill Wittman, page 281.

Jim Whitmer, page 285.

Mimi Forsyth, page 289.

Robert Fried, page 292.

James L. Shaffer, page 295.